C000171813

BORNEO
BOYS

By the same author

Drop Zone Burma: Adventures in Allied Air-Supply 1943–45
(Pen & Sword Books, Barnsley, 2008)

Lifeline in Helmand: RAF Battlefield Mobility in Afghanistan
(Pen & Sword Books, Barnsley, 2010)

Drop Zone Borneo – Life and Times of an RAF Co-Pilot,
Far East 1962 - 65
(Pen & Sword Books, Barnsley, 2010)

BORNEO BOYS

RAF Helicopter Pilots in Action –
Indonesian Confrontation
1962–1966

Roger Annett

Pen & Sword
AVIATION

First published in Great Britain in 2012 by
PEN AND SWORD AVIATION
an imprint of
Pen and Sword Books Ltd
47 Church Street
Barnsley
South Yorkshire S70 2AS

Copyright © Roger Annett, 2012

ISBN 978 1 78159 010 2

The right of Roger Annett to be identified
as the author of this work has been asserted by him in accordance
with the Copyright, Designs and Patents Act 1988.

A CIP record for this book is available from the British Library.

All rights reserved. No part of this book may be reproduced or transmitted
in any form or by any means, electronic or mechanical including
photocopying, recording or by any information storage and retrieval
system, without permission from the Publisher in writing.

Printed and bound in India
By Replika Press Pvt. Ltd.

Typeset in Plantin by
CHIC GRAPHICS

Pen & Sword Books Ltd incorporates the imprints of
Pen & Sword Aviation, Pen & Sword Family History, Pen & Sword Maritime,
Pen & Sword Military, Pen & Sword Discovery, Wharncliffe Local History,
Wharncliffe True Crime, Wharncliffe Transport, Pen & Sword Select,
Pen & Sword Military Classics, Leo Cooper, Remember When,
The Praetorian Press, Seaforth Publishing and Frontline Publishing

For a complete list of Pen and Sword titles please contact
Pen and Sword Books Limited
47 Church Street, Barnsley, South Yorkshire, S70 2AS, England
E-mail: enquiries@pen-and-sword.co.uk
Website: www.pen-and-sword.co.uk

Contents

Foreword

by

Wing Commander F.D. Hoskins
OBE RAF (Retd)

During the Borneo Confrontation the Army's operational radio traffic sometimes clashed with similar traffic in Vietnam and on at least one occasion the British officer was told to 'Get off the air! Don't you know we're fighting a war here?' The response was, 'So are we, but we're winning ours!' And we did win our war in Borneo, even though it was officially not a war but only a 'confrontation'. Perhaps because it was not called a war is why it has never received the level of public recognition given to the conflicts in Korea, the Falklands, Iraq and Afghanistan. Nevertheless, when men are seeking to shoot at each other at the behest of politicians, and some are killed, then surely it is a war.

No one service or unit can claim that they alone were responsible for winning, but that the war in Borneo was won by the British and Commonwealth forces was certainly helped in no small measure by the use of the helicopters of all three services. The Royal Air Force contributed four squadrons of Whirlwinds, Nos 103, 110, 225 and 230, and one squadron of Belvederes, No. 66. Helicopters not then being at the top of the RAF's priorities, many of the pilots were officers with some seniority as flight lieutenants but without prospects of promotion, or else Master Pilots and some sergeants, a group evidently not deemed suitable to fly the latest jet aircraft. This situation changed so that, by the mid-1960s, younger officers, even those only recently awarded their wings, began to be allocated to helicopter squadrons, thus gradually replacing the old regime – but not before learning from those men who had done an excellent and very valuable job, largely without the thanks and recognition they so richly deserved.

In 1965 I was privileged to be appointed to command No. 103 Squadron, based at Seletar, in Singapore, but with most of the squadron in Borneo, operating from what had previously been the purely civil airfield near Kuching and from several forward bases. Shortly after my arrival No. 225 Squadron was disbanded and its pilots transferred to my squadron and to No. 110 Squadron. Thus I saw some of the phasing out of the old and the introduction of the new and younger pilots, some with fixed-wing squadron experience, but most without.

These were interesting and exciting times and the flying in Borneo was demanding, not least because of the weather, the terrain, poor radio coverage and the poor quality of the maps available until late in 1965. Sometimes tasks required two helicopters but more usually operations were carried out by just one, so of necessity pilots were sent out either alone or with a crewman, although there were not enough of the latter for every sortie. As a squadron commander I was therefore faced with having to trust youngsters to take a valuable Whirlwind from Kuching early in the morning with the prospect of returning late in the afternoon after using their own judgement and initiative to carry out their assigned tasks well beyond the possibility of supervision by more senior and experienced officers. They responded magnificently to this trust and I was, and still am, filled with admiration for them.

It is thus particularly pleasing that Roger Annett is not only telling the story of our helicopter operations in Borneo but has chosen to base it on the exploits of some of what he terms the 'Borneo Boys' – and the way they undoubtedly, and quickly, became 'Borneo Men'.

Fred Hoskins

Pimperne
April 2012

Author's Note

A substantial team has contributed to the research for this book. Up in front come the twenty-four veterans of the Borneo Campaign who gave their time to meet the author, to open up their long-term memories for stories and their attics for photos and memorabilia, and to proof-read and embellish their accounts as transcribed by him. In support is a bevy of writers – the dozens of junior officers who wrote up the history of the conflict in real-time for RAF, Army Air Corps and Fleet Air Arm Operational Reports.

That assigned duty had a mixed appeal. To some it was a bind, a task that kept them away from the bar of an evening – to others it was an opportunity to indulge a creative urge. To all, having to bash away at a low-tech typewriter in the heat of the tropics, perhaps on a trestle table in a jungle forward base, attacked by mosquitoes and assailed by the roar of drenching rain on a canvas or 'wriggly tin' roof, it was a challenge. As a result of their efforts a full picture of operations, together with insights into life on active service is held at Armed Forces' museums and in the National Archive at Kew, available for authors, historians and descendants alike. For that, I am grateful to those perspiring scribes and their diligent curators.

I am also indebted to my patient wife Jenny for once again making the first editing assault on initial drafts of the manuscript, and to the staff at Pen & Sword for their support, encouragement and production skills.

The hope is that the resulting *Borneo Boys* achieves its aim in providing a worthy tribute to the veterans of the British and Commonwealth helicopter campaign that led to the survival of the nascent Malaysia.

Roger Annett

Marlow
Buckinghamshire
April 2012

Introduction

In May 2011 two dozen veteran RAF helicopter pilots are gathered together for a reunion at HMS *Heron*, the Royal Naval Air Station at Yeovilton, in Somerset. They have a loose association, now ninety-strong, which they've dubbed 'The Old Rotors', and for the past ten years they have made an annual visit to a military base, followed by an evening 'bash' in a local hotel.

The whole show is organized by a veteran of the 1960s Borneo Campaign, Wing Commander (retired) Colin Cummings. In 1966 he spent formative months of his young life as a Supply Officer on the island base of RAF Labuan, off Brunei, directly supporting RAF, Fleet Air Arm and Army Air Corps rotary operations against marauding Indonesian forces over in Borneo. He put in many hours airborne over the mangrove swamps and jungle and is a confirmed rotary man.

Many of the Old Rotors are veterans of the Borneo Campaign and memories are stirred at the helicopter section of Yeovilton's Fleet Air Arm Museum, where a continuous video loop depicts the Navy's rotary history. Rotors beat overhead as presentations are given by two of the Naval Air Squadrons with Confrontation in their battle-honours, 845 and 846.

At the evening dinner the Guest of Honour is the Air Vice Marshal recently appointed to run Joint Helicopter Command in Andover, the nerve centre of all three Services' rotary assets, vital in today's counter-insurgency operations. He and the veterans have more in common than they might have expected and there's widespread support for an account of the equally important contribution made by helicopters to the Borneo Campaign.

In the following months many Old Rotors, blessed with logbooks and memorabilia, flock to the cause. They are excellent raconteurs, and it turns out to be a cracking good story.

South-East Asia

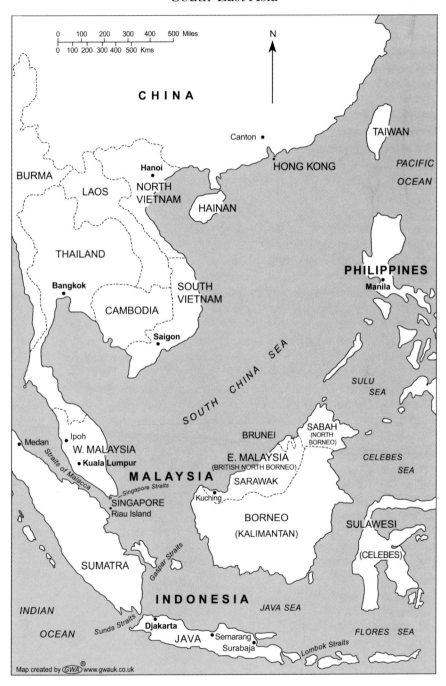

The Borneo Frontier: 1st Division Sarawak

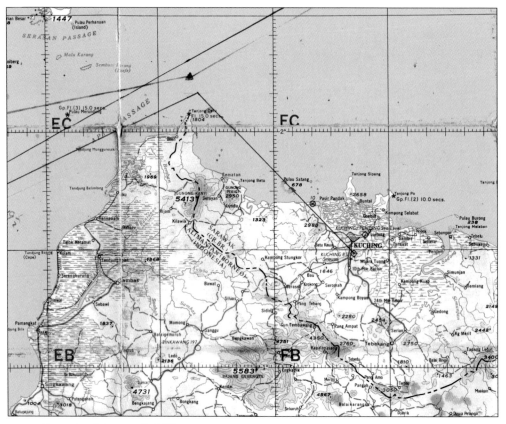

Operational Aeronautical Chart. Crown Copyright 1957

The Borneo Frontier – Sabah Interior

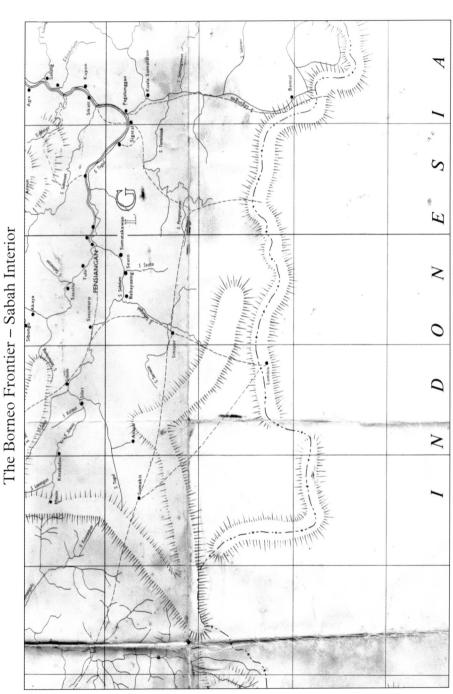

Operational map as issued. Crown Copyright 1963

The Borneo Frontier – Sabah Interior

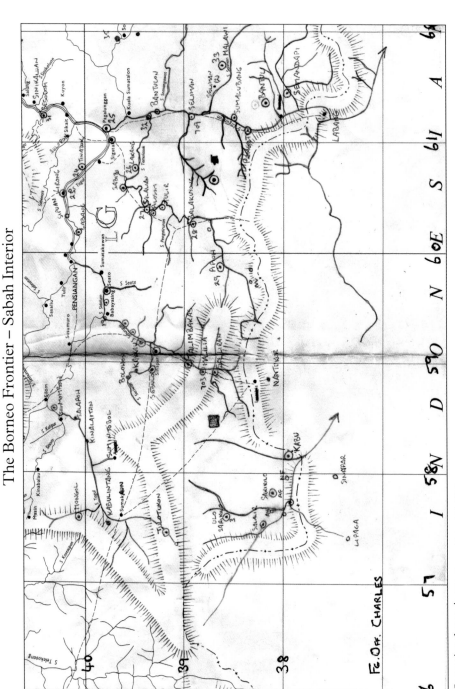

Operational map in use. Crown Copyright 1963

The Borneo Frontier – 2nd–5th Divisions Sarawak, Sabah and Brunei

Glossary

AAC	Army Air Corps
AATDC	Army Air Transport Training and Development Centre
AD	Air Despatch
ADIZ	Air Defence Identification Zone
AFC	Air Force Cross
amah	domestic help
AOC	Air Officer Commanding
APO	Acting Pilot Officer
ATC	Air Training Corps
ATC	Air Traffic Control
ATOC	Air Transport Operations Centre
attap	palm tree
AUW	All-Up Weight
basha	hut
BMH	British Military Hospital
batu	the rock of …
Casevac	Casualty Evacuation
CCF	Combined Cadet Corps
CCO	Clandestine Communist Organization
C-in-C	Commander in Chief
CFS	Central Flying School
CFS(H)	CFS Helicopter Wing
CLARET	codename for clandestine patrols
CO	Commanding Officer
DZ	Drop Zone
Dayak	loose term for the indigenous races of Borneo
DFC	Distinguished Flying Cross
dhobi	Hindi for laundry
ETPS	Empire Test Pilots' School
FAA	Fleet Air Arm
FEAF	Far East Air Force
FTS	Flying Training School
GHQ	General Headquarters
GPMG	General Purpose machine gun
GR	Gurkha Rifles

HF	High Frequency
HMS	Her Majesty's Ship
HQ	Headquarters
Iban	dominant *Dayak* race in Sarawak
IBT	Indonesian Border Terrorist
IOT	Initial Officer Training
ITV	Independent Television
Jungly	Royal Navy helicopter pilot
kampong	village or hamlet
KD	Khaki Drill cotton fabric
kelong	wood-built offshore fishing platform
KKO	*Korps Kommando Operati* (Marine Commando)
KL	Kuala Lumpur
Konfrontasi	Confrontation
Kosbies	King's Own Scottish Borderers
LP	Landing Point
LZ	Landing Zone
MAOT	Mobile Air Operations Team
MC	Military Cross
Medevac	Medical Evacuation
NAS	Naval Air Squadron
NCO	Non-Commissioned Officer
OC	Officer Commanding
OCU	Operational Conversion Unit
OR	Other Ranks
pa	river
padang	field
parang	30cm-long hunting knife
PMC	President of the Mess Committee
PoW	Prisoner of War
PPL	Private Pilot's Licence
PSP	Pierced Steel Planking
QFI	Qualified Flying Instructor
QHI	Qualified Helicopter Instructor
RAR	Royal Australian Regiment
RASC	Royal Army Service Corps
RCC	Regional Control Centre
RAAF	Royal Australian Air Force
RAF	Royal Air Force
RFC	Royal Flying Corps
RN	Royal Navy
RNAS	Royal Naval Air Station

GLOSSARY

RNVR	Royal Naval Voluntary Reserve
RNZAF	Royal New Zealand Air Force
RM	Royal Marines
RMAF	Royal Malaysian Air Force
RMC	Royal Marine Commando
RPM	revolutions per minute
RV	rendezvous
SAC	Senior Aircraftman
SARBE	Search And Rescue Beacon Equipment
SH	Support Helicopter
SHNAP	Seletar Helicopter Night Approach Pattern
TNKU	North Kalimantan Nationalist Army
UAS	University Air Squadron
UN	United Nations
USL	Underslung Load
SAR	Search And Rescue
SAS	Special Air Service
SBS	Special Boat Squadron
semut	ants
SH	Support Helicopter
SLR	Self-Loading Rifle
SMG	Sub-machine gun
SRT	Short Range Transport
tanjong	cape, promontory or headland
UHF	Ultra High Frequency
VHF	Very High Frequency
VIP	Very Important Person
VSO	Voluntary Service Overseas
Wings	RAF pilot badge

Prelude

It's midday on the island of Borneo. The equatorial sun beats
down on tropical rivers, swamps, and jungle. Morning mists are
burning off and before long there'll be towering rainclouds. On
the coastal plain of the state of Sarawak, a couple of RAF
helicopter pilots are hunched over a trestle table in the
sweltering wooden cubicle that serves as Operations Room for
103 Squadron RAF at Kuching Airport. Brows furrowed and
pens in hand, they're writing up the dawn missions that have
taken them today, 28 September 1963, to helipads within
shooting distance of the Indonesian border, not more than
twenty miles away to the south.

*Crest of 103 Squadron
RAF: motto translates
as 'Touch me not'.*
(Crown Copyright)

   With a shuffle of flip-flops the *char wallah* arrives, bearing
much needed egg butties and strong tea. The two aviators
stretch out their legs, light up cigarettes and swap stories of the
morning's action. In rumpled green army-style combats and jungle boots, these
fellows don't have the buttoned-down look of your average peacetime RAF
officer. For these young chaps, neither of them much more than twenty-one
years of age, are in the front line.

Sarawak: morning mists and mountains. (Colin Ford)

PRELUDE

Detached from their permanent base, at RAF Seletar on Singapore Island, 400 sea miles to the west, their job is to service the British and allied soldiers defending the Sarawak border against Indonesian insurgents. Of greater concern to them than military protocol is the keeping together of body and soul in a harsh and hostile environment – and doing their job.

It's a tough and sweaty one. Throughout most available daylight hours, these tyro first-tour pilots sit perched in the cockpit of a Westland Whirlwind Mk 10 single-rotor and single-engine helicopter, lifting troops, supplies and casualties in and out of forward bases and the tightest of jungle clearings. It's high-risk stuff – in the hot and often high expanses of Borneo their aircraft turn out to be somewhat deficient in power. On top of that, there's the challenging tropical weather and rugged terrain. And they're at war – a real, shooting war.

The Federation of Malaysia, comprising peninsular Malaya, the island of Singapore, and the states of Sarawak and Sabah in the northern, ex-British part of Borneo, came into being just a fortnight ago and the President of Indonesia, the populist nationalist Achmed Sukarno, is incensed. He had in mind a different federation, one comprising the 3,000-mile-wide archipelago of Indonesia, the equally widespread Philippines, together with Malaya and British Borneo. He has vowed to destroy Malaysia and to eject the British 'colonials'. He has worked his people into a frenzy – a mob has just sacked the British Embassy in the capital, Djakarta, and RAF transports from Singapore have mounted a dramatic evacuation of 400 British nationals. Sukarno's 'Confrontation' against Malaysia is gathering pace.

The government in London has honoured treaty obligations with the ex-colonies and reinforced its armed presence on the 1,000-mile Borneo frontier with Indonesian Kalimantan. At some 210,000 square-miles the latter is roughly three times the size of the Malaysian part of the island. No more than 3,500 British, Gurkha and Malayan ground troops are currently holding the front – not nearly enough for security, spread out as they are at one soldier for every 300 yards of mountainous border. On the Kalimantan side are reportedly encamped double that number of Indonesian regulars, the majority facing Kuching and many of them battle-hardened paratroops. They are supported on both sides of the border by many more local irregulars, Sukarno's guerrilla force. The defenders can survive only by mounting foot patrols from strongly-protected forts, re-supplied by air. Tactical transports and helicopters have the potential to give the British and their allies, in this almost roadless terrain of jungle, rivers and swamp, a commanding degree of battlefield mobility.

But the Far East Air Force (FEAF), although furnished with a fair number of transports, has all too few rotaries available for the job. So the helicopter squadrons at Seletar are being reinforced with more machines and the pilots to fly them. Many of those are brand-new young recruits.

At an age when their schoolmates back home are up at university, articled to solicitors, apprenticed to a trade, or working in the City, these lads are in the front line of battle. They sleep in foetid tents or *attap basha*-huts in the racket of the tropical night, before emerging at crack of dawn to grab a bite of breakfast and a tasking sheet. Then they wind up their helicopters, load up with soldiers and ammunition and fly them off at treetop height to remote jungle clearings. Usually alone in their cockpits, without a navigator and only a compass for navigation aid, they have to rely on their skills at map-reading to find their way – and in this largely unsurveyed territory, the maps they're given are primitive in the extreme, with large areas of plain white paper. To cap it all, on the border they come within range of Indonesian heavy machine guns. This is the work of the 'Borneo Boys'.

★ ★ ★ ★ ★

Butties, tea and reports finished, the two pilots, Flying Officers Colin Ford and Sam Smith, colleagues since joining up, haul themselves to their feet, ready for the next mission. But Flying Officer Al Philips – one of the older guys on 103 Squadron with a tour on the Hastings transport fleet under his belt – strides importantly into the room.

'It's all been changed,' he announces.

The situation is that within a few hours, the Kuching detachment of three Whirlwinds is to embark on the Royal Naval Commando Carrier HMS *Albion*, for immediate ferrying to the RAF base on the coastal island of Labuan, 800 miles to the north-east.

'Reinforcements are needed up there,' he says. It seems that Indonesian insurgents are ramping up their attacks and the 110 Squadron Whirlwinds currently covering the area are in need of some back-up. A Fleet Air Arm (FAA) squadron, 845 with Wessex helicopters, is flying in from *Albion* to replace the Whirlwinds here in Sarawak.

Re-energized by the prospects of a ferry trip and a change of scene, the pilots grab their flight bags and make their way to their quarters in the Semengo Camp army barracks, just outside the airport. They've been on detachment a full month and the personal kit they brought with them takes a bit of finding – if it's not in their meagre wardrobe space it's probably out for laundry with the local *dhobi* girls. They track down the khaki drill (KD) kit they wear when not flying, and the slacks and shirts for evenings on base and rarer off-duty hours downtown. Then there's the all-important change of flying kit. By now, to everyone's relief, the RAF standard-issue blue flying-suit – much too hot and heavy – has been ditched in favour of lightweight jungle-green shirts and combat trousers from Army Stores.

Before take-off, scheduled for 1600, when it's expected that the afternoon storms will have eased, Al Philips finds time to convene a briefing on deck-landing – the two lads have not done one of those as yet. After another hasty snack from the airport café, they trudge out into the late-afternoon sun (the storms have eased) and are met by the ever-present stench of rotting jungle vegetation mixed with the heady aroma of aviation fuel that characterizes a Borneo air-base.

Their machines stand ready on the extended airport dispersal, recently constructed out of pierced-steel planking (PSP) to absorb the dramatic increase in military traffic. The Whirlwinds have been refuelled and checked over by the detachment team of two dozen ground crew engineers, who work long hours in their tented base, in baking sun, steam-bath heat and drenching rain. Nevertheless, like the professionals they are, the airmen circle their aircraft to make sure that no panel is loose, all vent covers are removed, and there are no tell-tale seepages of oil.

Bags stowed in the freight cabins, each already occupied by one of the RAF men coming along as crew, the pilots clamber up the three footholds on the sheer eight feet of fuselage wall below the cramped cockpit. Hauling their heavy navbags, 'bone-dome' flying helmets and themselves through the side window apertures, they strap themselves into the right-hand seat of two. It's hot and airless in there, but soon they'll have the relief of being up at a slightly cooler 1,000 feet.

Plugged in to the intercom, they run through their pre-start checks. Hands fly across front, overhead and central instrument panels, checking dials, switches and levers in routines that are by now second nature. The leader calls for the lads to check in, and with all on-net, gives the signal to start engines. The electric starter motors begin one by one to whine, and at 5,000 revolutions per minute (rpm) 'Avtur' fuel, kerosene refined for aviation use, sprays into combustion chambers and ignites. Hot gases surge through the turbines and the single Bristol Siddeley Gnome engines wind up to a ground idle speed of 14,000rpm in a high-pitched, rasping roar. Rotor brakes are released and the blades whirl steadily up to their constant 220rpm, adding a 'thwack, thwack, thwack' to the din. Each pilot confirms to the leader that after-start checks are complete and, tuned in to the Kuching airfield local VHF channel, Al calls for clearance to depart, en-route HMS *Albion*.

From the 2,000-yard tarmac airstrip, the Whirlwinds lift off. The pilots cant rotors forward to dip the nose and gain airspeed before climbing into the West Sarawak sky. Behind them, down to the south, storm clouds are lingering, but up ahead, over the ocean, it's gin-clear. At cruise-climb speed, the loose-trail formation (at a comfortable separation of fifty yards) clears the airfield, before flying over the native wooden huts on the outskirts of Kuching, and abeam the imposing colonial-style buildings and open markets of downtown. This was the previous capital of the ruling family of British Rajahs Brooke and now it's the administrative centre of Sarawak, an independent state in the new Federation.

Once over the broad Sarawak River, where a fleet of *sampans* criss-crosses the muddy waters and the former Sultan's palace, the *Istana*, shines out among its trim green lawns, the leader sets course for the coast. The *Albion* is steaming some thirty nautical miles out, en-route Labuan. The estimated flight time for the Whirlwinds to get to her is half an hour.

The route to the sea, now less than ten miles away, takes the Whirlwinds over the maze of estuaries that marks the edge of the coastal plain. Half-a-dozen sizeable rivers drain off the border-mountains to the west, south and east of Kuching. Up ahead, the heights of two headlands guard the track through to the South China Sea. To starboard is the picture-postcard Tanjong Po, surmounted by an oriental-style lighthouse. Up there is a landing-point (LP) familiar to the helicopter pilots – it's a regular re-supply run, as is the taller, hump-back ridge to port. The wooded and rocky Tanjong Sipong, close-on 3,000 feet high, is home to an army post, a refuge for a watch-keeping party. They are tasked with giving early warning of possible seaborne marauders from Indonesia, which is not more than two dozen miles around the coast to the west. The pristine beaches alongside the headland host boat-parties from Kuching, as well as serving as an LP for Whirlwinds and a dropping-zone (DZ) for the air-supply RAF transports that keep the soldiers in rations, fuel and beer.

RAF Whirlwind 10 at Tanjong Po lighthouse. (Fraser Skea)

PRELUDE

The formation clatters on past the headlands and sets course over what for the pilots is an unnatural element, the 'oggin', and without a ship in sight. They are used to map-reading their way across hundreds of square-miles of West Sarawak terrain, picking out rivers, streams, high ground and villages to find their way. But out here map-reading is not an option. And although they've been given the winds forecast for over the ocean and have worked out a course to steer, there's no radar to check track made good.

They are listening out on UHF, seeking to make contact with *Albion* and get a radio-directional steer. The helicopters are eating up the nautical miles at ninety per hour and should be within range – Al Philips decides to press the transmit switch and call the ship. The response is immediate – *Albion's* flight-deck control is reading them loud and clear and has them on the radar. An assured naval voice gives a steer of 020 magnetic and a range of twenty miles, adding that the RAF Whirlwinds are 'welcome aboard'.

Sam is behind the leader and at the tail sits Colin, who can take a few moments to look around him. To starboard, the distant horizon is lined with the dull green of mangrove swamp, guarding the many deltas of the longest waterway in British Borneo, the mighty Rajang. This river leads to Sibu, the second town of Sarawak and a frequent destination for the Kuching Whirlwinds – over there, 100 sea-miles away, the squadron operates a forward base. Fifty miles to the west lies Tanjong Datu, a prominent headland which marks the border with Indonesia, and two-score miles beyond that, on the farthest horizon he can make out the grey smudges of the Seresans – on the very outskirts of the Indonesian archipelago of some 30,000 islands. The *Albion* would have threaded its way through those two hostile hotspots on its transit from the Naval Base on Singapore Island to the Borneo coast.

Colin scans the expanse of the bay – still no carrier and there's a lot of sea out here... Yes, there she is! A low grey shape lying off to starboard – unmistakable with flat top, tower, and long-range search radar at the mast-head. A broad wake streams out behind her as she steams along at her usual 20 knots, on a heading of just north of east for Labuan. It's taken not much more than twenty minutes to reach her and he'll be on board in no more than five. It's time to get mentally tuned for landing.

The leader makes a wide starboard turn around the stern of the ship, dropping down to approach height and speed and moving forward to formate on the bulk of the carrier. As they come up on the port beam, the landing area down below to starboard looks reassuringly large – at first sight, not much shorter than some of the dirt-strips in the Sarawak forests. The sea-state's been given as flat calm, so there's no heaving deck to deal with and it should be a piece of cake – just a matter of keeping focused.

There are nine landing-spots marked out along the length of the ship. Al Philips, called in by the Flight Deck Officer to land on Number 3, edges his machine forward, flying parallel to and fifty feet above the level of the deck, until he comes abeam that marker. The other Whirlwinds, as briefed, hold off well clear, in line astern to port, free of each other and any turbulent, 'dirty' air.

Following the naval marshaller's signals, the leader then crabs to starboard, coming to a steady position amidships above the 2-inch armoured steel-plating. Head-on into the wind streaming over the prow, his indicated air-speed is 25 knots. He comes stationary over Spot 3 and, when given the signal, lowers the wheels of the Whirlwind to the deck. Chocks in, engine off and blades winding down, his aircraft is swarming with ratings. Rotor brake on – it's gone like a dream. Sam makes it safely to Spot 2 and now it's Colin's turn.

Al said at the briefing they'd land us like his – aft to for'ard, to keep rotors in clean air over the deck... Here we go – bring the Whirlwind alongside, then to starboard and finally forward to Spot 1 ... Difficult references up here in the bows ... Can see the deck to the right – nothing at all to the front... But there's the signal to land, so it's collective lever fully down ... The wheels bump firmly onto the steel-plating and stay there.

Colin gets the chop sign from the marshaller and, as the engine winds down, the crewman and naval ratings are up on the fuselage, ready to fold the three blades of the rotor as soon as it stops. After-landing checks complete, Colin's off through the window hatch and down the side, his jungle boots hitting the deck less than thirty minutes since lift-off from Kuching.

Their combats billowing out in the 20-knot gale, the three RAF men gather by the bridge where they meet two 110 Squadron pilots who flew their Whirlwinds onto the ship in Singapore, bound for Brunei to replace a pair of ageing Bristol Sycamores. For the two young tyros it's a moment to savour. Just a few months after gaining their RAF Wings, they've pulled off deck-landings underway on this famous ship. The wide sea, the towering bridge, and the arc of tropical sky make a splendid sight.

The leader's machine, rotors securely folded, has been rolled onto one of the two aircraft lifts and is sinking to the hangar beneath the deck. The others are well on the way. Reunited with their flight-bags, the visitors follow a welcoming naval lieutenant down below, to what is at least for the RAF men, the alien world of one of Her Majesty's ships at sea.

The lads spend an hour getting their bearings, and becoming attuned to the sounds of a warship – hissing steam, clanging bulkhead doors, squawking klaxons and all – before, smart in their KD uniforms, they are generously entertained in the air-conditioned comfort of the Wardroom by their hosts. There's a good deal of Borneo stuff to talk about but before long they're ready to climb into their bunks and fall asleep to the beat of *Albion*'s steam turbines and powerful twin-propellers.

HMS *Albion* was commissioned in May 1954, as a conventional carrier with a complement of two dozen naval fighter aircraft, which she first launched in anger in the 1956 Suez Crisis. Helicopters figured minimally in her order of battle then – just the single Search and Rescue (SAR) Westland Dragonfly. But in January 1962 she was re-commissioned as a sister ship to the Navy's first Commando Carrier, *Bulwark*, and embarked 845 NAS with Wessex helicopters, and 846 with Whirlwinds.

In her role of transporting Royal Marines and flying them into action, *Albion* turns up any place, any time – often at dawn. This, and her paintwork have earned her the nickname of the 'Old Grey Ghost'.

Lately she's been shuttling the length of the Borneo coast, embarking and disembarking aircraft and men en route. On this northern leg it will take two nights' steaming to cover the remaining 600-odd nautical miles up to Labuan. During the day, the RAF men take a guided tour, checking out the oily, noisy and well-drilled action in the depths of the cavernous engine-room, and calling in on their precious Whirlwinds in the hangar. Climbing the tower to the Bridge, they watch the green and swampy coast of Sarawak creep by on the horizon to starboard. They are also treated to an air-show as three more of their squadron's Whirlwinds come whirling over from Sibu to join the *Albion*, led by Flight Lieutenant Bill Oliver. Bill, a former army officer and veteran of the Korean War, is their Flight Commander. With him in the formation is Flying Officer Mick Charles, another first-tour colleague of Colin and Sam from training. The Labuan-bound Whirlwind party is now all present and correct on board.

By the second evening the ship is tracking along the shores of the Sultanate of Brunei. The three Borneo Boys, standing on a companion-way beneath the

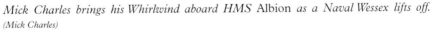

Mick Charles brings his Whirlwind aboard HMS Albion *as a Naval Wessex lifts off.*
(*Mick Charles*)

Kelong fishing platform: Sea Dayak home and workplace. (Google Images)

overhang of the flight-deck are able to make out the twinkling lanterns of native *kelongs* – wooden fishing-platforms that are home and workplace for native Sea *Dayak* communities. They can also spot the burn-off flares of refineries. Brunei is an oil-rich British Protectorate whose rulers have decided not to join the Malaysian Federation but where, not quite a year ago, in December 1962 an Indonesian-inspired rebellion against the Sultan started this whole business of Confrontation.

The *Albion* had taken part in that action when her embarked FAA helicopters flew ashore to support British forces flown in to quell the uprising. They broke the back of the attempted coup before the year-end but in the following months Indonesian raiding parties have regularly crossed the border into Sarawak, and defending British troops have dug in. It's a war – undeclared, but a war nevertheless.

★ ★ ★ ★ ★

At dawn on the last day of September 1963, the three tyro Whirlwind pilots are back in their flight-kit, bags packed, ready to re-enter the action in Borneo. They have been briefed that lift-off from *Albion* is to be at 0800 which, counting back from engine-start at 0750, means that they are to be ready-on-deck at 0730. Their day begins with weather and ops briefing at 0630 (morning mist but fine later, all quiet over Brunei Bay) followed by a generous naval breakfast and a warm leave-taking from their hosts.

By this time, the ship is hove-to, lying at anchor off Labuan. On deck, the Whirlwinds are standing with rotors unfurled, attended by the RAF crewmen and the naval ratings on flight duty. These seamen know all about 'choppers' and their challenges, they're a significant part of Commando Carrier working life.

The two Brunei-bound machines are up-front on Spots 1 and 2 and behind them is the six-ship formation routed to Labuan. Colin, Sam and Mick are happy to be back in the cockpit, going through all the familiar drills and routines. Right on time, the Whirlwinds' engines screech into life. A minute or two later the rotors spin, and at 0800 precisely, one by one, the aircraft clatter off the reassuring bulk of the *Albion*.

The Brunei pair climbs away in the morning mist, turning to the right for Brunei. Bill Oliver leads his charges to the left, and within minutes makes landfall over the Labuan beaches. Flying on over the few hundred yards of scrub between sea and airport, the formation reaches the PSP landing spots to

RAF helicopter dispersal and tented base, Labuan 1963. (Colin Ford)

Labuan Airport 1964. Foreground: control tower and Airport Hotel. Middle ground: civilian DC-3 airliner, RAF Valetta, Shackleton, Pembroke and three Javelins (one on QRA). Background: the mountains of Borneo. (Colin Ford)

starboard of the long concrete runway. Settling alongside the tented base of 110 Squadron, the Whirlwinds are taken in charge by the airlifted ground crew of 103, who are already toiling to erect more canvas of their own.

Without alarms, but with a considerable helping hand from the Royal Navy, the transfer from Sarawak has been successfully completed. For the Borneo Boys it's back to crude airstrips and makeshift clearings – and the heat, sweat and hazards of jungle war.

* * * * *

The Old Grey Ghost, having embarked the Sycamores from Brunei, weighs anchor and steams back to Singapore from where, after some respite and tender loving care in the Naval Dockyard, it will be onwards to North Africa. In Tobruk there'll be RAF Whirlwinds and Belvederes to pick up and, after a 10,000-mile round trip, she'll have them back in the Far East by New Year 1964. Then she'll resume her routine of ferrying troops and equipment, light aircraft and helicopters to and from Borneo – a lifeline in the struggle against the jungle guerrillas.

Chapter 1

The Brunei Rebellion

Tensions in the oil-rich sultanate of Brunei had been building since the Second World War when, early in 1942, the Japanese Imperial Army invaded South East Asia. As they pushed west, they occupied the whole of Borneo, establishing bases at Tarakan on the east coast and Labuan on the north-west. They imposed a brutal regime on both the British and Dutch colonies and it was not until 1944, as the tide of war in the Pacific was on the turn for the invaders, that the Allies could strike back.

One Englishman, the anthropologist and Specialist Operations Executive (SOE) recruit Tom Harrisson, together with three Australian soldiers parachuted into the northern highlands of Borneo to recruit tens of thousands of willing native head-hunters into a guerrilla force. These *semut* (ants) harassed the Japanese with British-supplied shotguns, their indigenous razor-sharp *parangs* and poisonous blow-pipe darts softening them up for the liberating Australian battalions that arrived in 1945. Pursued up the rivers to the mountains, the hapless occupiers suffered heavy losses before the atomic bombing of their homeland gave them the relief of surrender in August 1945.

In British Borneo, 200 years of imperial rule had been relatively liberal, the colonial administrators respecting the free-trading traditions and animist beliefs of the multitude of tribal groups and when British administrators returned to Sarawak, Brunei and British North Borneo affairs reverted much to the earlier *status quo*. However, the southern three-quarters of the island, Kalimantan, along with most of Indonesia, had been the preserve of Dutch colonials, hated for their cruelty and oppression. A populist political leader, Dr Achmed Sukarno, used the post-war power vacuum and surrendered Japanese weapons to seize control in Djakarta. It took four divisions of British and Indian troops, supported by around one hundred RAF aircraft, to restore order, enabling the Dutch to return to the Netherlands East Indies at the end of 1946.

To the Indonesians, the British were now bracketed with the Dutch as colonial oppressors and when, in 1949, backed by the United Nations, the nationalists threw out the Dutch and gained their independence, Sukarno, now head of state, became intent on disposing of British rule over northern Borneo.

His resolve was strengthened when Communist insurgents appeared to gain the upper hand over the British in the 1950s Malayan Emergency.

Sukarno had in mind a Confederation of Malay states in South East Asia which he dubbed 'Maphilindo' – a combination of Malaya, the Philippines and Indonesia. He lobbied the United Nations and the United States for support and found some sympathy – the Americans in particular saw the potential that such a power-bloc might have for stability in the Pacific Rim. In response, the Malayan government under Tunku Abdul Rahman, encouraged by the British, developed a counter-proposal – for a Federation of Malaya, Singapore and the British Borneo states, 'Malaysia'. Sukarno saw this as a direct challenge from colonialists and was determined to thwart the Tunku's plans. He saw an opportunity for direct action in Brunei.

A Sultanate of two enclaves amounting in total to just 2,226 square-miles, Brunei sat between the British colonies of Sarawak and North Borneo, facing Labuan Island across the bay to the north. It was rich in agriculture and timber, and extracted four million tons of crude oil annually. Much of this was refined under concession in the coastal town of Seria by Shell Petroleum, a British company. The oil brought immense wealth to the Sultan and his entourage, but nonetheless, the majority of the 85,000 population, the Malays, revered him. Most of the Chinese, who made up one quarter of the inhabitants but

Riverside longhouse. (Colin Ford)

2

were denied citizenship, may have harboured some resentment, but generally prospered in trade and commerce. The various indigenous tribes, isolated in longhouse and *kelong*, were remote from politics.

But Sukarno, seeking not only to destabilize project Malaysia but also to seize the oil and its revenue, succeeded in gaining the support of the militant wing of the popular People's Party, the so-called North Kalimantan National Army (TNKU). Fronted by a local firebrand politician, A. M. Azahari, this force cobbled together fifteen companies of semi-trained 'volunteers' armed with a few Indonesian machine guns as well as a couple of hundred shotguns remaining from the wartime *semut* action. They were backed by 8,000 untrained but enthusiastic *parang*-wielding supporters. At two in the morning of 8 December 1962, the rebels rose up, attacking and occupying the police station in Brunei town.

Their objectives were to capture the Sultan and install him as a figurehead before looting supplies and further weapons from police stations. They planned then to capture oilfields and European hostages to use as bargaining counters with the British. Their long-term aim was an independent People's Republic of Borneo. As a plan it was sound, but their line of command was weak (at the time of the uprising, Azahari was safely ensconced in Manila) and, crucially, the mass of the armed supporters were not made aware of the time and date of kick-off. In addition, the TNKU had failed to target Brunei airfield, situated in a key position just north of the town, on the river and no more than ten miles from the sea.

Although the timing of the uprising had taken them by surprise, British and Malay commanders and local administrators had for some time been preparing for trouble. Sukarno's threats against the proposed Malaysian Federation had prompted a build-up of forces in the British sovereign bases of Singapore, which comprised three RAF airfields, the Naval Base of the Far East Fleet, the FAA air-base and a half-dozen barracks of regular British and Gurkha troops.

As news of the rebellion reached the British High Command in Singapore, events moved fast – even though it was a largely off-duty Saturday – and within hours two companies of King Edward's Own Gurkhas and 1st Royal Green Jackets boarded Beverley transports of 34 Squadron RAF for the four-hour flight to Labuan. Overnight, they were inserted unopposed at Brunei Town airfield and fought their way through the streets before setting off on the sixty-mile road to Seria. There, the rebels had reportedly captured Anduki airfield and the refinery and taken their European hostages – the police station, however, was holding out.

It was monsoon season and a disrupting seventeen inches of rain had fallen in four days, but, nevertheless, the convoy made good progress but were held up by a rebel strongpoint at Tutong. It became clear that to relieve the serious situation at the refinery a flanking attack was needed. It came on Monday 10th in the form of a Beverley transport of 34 Squadron RAF, which braved the weather and rebel machine-gun fire to insert ninety men of the recently-arrived Queen's Own Highlanders at Anduki airstrip. The captain, in an outstanding display of airmanship, managed to land, discharge the warrior Scotsmen, and roar back into the air within the length of the saturated, jungle-fringed strip – all inside a remarkable ninety seconds. At the same time, five Twin Pioneers of 209 Squadron landed two dozen more Highlanders on rough ground behind the police station. Seria was cleared of rebels, and all hostages were released unharmed, within two days.

Meanwhile, on the day of the uprising, HMS *Albion* was on the Indian Ocean, five days out of Mombasa en-route the Far East, carrying the men of 40 Commando Royal Marines and their equipment. Also on board were the Wessex Mk 1 helicopters of 845 Naval Air Squadron (NAS) and Whirlwind Mk 7s of 846, flown by 'Junglies', a term coined by Lord Louis Mountbatten for the courageous pilots who operated early marks of Whirlwind in Malaya.

The ship received a signal from the C-in-C Far East Station: 'Proceed with full dispatch Singapore'. The engineers wound up her turbines to record speeds and she ploughed her way to the Singapore Naval Base in four days, arriving on 13 December and staying just long enough to embark a further Commando, 42. Within five days of receiving the first signal, she anchored off Kuching and disembarked 40 Commando, who took up positions along the Indonesian border. The following day, 846 NAS Whirlwinds flew into Seria, and the Wessex of 845 into Brunei, where they and 42 Commando were straight into the action. Theirs was to be the first of many helicopter-aided operations in the Borneo Campaign.

Eighty-nine Marines famously made a river assault at Limbang from two un-armoured and unarmed lighters pressed into service as landing craft. In a brisk fire-fight, the town was cleared of upwards of 350 rebels and the Resident, his wife and six other hostages were rescued in the nick of time. The TNKU force was routed with fifteen dead and eight captured (42 Commando losing five and suffering eight wounded) and the back of the rebellion was broken. Tom Harrisson, now resident in Sarawak, had roused his old friends the irregulars and, armed with shotguns and spears, they now moved in to cut off the rebels' escape routes.

The naval helicopters were tasked with troop lifts and casevac, together with interceptions of suspicious water-borne craft, and flew close on 2,000 sorties in the first twenty-six days. It was a sign of devolved authority to come that *Albion*'s commander, Captain Madden, directed the army bosses on the spot to use the helicopters as required, without the necessity of referring back to him. The Junglies were to remain in the challenging monsoon conditions of Brunei for six weeks, before flying off to the *Albion* for rest and repair.

Within days, there was a score of helicopters in action, as four brand-new

RAF twin-rotor Bristol Belvederes of 66 Squadron, and the same number of ageing Sycamores of 110, as well as Westland Scouts of 656 Squadron, Army Air Corps (AAC) found their way up to Brunei to join the fray. Some were ferried by *Albion*, others were loaded into Beverleys in Singapore and flown north but three of the Belvederes, fitted with internal overload fuel-tanks, managed a dawn running-lift-off from RAF Seletar to pioneer a historic flight of 400 nautical miles over the South China Sea to Kuching. They did that in four hours and, after refuelling and refreshment, rattled their way another 400 miles up to Labuan before nightfall.

Crest of 66 Squadron RAF: *motto translates as* 'Beware, I have warned'. *(Crown Copyright)*

Working closely with army commanders, helicopter support greatly assisted in bringing the main action in Brunei to an end by the turn of the year. There was no further organized aggression from the TNKU, but it took until the middle of May 1963 to round up the entire rebel force, estimated at 5,000 strong.

There had been little sign of Indonesian direct involvement during the Brunei Rebellion. British Intelligence Staff reckoned that Sukarno had threatened to send in volunteers but the uprising had collapsed before he could act. Nevertheless, the torrent of vitriolic propaganda from Djakarta continued and, in April 1963, Sukarno made public his policy of *Konfrontasi* against the proposed Malaysia. He gave notice of his intentions when a party of thirty Indonesian Border Terrorists (IBTs) crossed the frontier south of Kuching, attacking the police station at Tebedu. The small defending force of Malay Border Scouts was taken by surprise, the raiders killing a corporal and wounding two policemen before looting the bazaar and making their way back over the border.

Daggers had been drawn. The build-up of forces gained pace on both sides.

Chapter 2

Tern Hill Tyros

Despite being caught on the hop by the Brunei rebellion, British forces and their indigenous allies managed to prevail in the action without heavy casualties, and took heed of the lessons learnt. The first was the need for a joint command structure, the better to co-ordinate the various Army, Navy and Air Force assets available. As a result, by 19 December 1962, a Joint HQ had been established at a girls' school in Brunei town, reporting directly to the C-in-C Far East. Appointed as first overall Director of Operations was Major General Walter Walker, who had learnt his jungle warfare principles as a Gurkha Brigade Commander in Malaya.

The second lesson was that a surveillance and reconnaissance capability was urgently needed – timely and accurate intelligence was essential in denying the enemy the advantage of surprise. Thirdly, winning the 'hearts and minds' of the Borneo tribal groups over to the defenders' cause would assist in gathering that intelligence and ensure that tribesmen were supportive of, not hostile to, British troops on jungle patrols. Fourthly, Walker knew from his time in Malaya that to dominate the jungle, his forces must operate from secure bases – plans were laid to establish a series of forts along the border.

And finally, it was obvious that the rotaries of the Army, Navy and Air Force could, with their inherent speed and flexibility, ensure the maximum of mobility in this battlefield of mountain, jungle and swamp. Walker needed more helicopters.

As part of that rotary reinforcement, orders were placed by the then Air Ministry for Whirlwind HAR Mk 10s, a development of the machines which since the early 1950s had been manufactured by Westland Aircraft in Somerset for the Royal Navy, under licence from the American Sikorsky Corporation. RAF Flying Training Command was tasked with sourcing the pilots to fly the new machines.

Up to then, 'choppers' had been considered by career-minded officers as being well off the beaten track and, as a result, they were crewed by NCO pilots and older air-crew officers nearing the end of their service. A fresher, as well as larger intake was needed. Pilots who had completed their first tour on fixed-wing aircraft were targeted, as were others entirely new to the service, detailed for helicopters after fixed-wing *ab initio* training. These were the Borneo Boys.

★ ★ ★ ★ ★

Colin Ford was among the first of the new joiners. Colin was born in December 1941 in Rawalpindi, where his father served with the British Army in India. The Ford family returned to England in 1945, and in due course Colin gained a place at Westcliff High School for Boys, in Essex. But army postings moved his father and family to Germany and he was sent to board at Prince Rupert School in Wilhemshaven – an experience, he says, which helped prepare him for later institutionalized life. At the end of the posting, Colin returned to Westcliff for 'A' Levels. With one brother in the Army and another in the Navy, and having a yearning since an early age to fly the Vampire jet, the RAF was his obvious choice. He was offered a commission on the Supplementary (Flying) List, and looked forward to his coveted pilot training. But the first stage was Initial Officer Training (IOT) and in November 1960, aged eighteen, he reported for boot camp at RAF South Cerney, north-west of Swindon.

On the same course as Colin was Ian Morgan, also eighteen years old. Born in Middlesbrough, North Yorks, where his father was a Teesside steel works engineer, Ian was sent away to boarding school in the remote Barnard Castle, where he joined the CCF. But that was all-army, and Ian had no thought of the RAF until a chum persuaded him in 1960 to join him on a trip down to Hornchurch, where he was to take the pilot-aptitude tests. Ian thought that sounded like fun, particularly the flying and the prospect of travel, and applied. He was offered a place at the RAF College, Cranwell, provided he gained two A-levels. Passing just the one, Biology, he also took the Direct Entry Commission route, signing on for a sixteen-year stint.

On graduation from IOT, Acting Pilot Officers (APOs) Morgan and Ford went on to No. 2 Flying Training School (FTS) at RAF Syerston in Nottinghamshire, and the newly-introduced Percival Jet Provost Mk 3 trainer. The flying was often disrupted by the fog which regularly crept in over the River Trent, and there was a a drop-out rate of around 33 per cent, but both lads took naturally to the air. They enjoyed the social life too – the Cranwell cadets who joined them in the local pubs had to be back in college by 11pm but the Syerston boys had no such restriction.

Ian and Colin moved on in March 1962 to No 8 FTS Swinderby, Lincolnshire, for advanced flying training on Colin's yearned-for Vampire T 11. Before long, it was time to make a choice of posting. Both began to weigh the odds on being sent to join the V-Force. They reckoned that to be highly likely, and for them, 'a sentence to sit for hours in a cramped nuclear-bomber cockpit at the end of a Lincolnshire runway waiting for the Third World War to start'. So when the word went out for six volunteers for advanced flying-training on the twin-piston-engine Varsity, Ian and Colin were the first to hold their hands up.[1]

At the RAF Oakington Ground School, the patient 'Chiefy' Swift led the new boys through the mysteries of the four-stroke cycle, engine-oil coolers and constant-speed propellers. Social life in the pubs and clubs of Cambridge was a delight, as was actually flying the Varsity. This was demanding, particularly the perils of single-engine landing practice, and the glide approach, but mastering twin-engine operation was highly rewarding. For one thing, on their 'solo' trips, they had a colleague as co-pilot and were able to note each other's actual abilities – as opposed to the self-conscious 'blagging' there had been in the Jet Provost and Vampire Crew Rooms.

After twenty months and 250 hours flying in three aircraft types, Ian and Colin passed out from Oakington on 16 November 1962 as full Pilot Officers, proudly sporting the 'Wings' presented to them by the Mayor of Cambridge. But their training was not over yet. The call had gone out for helicopter pilots and the two lads were posted for rotary conversion. They got their Wings on Friday, had the weekend off and on Monday reported for the basic course at the Central Flying School Helicopter Wing, CFS(H) at RAF Tern Hill in Shropshire.

★ ★ ★ ★ ★

Following in the footsteps of Colin and Ian on IOT, less than one month later was another straight from school, Mick Charles. Born in Oswestry in October 1941, he had military service in his lineage. His builder father had been in the early RAF after the First World War and the RNVR in the Second, and his much older brother flew post-war Hornets and Spitfires. After Oswestry School, instead of taking the planned farming option, still aged just eighteen Mick applied successfully for RAF aircrew. He was awarded a Direct Entry Commission on the Supplementary List.

Graduating from South Cerney in April 1961, APO Charles went for basic flying training on the piston-engine Percival Provost at No 6 FTS, located firstly at RAF Tern Hill and then at Acklington in Northumberland. He progressed to RAF Oakington for forty hours advanced on the Vampire before becoming another transferred to the Varsity.

During the Varsity phase the students had had to state their preference for first operational posting, the choice being between Coastal Command Shackletons, Transport Command Beverleys and helicopters. He made his selection in that order but was coaxed into accepting rotaries. At least, he reckoned, they sounded different. He gained his Wings and in November 1962, found himself on the same course as Colin and Ian at Tern Hill.

★ ★ ★ ★ ★

They were the first of the new breed. The course consisted of a mixture of a few flight lieutenants who had completed tours on fighters, bombers or transports, and those who had joined the RAF straight from school, Ian, Colin and Mick among them.

Among the lads there was by now no lack of motivation to succeed on the course. Opportunities for front-line action on helicopters were many, from SAR in the UK and the Cold War front in Germany, to policing unrest in Aden and Cyprus. Also, there was the exotic Far East – snippets of news were beginning to arrive, telling of the part played by rotaries in the Brunei Rebellion. New types such as the twin-rotor Belvedere and the turbine-powered Whirlwind 10 beckoned but first they had to master the alien world of the helicopter cockpit.

Basically, the students were told, all rotaries are inherently unstable. With normal fixed-wing aircraft, the lay-out of control surfaces is designed for the airframe to be self-correcting – when disturbed by turbulence, everything tends to return to its previous path. In the helicopter, none of that applies. It's little more than a box hanging below a variable-pitch main rotor which, with blade-tips whirling around at 400 knots, has all the eccentricities of a gyroscope. With no auto-stabilization devices, what the helicopter pilot of the early 1960s had to do was persuade a series of competing force-vectors to maintain a satisfactory balance and proceed in the required direction, at a given height and speed. To achieve that, he had three flying controls.

The collective lever, positioned below the left hand, governed the angle of attack of the rotor blades – pull it up and the pitch increased and you went up, push it down and *vice-versa*. It also incorporated a twist-grip throttle, used to vary fuel-flow to the engine and keep rotor-rpm within limits – quite a trick when all other control movements were tending to speed the thing up or slow it down.

The right hand gripped the cyclic stick. Positioned between the pilot's knees, this in essence acted like a fixed-wing joystick – left hand down and you went left, and again *vice-versa*. Push it forward and the nose dropped, and so on. The cyclic was linked to a swash-plate mechanism beneath the main-rotor bearing which cleverly varied the angles of attack differentially as the blades went round, pushing the machine left and right, and the nose up or down, as required. But unlike a joystick, the cyclic could never be left to its own devices. To maintain that vital balance, it had to be gripped by the pilot at all times, in the air or on the ground – let it go and the stick fell over, followed by the aircraft.

Finally, foot-pedals varied the thrust of a tail-rotor, set vertically at the rear of a tail-boom so as to balance lateral forces in forward flight and give the pilot directional control in the hover.

Mastering all those inter-related controls and becoming a helicopter pilot could be compared to acquiring the skills of a circus juggler balancing on a unicycle. There was an age-old trick that could give the tyro a feel for it – circling one hand over the head while patting the other against the tummy. That was the nut that the Tern Hill students had to crack, and they first had to do it on the most cantankerous of basic trainers, the Bristol Sycamore.

The Sycamore first flew in July 1947, the earliest of all-British helicopter developments. It did sterling service throughout the 1950s in the casualty evacuation role in the Malayan Emergency, despite the power limitations of its Alvis Leonides radial engine in the hot and high environment. It was a machine that tested the skills of experienced pilots, let alone the *ab initio* guys. Ian Morgan remembers it well:

> This aircraft was hard work to fly – it was a bone-shaker with manual controls, and a twist-grip throttle on a single, centrally-mounted collective. Although the collective could be clamped in a selected position, the cyclic had to be hands-on at all times. But I had a nice, experienced chap as instructor, a veteran of the Second World War and of helicopter ops in Malaya. Every sortie, he insisted on practising forced landings – I really thought that a bit over the top as the faithful Leonides never even coughed at me.

Mick Charles was happy to be reunited with the Leonides, which he knew from the Piston Provost:

> The slightest variation of rpm was easy to hear – you could fly the Sycamore by ear! But apart from that, it could be hard work. During solo consolidations we students were not cleared to park the aircraft at dispersal – we were told to land on the grass, so the instructor could come out and safely take it the rest of the way.

Colin Ford adds:

> The critical step was learning to hover. My instructor would always make sure there was time for a few minutes' practice at the end of a forty-minute lesson. First, he'd give you just the cyclic, telling you to hold the heli on the spot – not at all easy, at first. Next time, it would just be the collective, to fly at a steady height – not too difficult. Then, it was holding the heading with the pedals – quite straightforward. But

10

things became significantly more difficult when handling all three flying controls together and at the same time trying to maintain rotor-rpm with the throttle. It was extremely tiring and tricky. But then one day everything seemed to click and you could do it – just like finding as a kid you could ride a bicycle. Early attempts at hovering were sometimes known as 'parish-flying' – in other words, keeping the aircraft within the airfield boundary!

Not all the students managed it. Ian Morgan remembers one who didn't:

There was one fatality, a New Zealand guy, Flying Officer 'Kiwi' Watson. He was one of three or four every year who were given basic flying training in NZ at the RAF's expense before coming over to an RAF OCU for fixed-wing or Tern Hill for rotaries. The accident is thought to have happened when he got into difficulties practising torque turns in the Sycamore.

For a torque turn, you got up to full speed downwind, and pulled up into a steep climb whilst at the same time closing the throttle. When the rate of climb fell to zero, you opened the throttle fully and the torque effect of the rotor spun the aircraft round into the equivalent of a stall turn. Now facing upwind, pointing at the ground, you gained airspeed in the dive and recovered to straight and level. It was in essence an aerobatic manoeuvre and required good coordination. It was a hairy exercise, the helicopter equivalent of spinning.

Despite the indiosyncracies of the Sycamore, and running into the infamously cold and snowy winter of 1962–63, all three lads completed their fifty hours. They had successfully mastered the techniques of rotary operation and gained a reward unique in aviation – the ability to fly forwards and backwards, upwards and downwards, as well as sideways and turning on the spot.

They moved on to the final part of their operational conversion, fifty more

Bristol Sycamore at RAF Tern Hill in Training Command Colours...

(Rick Atkinson)

... and a Westland Whirlwind in the same.   *(Crown Copyright)*

hours on the Whirlwind 10, the latest in the line of much-needed rotaries being delivered to the RAF. The Whirlwind series had followed a development path that was far from smooth.

* * * * *

In Second World War Britain, large-scale military demand had been the catalyst for rapid development of fixed-wing aircraft, but rotaries hadn't achieved an effective operational punch and had been kept on the back burner. The focus of military progress for helicopters was in the specialized fields of the Royal Navy, anti-submarine work and sea rescue, and post-war, development of the AAC gave the soldiers leverage in tactical troop movement and logistic resupply. The effect was that the Air Force was left with no rotary role, and the Army's and the Navy's requirements dominated Britain's limited manufacturing capability.

The RAF therefore faced emergencies worldwide with nothing in the rotary operations area but theoretical plans. There were no arrangements in place for acquiring the helicopters which could put them into action. When conflicts arose, the junior Service had to buy whatever was available in the market. Then came the Malayan Emergency.

In 1948 Communist terrorists began to infiltrate the Malayan peninsula, and British forces in the colony found themselves faced with an increasing need to police many square-miles of mountain and forest. This prompted the Air Ministry to unearth a study on the possible use of helicopters in casualty evacuation, which led to the Ministry of Supply investigating what was available to carry out such a task. They came up with the British-designed Bristol 171 Sycamore, but that machine was not expected to be available before 1951 at the earliest. The Admiralty, however, had a batch of the Dragonfly, a British version of the American Sikorsky S-51, in production, under licence at Westland Aircraft Limited in Somerset, the only significant manufacturer left in Britain at the time. After much arm-twisting, the Navy agreed to release three of them to the RAF.

These Dragonflys were sent out to FEAF for evaluation by the brand-new Casualty Evacuation Flight at Kuala Lumpur. Despite a lack of power in tropical conditions, and the paucity of training and experience of the assigned three pilots and thirteen ground crew, they operated with resounding success for the trial period of twenty months. During that time they evacuated 265 casualties and lost just one aircraft to the unforgiving jungle. Against all the odds the flight grew into a squadron, number 194, and widened operations to a full range of tasks, from troop carrying, through tactical reconnaisance and casevac, to SAR. What was becoming apparent was the potential of the helicopter in the battlefield.

The Royal Navy entered the Far East theatre in January 1953, operating ten American-built Sikorsky S-55s from their Sembawang air-base on Singapore Island, where they were joined by 194 Squadron. Two months later the first Sycamore arrived and, despite difficulties with its wooden rotor blades in the tropical conditions, the aircraft came through its three-month trial. The more powerful Sycamores started to replace the Dragonflys within the year and by 1956 that gallant machine had been withdrawn from Malaya.

Meanwhile, the S-55s operated by the Navy had taken over the trooping role in its entirety, by the end of 1953 carrying over 12,000 men. The aircraft impressed with its pilot-friendly handling characteristics. The design was the first from Sikorsky which had the engine housed in the nose with the pilots above and behind it, allowing for a relatively spacious cabin immediately below the rotor-head, roomy enough for ten passengers. This removed the awkward business of centre-of-gravity adjustment under load which had bedevilled the Dragonfly. But performance in hot and high Malaya proved disappointing. An aircraft which could carry ten passengers on a cool day over Salisbury Plain could at times scarcely lift more than a couple in Malaya. More power was needed and it came in two stages. Two marks of piston-engine machines, now known in Britain as the 'Whirlwind', were built for the Navy under licence by Westland – the Mk 3 with the American Wright Cyclone powerplant, and the Mk 5 with a more powerful version of the engine in the Sycamore, the British Alvis Leonides.

In due course the demand for more, and more advanced, RAF helicopters in Malaya (the Naval squadrons were becoming hard-pressed) won the Air Ministry funds for its own Whirlwind variants from Westland. The first flew at Weston-super-Mare in August 1953, followed by ten production aircraft which entered RAF service as the Whirlwind Mk 4. Powered by the supercharged Wasp, they did sterling service in Malaya. But they were kept in business only through the efforts of the maintenance crews – in the tropical conditions the new aircraft were bedevilled by technical problems, particularly with the engines. In its best year, 1956, serviceability of the RAF Whirlwind force was no higher than 41 per cent, and in 1957, it was out of the line on no fewer than four occasions.

But, in August that year, the granting of Malayan independence produced a dramatic improvement in the security situation, the Chinese terrorists losing what little support they had from the indigenous population. This enabled the ageing Naval S-55s to be withdrawn from service and the RAF Whirlwinds and Sycamores now had the field to themselves in the Far East.

The Malayan Emergency was declared at an end in 1960. Since the start of the campaign in 1952, Navy, Army and Air Force helicopters had between them lifted more than 110,000 troops, carried some 19,000 passengers and hauled half a million pounds of freight. Five thousand casualties had been evacuated and the rotaries had successfully carried the offensive to the terrorists' jungle hideouts, a major factor in their defeat. The case for the helicopter in battle had been decisively made.

By now pressure for RAF helicopters elsewhere was growing, both for security operations in the Middle East and for SAR units at home. An Air Ministry survey showed a net shortage of Whirlwinds, and into the gap in 1960 flew the Mk 10. After further frustrating delays the first machines were at last deployed to 110 Squadron in 1963, at RAF Seletar in Singapore.

★ ★ ★ ★ ★

The Whirlwind's Gnome gas-turbine engine was one of the first with an electronic analogue computer as part of the fuel control system. This controlled fuel flow during acceleration to prevent engine surge and took the hard work out of rotor-rpm control, which was now fully automatic. But instrumentation was basic, the only indication of power for the pilot in the first years of the sixties being a fuel-flow meter. Also, as with the Sycamore, the cyclic stick had to be held at all times. This led to difficulties in operating the instruments on the central console if you were right-handed, and vice-versa if you were in the other seat and left-handed.

Mick Charles discovered other challenges:

With a turbine, it was much more difficult to hear the variations in rpm. And, as in all helicopters, you had to be wary of ground-resonance. With the wheels on or near the ground this could build into an uncontrollable instability that could, and on occasion did, tip you over, with disastrous results for the rotors.

A further possible pitfall for a trainee was 'ground effect'. This occurs within a rotor's diameter of the surface on ascent and descent. Downwash blows the bladetip vortices outwards which extends the clean area of the aerofoil and increases lift, thus reducing the power needed to maintain height. All to the good, as long as the pilot is aware and knows how to react.

Engine failure was another hazard that gave rotary students particular pause. Ian Morgan had one, fortunately in dispersal. 'The drive to the HP pump failed – a possibility always somewhere in my mind on Whirlwind sorties from then on.'

But there were no further mishaps, and Ian, along with Mick and Colin, all now promoted to Flying Officers, graduated as fully-qualified helicopter pilots on 8 May 1963.

They were all sent off to the Joint Warfare Establishment at Old Sarum to learn about Short-Range Transport (SRT) Operations with the Army. In the the words of Colin Ford, 'It was a fun two weeks – gave us a chance to fire field-guns at Larkhill and drive armoured vehicles and tanks around the ranges at Warminster.'

Postings had come through and for Mick, Ian and Colin, together with Sam Smith, another straight-from-school colleague at South Cerney, it was to be 110 Squadron at the RAAF base at Butterworth in Malaya – to fly the cantankerous Sycamore.

However, on their fortnight's embarkation leave, they received welcome news. The Singapore unit of 110, B Flight, based at RAF Seletar, was to be re-equipped with the Whirlwind Mk 10, and the four Tern Hill tyros were selected to be part of that. So, on a sunny mid-June day, it was with more than some excitement that the four young officers climbed the steps of a Transport Command Comet 4B at RAF Lyneham in Wiltshire. They were off to the sharp end of things. And in the exotic Far East to boot, where the action in Confrontation was building up into a fair old storm.

Chapter 3

The Sharp End

During the Brunei Rebellion, the worst of the hazards facing the security forces operating out of Labuan and Brunei had been torrential rain carried on storm-force winds. In the first month of 1963 the violent weather continued, adding flood relief and SAR to the helicopters' already-crowded tasking sheets. This was the onslaught known as the North-East Monsoon.

Borneo was, and is in the path of an airstream which the meteorologists call the Indo-Australian Monsoon. Upper air currents in the Himalayas trigger strong north-easterly winds. These blow down over Thailand and the east coast of Malaya, picking up a full weight of moisture from the China Sea, and hit the island anytime in October. Mount Kinabalu, soaring to over 13,000 feet, assisted by the interior ranges deflect the stream down towards Australia, but not before the ascending saturated air cools, triggering storms. In the prosaic words of the metmen, 'The effect is to create a cyclonic vortex over Borneo, which together with descending cold winter air from higher latitudes, causes significant weather phenomena in the region, lasting from October to January.'

The rotaries thus had frequently to cope not only with very heavy rain and poor visibility but also a low cloud base and squally winds, all limiting their operational effectiveness.[2] General Walker was telling everyone who would listen that he didn't have sufficient numbers of helicopters given the difficulties and size of the Borneo theatre of operations. Making matters worse was the fluctuating serviceability of the somewhat fragile machines. They were being maintained at the end of a supply chain of up to 1,000 from Singapore, and close on 7,000 more from the UK. He was promised reinforcements but, until they arrived, he had to make sure he made the most of the meagre force he had.

The Sycamores of 110 Squadron RAF, conspicuous in their all-yellow SAR paintwork, despite being plagued by rotor-blade problems and shortage of spares managed 266 sorties out of Brunei that January, six of those being casevac missions. But this long-serving aircraft was pushed to carry much more than a couple of passengers at a time, and could lift only minimal freight.

The much newer twin-rotor medium-lift Belvederes of 66 Squadron were far more powerful. With full fuel tanks the machine could lift a payload of 1,500lb internally or as under-slung freight, or a patrol of seven fully-armed men, at 120 knots over an operating radius of 200 nautical miles. Over shorter distances, the tanks-full load of 4,000lb of Avtur decreased and the disposable load increased to a maximum of 6,000lb or eighteen troops. From their Brunei base, the four machines in January transported 158,000lb of freight, together with 729 passengers.

The half-dozen AAC Scouts were brand new and as such suffered badly from teething problems. When serviceable they had space only for three or four soldiers but, on Sarawak detachment from their base at Kluang in peninsular Malaya, they showed their worth in communication and reconnaissance tasks.

Unofficial Crest of 110 Squadron RAF. This version was created in 1966 by Sergeant Pilot Ayris in Borneo. He added the shower and replaced the official motto Nec Timeo Nec Spermo (I neither fear nor despise) with one from flying-boat days: Aqua Fervens Constans Borneus (Always in hot water in Borneo). (Fred Ayris)

Full use was made of the carrier-based Naval Air Squadrons. The Junglies were re-mustered from Commando duties, establishing their base at RNAS Sembawang (they called it 'Simbang'), a grass airfield between the Naval Base and RAF Seletar in Singapore. They were then ferried on *Albion* to operate six-month 'roulement' detachments at Labuan, Sibu, and Kuching. But, in January and February 1963, turbine failures in their single Napier Gazelle engine led to two Wessex crashes. In the second of these, a 66 Squadron Belvedere lifted the 4,500lb of the fuselage to a barge for return to *Albion*. In the same month the Belvederes hauled two downed naval Whirlwinds direct to the carrier's deck. These setbacks not only resulted in the navy pilots establishing the practice of flying in pairs over the jungle but also slowed their work rate to ninety-six sorties in January and 125 in February. Then an engine modification programme led to the complete withdrawal, albeit temporary, of the Wessex at the end of March.

Despite the loss of those two Whirlwinds, 846 NAS succeeded in extending their detachments to the hotspot of Tawau on the eastern coast of Sabah. When 845 returned to Borneo in April, it was to embark *Albion* for Kuching, to work with 2nd Battalion/10th (2/10th) Gurkha Rifles and A Company 40 (RM) Commando. They established a forward base at Belaga, a longhouse village lying in the upper reaches of the Rajang, fully seventy miles from the Borneo coast.

The Junglies were even more in demand when on 4 May, Belvedere operations came to a sudden and tragic halt. Thirty minutes after take-off on a supply sortie to Ba Kalalan, XG473 crashed near Lawas, killing the four soldiers and two civilians on board as well as the crew of three. The entire fleet was grounded for two months.

On its way to assist the stricken Belvedere, a 110 Squadron Sycamore had also gone down. In this incident, the pilot managed a controlled auto-rotating forced-landing in swampy ground and he and his crew, and later their machine, were lifted back to Brunei by a naval Wessex.

Despite that loss, the Sycamores, with little in the way of navaids, had by June extended their range as far as Long Semado, a challenging three-hour round-trip from Brunei, as well as to Sepulot and Pensiangan, even more remote in deepest Sabah. That month, they completed 151 sorties, many of them into primary jungle close to the border, carrying some 200 troops and over 3,000lb of freight.

And so it continued, with the Joint HQ juggling its limited RAF, FAA and AAC rotary assets to achieve maximum operational effect – leverage that became more and more essential as the sabre-rattling from Djakarta grew increasingly frenzied.

★ ★ ★ ★ ★

Sukarno had at his disposal a powerful air force, operating aircraft supplied by America, Russia and Britain itself, and a multi-purpose flotilla of Russian-built naval ships manned by 34,000 men, of whom 9,000 were Marines. His army numbered 300,000 regular troops in 134 battalions, together with 3,000 Commandos. British Intelligence reckoned that perhaps 6,000 of these soldiers had been positioned by mid-1963 to within twenty miles of the Borneo border, with a concentration in the 1st and 2nd Divisions of Sarawak, where they operated, in the words of Walter Walker, 'within five fighting days' of Kuching.

The British defending force could depend upon the Royal Navy's Far East Fleet under Admiral Sir Varyl Begg to keep Indonesian ships in port but, in late 1963 General Walker had just five infantry battalions to defend the 1,000 miles of mountainous jungle border. In this land of rivers and tracks, and very few roads and airstrips, helicopters were essential for these troops' mobility, a prerequisite for immediate reaction to hostile incursions. But there were only a dozen troop-carrying rotaries available. It seemed that the odds were very much in favour of the aggressor.

But for border surveillance, Walker had been sent a squadron of 22 Special Air Service (SAS) Regiment infantrymen, supported by the No 1 (Guards) Independent Parachute Company, the pathfinders for the Paras. He knew what they could do from his Malaya days, and a system of four-man patrols was set up. In due course they operated out of strongpoints established every 10,000 yards or so along the border. Supplied by air, they came to be self-sufficient for weeks rather than days. Formed in the same mould as those elite groups, the Gurkha Independent Parachute Company was deployed to Sarawak to train and subsequently command a new unit, the native *Iban* Border Scouts, raised by Colonel John Cross of 7th Gurkha Rifles.

Logistics, as always, were crucial and a dependable chain of supply was established. Cargo ships carried bulk and heavy goods to Labuan, Sibu, Kuching, and Tawau, where the Royal Army Ordnance Corps (RAOC) broke them down into air-transportable loads, either for land-on delivery forward by Twin Pioneer, or airdrop from Beverleys and Hastings. Helicopters and long-boats then carried the essentials of jungle living and fighting further forward to the patrols.

To gain the goodwill of local tribes, it was a rule that each patrol should include one man with basic medical training, ready to perform what, for the natives, were apparent miracles with aspirin, penicillin, bandages and ointments. And room was always found in the corner of a knapsack for gifts to the village headmen.

By these methods, Walker aimed to 'dominate the jungle' and lessen the odds against the defenders but to achieve this aim, more helicopters were a pre-requisite. More were indeed coming – Whirlwind 10s were on the Indian Ocean and would arrive within weeks. And in June, the pilots to fly them began to arrive.

★ ★ ★ ★ ★

On 13 June 1963, after a journey of two days, in a series of hops from one staging-post of the Old Empire to another, four young men clambered off the Transport Command Comet to plunge into the perfumed, steam-bath atmosphere of night-time RAF Changi. It was midnight before Mick, Colin, Ian and Sam emerged from Movements Control, to find a service bus waiting to ferry them westward across Singapore to Seletar, one of the three RAF bases on the island, and the one that was home to the rotaries.

It took until one in the morning to motor through the cacophony of the thronging night-time streets of downtown, senses taking in the alien sights, sounds and smells of the colonial melting-pot, before they could unpack their bags in the spacious Officers' Mess on Seletar base, down by the twinkling *sampan* lights of the Straits of Johore.

Their rooms spoke of decades of history, colonial-style. Large, ventilated by king-sized fans rotating in the high ceiling and vents at top and bottom of the white-washed walls, they opened out onto a private verandah. Doors were of the oriental bat-wing mahogany type – louvred, as were the unglazed windows. These were the real thing – they were out in the Far East all right, in a world totally different from Tern Hill.

Officers' Mess, RAF Seletar...

... and a junior officer's room.

(pictures Mick Charles)

Climbing exhausted into mosquito-net covered beds they were soon off to sleep, despite the night-calls of frogs and cicadas.

★ ★ ★ ★ ★

The next day, revived by showers and a substantial breakfast they were picked up at 11 o'clock by officers of 110 Squadron and driven in bright sunlight along carriageways lined with fragrant *frangipani* and dark green tropical grass. Across the blue waters of the Straits lay the forested banks of the southernmost state of Malaya, Johore. At the northern end of the tarmac runway, their escorts pulled up outside the headquarters of the helicopter units. Newly-built in white-painted breeze-block, the single-storey building housed 66 Squadron operating the Belvedere, and B Flight of 110 with its shiny brand-new Whirlwinds.

In the squadron's air-conditioned office, the four newcomers were welcomed by the B Flight Commander, Flight Lieutenant Peter Davis, who brought them up to date. The first Whirlwind 10s had been received at Seletar in April, but although pilot-conversion was well advanced, the new machines had not yet seen operations over in Borneo. However, he had been given notice that the Flight was to prepare for a detachment of six aircraft to Kuching in Sarawak from 1st July.

Furthermore, he had also received notice that to reinforce the RAF's helicopter assets in Borneo, a new Whirlwind squadron, using the available number of 103, was to be spun out of 110. B Flight was to form the core of the new outfit – he would command it and the four tyros were to be part of it. The new squadron was to receive its badge, featuring a black swan, on 1 August.

This news surpassed the lads' best expectations. Necessary papers were perused and signed, colleagues met and flying kit issued. By the afternoon, the newcomers were free to go on leave for a couple of days' acclimatization.

They found their way back to the Mess, to be introduced to Mr Shafi the tailor, who measured them up for KD uniforms, and to Mr Wong the shoemaker and provider of suède desert boots. In the evening they made first acquaintance with *Tiger*, the world-renowned local brew before being taken off for a party at the Seletar Yacht Club. There, all four were invited to try water skiing from the beach below the Mess and the next day, exhilarated by the experience they decided that the key to attracting girls was the acquisition of a speed-boat – and perhaps a couple of MG roadsters into the bargain.

They didn't manage the speed-boat but in due course they did become proud MG owners. Ian's TD model was black and Mick's bright-red, while Colin Ford acquired an elegant maroon TF 1500. There were soon trips back across the island to the Chinese shops of Changi Village to check out state-of-

Mick Charles's MG TD roadster on a jungle jaunt. (Mike McKinley, the subsequent owner)

34 Squadron Blackburn Beverleys in the wet at Seletar. (Colin Ford)

the-art consumer technology and the latest in Far East casual wear. Life in the Officers' Mess was good, with *amahs* to do their *dhobi* and local cooks to give the basic English food a touch of eastern spice. The only drawback was that the runway ran right alongside the building – they found that Beverley transports running up their massive radial engines were not conducive to a good night's sleep.

Their leave over, the newcomers started a crash-course of theatre-conversion training. A stream of Whirlwinds Mk 10, camouflaged grey and green, was coming out of the Seletar Maintenance Unit, ready, after ground engine-runs and basic air tests, to be accepted onto the squadron inventory.

★　★　★　★　★

In mid-1963, 110 Squadron was busy on three fronts. The Sycamore detachment in Brunei continued, but now mostly tasked with communications work, the FAA bearing the brunt of the rotary burden in the continuing absence of the RAF Belvederes. The Squadron Headquarters base at Butterworth had received its first Whirlwind 10s and at Seletar final preparations were in progress for B Flight to split off into 103 Squadron on 1 August. But before that event, on 1 July as detailed, Pete Davis led six B Flight Whirlwinds onto *Albion* for ferrying to Kuching, to establish a new detachment for 'an indefinite period'.

Arrived off the Sarawak coast, for the Whirlwinds it was a thirty-minute flight from the carrier, down over the South China Sea to Kuching Airfield, some four miles south of the town and 400 sea-miles from Singapore. The helicopter crews sent on detachment had been selected from the older, more experienced pilots on the Flight, all of them married men on three-year tours, with families in quarters or hirings on the Seletar base. Waiting for them at Kuching were the 110 Squadron Engineering Officer, Flight Lieutenant Ryden, and the twenty-one men of the ground crew who had been flown in by Beverley.

All went to plan and at the end of the month, Pete Davis was able to write in his report:

> Successful month of operations – troop lifts and re-supply, with some aeromed missions. Hotter than Singapore but Whirlwinds coping – on average four to five out of six serviceable. Maps poor with no relief shown. Poor VHF and UHF – HF would help. Looking forward to becoming independent 103 Squadron 1st August

★　★　★　★　★

Whirlwind in low hover at Lombong clearing. (Mick Charles)

Whirlwind up-country in Malaya at Fort Betau, sharing runway with a 209 Squadron Twin Pioneer. (Mick Charles)

Meanwhile, the four new boys on B Flight in Seletar were learning the essentials of operating in a hot and high environment. July 1963 saw them on training sorties into and out of under-sized clearings in the mountainous jungles of up-country Malaya. There was a lot to it, as Colin Ford remembers:

> The mix on the squadron was of pilots with three, four or more tours on fighters, transports or maritime – and the four of us, just out of training. However, we were all pretty much equally new to the helicopter and I don't think we were looked down on.
>
> We had to learn to navigate over the jungle, deal with tropical weather and find safe entry and exit lanes into and out of LPs cut in hundred-and-fifty-foot trees. The closest training clearing, Lombong, was in the Johore jungle about twenty minutes, some thirty miles, north of Seletar. To get a wider look at the sort of terrain in which we'd shortly be operating solo, we flew – with our QHIs [Qualified Helicopter Instructor] – in a three-ship formation up-country to Kuala Lumpur and Ipoh. North of Butterworth we called in on the forts at Kemar and Betau – they dated from the Emergency. I've still got the fablon-covered map, with the red dots I marked with chinagraph pencil to indicate the fuel dumps.
>
> As well as the Short Range Transport (SRT) role, the squadron also provided area Search and Rescue cover – two of the squadron aircraft were in full SAR fit and painted yellow. For SAR, we flew as a crew of three – single pilot, navigator/winch operator and winchman. In the SRT role, and for other flights we might fly with another pilot or a crewman but often, we flew solo.
>
> If we needed to go away up-country we had a number of our squadron ground tradesmen who could go along as crewmen. They'd been given additional training on first level tasks and refuelling. I found them extremely resourceful guys who enjoyed the flying and getting away from base. I believe they were entitled to the princely sum of one Malaysian dollar per day as supplementary pay.
>
> But we were also trained to carry out basic maintenance in the field and as early as the first week of August, we began to be deemed 'fit for purpose' and given our self-authorisation certificates signed by the AOC. Those cleared us to authorize our own sorties when away from Seletar so we could now go off on our own into Malaya, sometimes for several days, and simply get on with the job.
>
> My first solo task proved to be a salutary lesson. I was detailed, at short notice, to carry a senior officer up-country to the Asahan Range, about an hour away. There, I was to wait a couple of hours and then return my pax to Singapore. The Seletar authorising officer assured me

I had enough fuel for the trip there and back. However, dodging thunderstorms and naively adopting climbing speed rather than cruise-climbing, the outbound trip took longer than planned and there wasn't enough fuel for the return leg. And, there was no fuel at Asahan. Much to the annoyance of just about everyone, I announced the very bad news that we would have to stay the night.

Next morning, a QHI flew in with a barrel of Avtur. He was, in fact, very understanding and, dare I say so, not unamused! I'd learnt the importance of knowing the fuel state and the lesson stuck. Never again would anyone plan my fuel load but me. Come to think of it, I'm still uneasy driving a car with the fuel gauge showing less than half-full.

In line with British treaty commitments to the Singapore government, the new pilots also experienced the excitement of operations in support of the Civil Powers, clattering their way down into exotic spots – among others, the colourful shopping arcades of Orchard Road, the green cricket pitch of the Padang, and the colonial Police Station on Pearl Hill.

But before going into action in Borneo, the four newcomers were sent for five days of training at the Jungle Survival School on Changi Beach, followed by five days living off the land in the forests of Johore. Immediately after that came the Escape and Evasion exercise, which entailed a night of being chased around the south-east coast of Singapore by determined and muscular men of the RAF Regiment. Ian Morgan made it to the RV point unscathed, while both Mick Charles and Colin Ford were caught, stripped and interrogated – but as valuable helicopter pilots they were treated fairly gently.

★ ★ ★ ★ ★

On 1 August 1963, B Flight of 110, including Flying Officers Morgan, Smith, Ford and Charles, duly morphed into 103 Squadron. It received its Black Swan badge and Peter Davis seamlessly took on the new outfit's command, having been promoted to Squadron Leader. His headquarters remained at Seletar, where the SAR, training, admin and maintenance units continued their tasks with no interruption.

For the Sarawak Detachment, nothing changed but the squadron's identity. Every day, missions were flown into the swamps and hills of the border areas – from Kuching into the 1st Division and from a forward detachment at Simanggang into the 2nd. The troops with whom they worked were frequently coming within small-arms' range of the Indonesians and this prompted Davis to call for Bren machine guns in Whirlwind cabins and for aircrews to be issued with steel helmets and armoured vests.

110 Squadron B Flight morphs into 103 Squadron 1 August 1963: far left, Officer Commanding Sqn Ldr Pete Davis, with Fg Offs Sam Smith (4th from left) Colin Ford (6th) Ian Morgan (8th) and Mick Charles (9th). (Crown Copyright)

By September, the four Tern Hill tyros were deemed to have completed their theatre conversion – subject only to a check-ride with the training pilot on arrival at Kuching. The detachment roster on 110 Squadron had been twenty-eight days out, twenty-eight back at base, but on the formation of 103, the roster had perforce been rewritten and the Borneo Boys' took temporary leave of their MGs and water-skis to take their turn of duty in Sarawak.

Chapter 4

Into the Fray

Sarawak had since 1864 been an independent state under the rule of the *Rajahs* Brooke, before the Second World War and the Japanese invasion intervened. On the eviction of the occupiers in 1945, it reverted to the status of a British colony, a highly unpopular move at the time. Shortly after his arrival, the first colonial governor was brutally assassinated. Kuching was the colonial capital and on the creation of the Malaysian Federation it was due to become the administrative centre of a recreated State of Sarawak. The town sat among the rivers which meandered, interspersed with extensive swamp, across the wide coastal plain. To the west and south the land rose to a border ridge peaking at 3,000 feet. This ridge stretched away for some 800 miles to the east, rising to 8,000 feet at the summit of Mount Murud, on the frontier with British North Borneo.

The country's natural resources were wood, fruit, palm oil and spices. At the coastal town of Miri, oil and natural gas were produced in considerable quantities and at Bau, in the far west, gold was mined. With a population of 51,000, Kuching was the biggest of half a dozen small towns. Three-quarters of the territory was under tropical rain forest, where the annual rainfall was 120–160 inches – there was a 'Wet' Season and a 'Very Wet' Season. The mean daytime temperature was 88 degrees Fahrenheit.

Helicopter pilots found themselves operating in close cooperation with army units over tough, rugged country with few roads – ideal for guerrilla warfare. All military personnel on the base were well aware of the threat from Indonesian forces, not much more than twenty miles away on the Kalimantan frontier. Sarawak's 48,000 square-miles were divided into five Divisions and the forces based in Kuching covered 1st and 2nd, facing, in mid-1963 an estimated 1,500 organized IBTs, supported by an uncertain number of Indonesian regular troops. In addition, there was the threat from around 24,000 Communist sympathizers, mostly Chinese, in Sarawak itself.

Sharing Kuching Airfield dispersals with the Whirlwinds were the forward detachments of the RAF transports – Hastings of 48 Squadron and Valettas of 52 – tasked with the airdrop of supplies to the jungle forts now being set up along the border. And alongside the 103 Squadron base was the HQ of another newly-arrived detachment from Seletar – the Belvederes of 66 Squadron were back in service.

* * * * *

The Belvedere squadron had had a troubling time in the three months since being grounded. At Seletar, three officers had been appointed to the harrowing duty of dealing with their dead colleagues' effects and the repatriation of their families. Two wives were soon back in the UK but the other was expecting a child and had to remain at the base hospital until the birth on 28 May. Not for nothing was the Belvedere known, well before this latest crash, as the 'Bristol Widowmaker'.

On the ground it was an ungainly-looking contraption – to Colin Ford, it looked rather like 'a giant pre-historic insect'. There was a story that, when the Belvederes first arrived in Aden, a ground crew man was heard to inquire, 'Sir, do we refuel it or does it just eat other helicopters?' Produced for the Navy, a requirement was the fitting of longer undercarriage legs at the front than at the rear, to enable a torpedo to be slung below the fuselage. The height of the cabin door meant that a long ladder was needed to get troops and freight in and out – not ideal for operations under fire. In any event, after trials, in which at ninety-two feet in length overall (from front of forward rotor to rear of the aft) it had a problem with aircraft carrier lift-wells, the Navy turned it down in favour of the Wessex. Thus, in late 1961, the twenty-five machines entered service with the RAF as its first tandem-rotor helicopter.

During its development and early service technical flaws in the control cables had proved hard to fix, as had problems with the unreliable engine-starting system. This was driven by a turbine that used Avpin, a high energy but at the same time very unstable fuel, always at some risk of explosion in operation. The only armour-plating fitted on the machine was behind the pilot's seat, not necessarily to guard against enemy ground fire but rather the explosive starter of the forward of the two Napier (now Rolls-Royce) Gazelle turbine engines. On top of that, a month before the Lawas crash airframe cracks had started to appear in the leading-edge of the tailfin.

That crash and subsequent grounding brought matters to a head. Rolls-Royce and Westland technical representatives were flown to Singapore to spearhead the necessary modifications. Minds were further concentrated by another starter explosion and fire at the beginning of June. It was not until the end of July that 66 Squadron was cleared once more for Borneo operations, mounting a three-ship detachment in Kuching, alongside the Whirlwinds of 103 Squadron.

In action from 1 August, the Belvedere began once again to carry the

'From 1 August 1963, the Belvedere began once again to carry the impressive loads of which it was capable.' *(Crown Copyright)*

impressive loads of which it was capable. During their first month in Sarawak, the three aircraft flew 112 operational hours, carrying 1,937 passengers and 96,000lb of freight.

★ ★ ★ ★ ★

Throughout September 1963, 103 Squadron performance in all units was hindered by a period of poor Whirlwind serviceability. The monthly target for each machine was forty hours but the Kuching aircraft were falling well short,

30

primarily through lack of spares. Nonetheless, time was found for the four tyros to complete their check-rides, be declared Theatre Qualified and rostered for operations. At first they were closely monitored by experienced pilots but they perforce quickly learned the rules of the game.

The first challenge they faced was the lack of decent charts. Aerial survey of British Borneo had been hampered over the years, both by war and by continual partial coverings of low cloud. As Mick Charles says:

> The maps we used on those Sarawak operations certainly were unsatisfactory, with great areas of white space with ten-kilometre grids but no contours, just hachures to show known high ground. They marked rivers, main towns – there weren't many – the odd village, and spot heights. But they could be in the wrong place or at the incorrect elevation. A particular danger for us rotaries, operating closer to it than most, was that the border's position was marked on all the charts as estimated.
>
> So flying had to be pretty much by day and visual, as we had minimal navaids – we just got to know the topography of the operating area as quickly as possible.
>
> We avoided going onto instruments and any enforced night flying had to be handled with the utmost care. We'd lift-off from high ground – a mountain top, say – into a known clear area with familiar sight-lines, such as the northern coastline. And then we'd let down into known terrain, referencing on light signals from the ground.

Radio communications were also a problem, as Mick further explains:

> The Whirlwind equipment fit was very basic. On the UHF and VHF radios we could only speak to main airfields or other aircraft. For a long time, we had no means of communication with army units. Navigation aids in the aircraft were limited to a Mark 4 compass[3] together with 'Violet Picture' – but that was simply a UHF homer with a left/right needle display which enabled us to home onto a SARBE[4] emergency beacon. When operating away from base, which was nearly all of the time, we were therefore on our own, with no Air Traffic Control, no one to talk to, no weather forecasts or any of the other support which is now largely taken for granted.

It seemed that RAF helicopters were not always top priority for supply with the latest equipment. There was the small matter of hands-free microphones – Colin Ford has the story:

When we went to Tern Hill in 1962, we discovered that we were expected to use Second World War tank drivers' mikes. These were fairly large, brown lozenge-shaped devices that half strangled you if worn too tight. Unfortunately, there weren't enough to go around so I did my first few trips in the Sycamore using an H-type oxygen mask – even worse. When we arrived in Singapore we found there was a shortage of mikes out there too. But in due course we were issued with the new Amplivox throat mike with two black circular pick-ups. We'd been told at Tern Hill that old throat mikes could sometimes be had for a few shillings down the Tottenham Court Road or at army surplus stores but at Seletar they were treated as V and A [Valuable and Attractive] items and issue was strictly controlled, by OC Flying Wing no less.

When using these mikes, we could talk normally, hands-free. We didn't produce that rather sibilant sound which comes from pursed lips in a mask – instead, according to the non-heli guys who listened in to us, we sounded as though we were gargling!

In the heat and thin air, extra care had to be taken with loading the aircraft for a mission. From base, as well as out in the jungle, weight carried was the responsibility of the pilot. Mick outlines the procedure:

Formal mission authorisation procedures were pretty much short-circuited – the man in charge was the client Company or Platoon Commander – and we needed to self-authorize, as it were. We reckoned that on ops, the basic weight of the

Whirlwind was five thousand, eight hundred and fifty pounds, plus two hundred for the pilot and emergency kit. With a maximum all-up weight of seven thousand eight hundred, that left seventeen-fifty for fuel, passengers and freight. Fuel was burnt on average at four-fifty pounds per hour and with minimum landing limit at two hundred – mind you, the fuel gauges were none too accurate – that gave you at the most some ninety minutes flying. All that meant that with a load of five soldiers and kit weighing twelve hundred pounds, which was pretty much our maximum, we only had a sixty-mile radius of operation.

Colin continues:

The real problem in calculating what you could carry was assessing the true weight of men, equipment and freight. First, you had to determine the weight of fuel needed for the sortie and you could then calculate the payload to stay within the maximum all-up weight. The Army would tell you how many men they wanted you to take, and we carried bathroom scales to weigh them, but operationally that was rarely possible. The same with freight. For example, we'd be tasked to carry 'chutes from airdrops back to base for re-use. There were guideline figures for these packs when wet or dry, but what is 'wet'? In reality there was no way of knowing the true weight of our loads.

The vital bathroom scales. (Martin Mayer)

The accepted practice was to make a best guess, load up, and then lift off to the low hover, where you'd check the margin between the power you were using and the max power available. Kit was then on or off-loaded until an acceptable power margin was available. It was somewhat rough and ready but it worked – we probably operated at max AUW most of the time.

On shuttle missions over a short distance, with engine-running refuels, the fuel load could be gradually trimmed to the bare minimum and that way, we'd progressively maximize the payload available.

Following my earlier Asahan experience, I personally always carried as much fuel as my task permitted. A barrel in my tanks was worth more than twenty barrels on the ground![5]

The only measurement of power was the fuel-flow meter. They weren't replaced with torquemeters until after Confrontation. But the Gnome had this excellent engine fuel-control computer, which removed the need to control rotor-rpm manually and made flying the Whirlwind so much easier than the Sycamore. Nevertheless, we practised failure of the computer as an emergency procedure and this called for a high level of throttle/collective co-ordination, markedly increasing overall pilot workload.

Crew room at Sibu Airfield 1963: 'egg banjo' business brisk. (Mick Charles)

INTO THE FRAY

Our squadron callsign in Singapore was 'Mike Oscar Mike Sierra Bravo' and in Borneo we used 'Mission' – both plus a number. And Kuching Airfield was codenamed 'Oasis'. Odd what you remember.

After a short period operating from Kuching, Mick Charles and Ian Morgan were sent up to the sub-detachment at Sibu, in the 3rd Division, which was established to relieve the naval Wessex squadron. It was a move that accelerated the young lads' development as self-sufficient pilots. Ian Morgan paints the picture:

> After spending the best part of three years in the closely-supervised world of Flying Training Command, it was quite a surprise to find ourselves operating in Borneo at the other extreme of the supervision spectrum. Going out on that September detachment, I'd flown just twenty-nine hours on the squadron, and only eleven of those were as captain. And seven days later, there I was, ferrying a Whirlwind with three ground crew passengers to Sibu, for eighty minutes over what was for me completely unknown terrain. I reckon I must have followed the coast and turned up the river Rajang to find the place.
>
> When we got there on the eighth, it was a hasty set-up of the detachment Ops Room and then straight into action. There was little time to get briefed on the big picture – all we knew was that Gurkhas were in contact with the enemy up on the border. Our first missions that same day were to lift some of them to the company base at Song and thence forward to a tight jungle clearing close to the frontier.
>
> There was barely any radio contact and we had just that G4 compass. You flew up the rivers where possible – on the starboard bank, the rule of the road – all the while looking out for shoals and clearings where you might just pull off an emergency landing, and perhaps then find a native track nearby. You got to know the waymarkers – unusual trees, rock formations or longhouses, that sort of thing.
>
> We carried on with that kind of work for three weeks solid. We were all now effectively self-authorising and had to decide when the weather was fit, what unserviceabilities we could fly with, what was the minimum fuel load we could safely get away with, how we were going to find our way to the next landing-site given that the map was blank in the area we were going to, and so on. It's fair to say that we all learned a lot quite quickly.

From Sibu, the Whirlwinds were tasked to fly up the Rajang and into the border mountains, most often solo, as Mick remembers:

Operating in the interior usually meant a couple of days on one's own so we pilots were checked out on basic maintenance – I remember that the rotor-head had a score of nipples that needed greasing every twelve-and-a-half hours' flying. And refuelling was a grind.

We carried a Zwicky pump – small but heavy, with an unreliable two-stroke motor. We'd drop that off at the appropriate up-country fuel dump. Then, as we needed more juice, we'd land alongside the airdropped forty-gallon drums which we'd previously stood on end to let any water settle to the bottom. But you never could tell, so we'd check for water all the same – a painstaking procedure using a tube, syringe and water-detecting pellet. Then, the Zwicky would take a couple of minutes to pump the fuel into the aircraft – hot work under the tropical sun and in high humidity.

By the time you'd pumped a couple of drums you were soaked. It was a relief to take off and climb to one thousand feet where the air was less humid and you could dry out.

The temperamental Zwicky pump in operation. (Rick Atkinson)

Colin expands:

> The temperamental Zwicky was the weak link in keeping our
> Whirlwinds flying and so we later carried a 'wobble' pump. This was
> rather like a small boat bilge-pump, actually worked very well but it took
> an awful lot of strokes over about a quarter of an hour to pump in a
> barrel of fuel. And it was of no use for a rotors-running refuel – the
> aircraft kept gaining on you!
>
> Later, a smaller wobble pump was fitted on the starboard undercarriage
> leg, but its fuel transfer rate was even slower so it needed even more strokes
> than the free standing version. Worse yet, it was quite fragile – I regarded
> it more as a final resort. Those refuelling pumps were critical to the whole
> Whirlwind operation. What we could do was limited by the need to refuel
> so often, and so tediously, with those flaky pieces of kit.

The new recruits had joined a squadron with an enlightened commander. As
Ian puts it:

> In Peter Davis we had the right boss for the time and place we were in
> – he was both unconventional and experienced. He'd joined the army
> towards the end of the Second World War and wore parachute Wings
> and the Military Cross.[6] In the 1950s Malayan Emergency, observing
> aircraft delivering supplies to his Gurkhas in the jungle, he evidently
> decided that flying might be a more amenable lifestyle and joined the
> RAF as a pilot, flying Hornet fighter-bombers in Malaya.
>
> He ran the squadron in a relaxed manner – he explained to me that
> as his group of young pilots were commissioned, they could be trusted
> to behave themselves as officers should. They also had their Wings, so
> they could be expected to do their job competently and with diligence.
> What supervision was needed? In any case, RAF rule-books were
> written on the assumption of fixed-base operations and in no way
> catered for the Borneo environment.
>
> The boss's Gurkha contacts were a real bonus – if we found
> ourselves up-country and in need of assistance, their units would always
> be ready to offer it. When we got to Labuan later on, they even let us
> have a Land Rover and driver.

Pete Davis's method seemed to work. Mick for one has nothing but positive
thoughts about his introduction to the Borneo action:

> It was a wonderful opportunity for a first tourist to learn how to operate
> independently with a minimum of support. We had to make our own

decisions, exercise our own judgement and plan tasks in the most efficient way in cooperation with army units. We had to learn fast how to make our own assessment of the weather and judge, as conditions deteriorated, when to turn back before it was too late. There were almost unlimited opportunities for legal low flying and we had a lot of fun in the process. And I came into contact for the first time in my life with different races, cultures, languages and religions. Those first weeks in Sarawak were a fascinating and mind-broadening experience.

★ ★ ★ ★ ★

Whirlwind 10 over oil-palm plantations in Sarawak 1st Division... (Colin Ford)

... approaching border range to south of Bau... (Dave Lanigan)

... and Landing Point hacked out on jungle ridge. *(Colin Ford)*

The weather worsens and... *(Mike McKinley)*

... a night-stop threatens. *(Colin Ford)*

As the Borneo Boys settled into the routines and excitements of Sarawak ops, the bigger picture in South East Asia was unfolding at speed. In August a UN fact-finding team had been transported by 103 Squadron around the 1st and 2nd Divisions, where in places they got a rough reception. According to Ian Morgan:

> In Brunei, they found widespread apprehension at becoming part of Malaysia. Few welcomed the idea of joining with Malaya and the other colonies in a Federation and losing the independence they had under their Sultan. In Sarawak they found some of the same. At least one of the local tribal chiefs was openly dismissive of being governed by an outfit ruled by the Malayan Prime Minister, Tunku Abdul Rahman, or 'Rothman' as he called him. To the surprise of the UN team, the same chief, rather than being governed by either Djakarta or KL, expressed a preference for remaining under British colonial rule!

But despite the somewhat equivocal findings of the survey, the British and Malayan diplomats carried the day. In the face of continuing threats from *Radio Djakarta* of dire action against Malaya and the British Borneo States if Malaysia came into being, the Federation was proclaimed on Sunday 15 September 1963 with the Tunku as Chief Minister. Sarawak and North Borneo (renamed Sabah) formed East, and Malaya and Singapore West Malaysia. The Sultan and his government, while wishing Brunei to remain a British Protectorate, perhaps with more than half an eye on those oil revenues, declined to sign up to the new arrangement.

There was much celebration in the streets of Kuala Lumpur, but those of Djakarta began to fill with protesting mobs. On the day following the proclamation, diplomatic relations were broken off with the new Federation and the Philippines followed suit. Encouraged by their leaders, thousands of Indonesian demonstrators stormed the British and Malaysian Embassies in the Indonesian capital and at the same time their consulates in North Sumatra were sacked. The British Ambassador decided to evacuate embassy staff and a fleet of RAF transports flew through heavy weather to Djakarta to lift some 400 British nationals to the safety of Singapore.

A state of undeclared war now existed between Malaysia and Indonesia and Britain informed the Tunku that under the terms of the Mutual Assistance Treaty, British forces were ready to assist in defending Malaysia's independence. The offer was accepted.

A Colonial conflict was thus transformed into an action waged on behalf of a Commonwealth ally. Supreme military authority was no longer with GHQ in Singapore but with the Malaysian National Defence Council in KL, chaired by the Tunku and linked to London by the British High Commissioner. Decisions were now to be implemented by a committee of all parties including the Malaysian Armed Forces and Police.

INTO THE FRAY

Ten days after the Djakarta evacuation, on 28 September, 150 Indonesian guerrillas mounted a surprise attack on Long Jawi, a village high in the headwaters of the Rajang river and just ten miles from the border ridge. The defenders – six men of the 1/2nd Gurkha Rifles, two Police Field Force signallers and twenty-one Border Scouts – fought bravely but were overwhelmed. The raiders looted the village and set fire to the police station. Five of the Scouts were killed, apparently after being taken prisoner. Trekking for four days through the jungle, the survivors brought word of the attack back to Base HQ, and counter-attack was immediate. Wessex helicopters of 845 NAS flew up from their new shore base at Nanga Gaat (on the Rajang and at over 100 miles from the coast, the most remote helicopter forward base in Borneo) to lift Gurkhas into ambush positions in the valleys above Long Jawi. The retreating guerrillas suffered heavy casualties.

This attack showed up the limitations of the Border Scouts. The *Iban* were subsequently partially disarmed (they kept their *parangs* and shotguns) and the Independent Parachute Gurkhas were concentrated in Kuching to operate in a 'fire brigade' role. It also further reinforced the need to engage the hearts and minds of the natives. It was learnt that Indonesians had infiltrated Long Jawi two days before the raid and not one inhabitant dared tell the defenders. But news of the insurgents' murderous brutality spread from longhouse to longhouse. Taken together with the immediate and effective British response, the *Iban* had been shown that it was to the Malaysian side that their support should be directed. From then on they came forward with intelligence on enemy movements, and with succour for the defending troops.

It was obvious to all that speedy counter-attack by the security forces depended on the ability to deliver helicopter-loads of fierce Gurkhas and Scotsmen without delay to the right spot. General Walker was quoted as saying, 'A single battalion with six helicopters is worth more in the jungle than a whole brigade with none.' The battlefield helicopter offered an insurance against the risk of ambush on a track or along a river, and provided speed, mobility and flexibility.

★ ★ ★ ★ ★

A particularly urgent need for helicopters was building in northern Sarawak and Sabah, where those countries' borders both met with that of Kalimantan. Up there tension was rising again. As Malaysia came into being, the 110 Squadron two-Sycamore detachment at Brunei, short of spares and pilots, was earmarked for closure, and two Whirlwind 10s were detailed to replace them. Plans were also worked up to have three 110 Whirlwind detachments operating

41

at each of Labuan, Brunei and Tawau by December. The Whirlwinds of 103 Squadron detached to Kuching were earmarked to transfer to Labuan as reinforcement.

Put on notice to replace 103 in Kuching was 225 Squadron, formed in January 1960 at RAF Andover with Sycamores and, since November 1961, operating the Whirlwind 10 at RAF Odiham in Hampshire.

As 225 Squadron could not be in place before mid-December, the Brunei HQ again shuffled its pack and the Wessex of 845 NAS were deployed to Kuching at the end of September 1963, allowing the 103 Squadron Whirlwinds and crews, Colin Ford, Sam Smith and Mick Charles among them, to fly off to HMS *Albion* – en-route Labuan and the special perils of north-east Borneo.

Chapter 5

The Pace Quickens

The island of Labuan, some fifty square-miles of level sand, coral shale and secondary jungle, was in 1963 blessed with a fine harbour at Victoria town, and 2,000 yards of concrete runway at the airport, where the Japanese-built control-tower was still in use. Over the sea to the south-east, lay mangrove swamps, behind which was the back-drop of the mountains of Sabah.

Old chums from 110 Squadron soon gave the newcomers the low-down on leisure-time possibilities on the island. If you were brave, you could stalk a giant monitor lizard in the bush, and there was swimming to be had at the beach below Shell Petroleum's mock-gothic Membedai Club – but beware the sandflies, the sewage pipe and the wrecked Jap motor-boat. All in all, the delights of the island were few, but a visit to Surrender Point, the Commonwealth War Graves Memorial and the Australian cemetery was a must.

Commonwealth War Graves Commission Memorial, Labuan. (Colin Ford)

Overhead Brunei Mosque. (Colin Ford)

But from their first briefing on the morning of their arrival, in the temporary Ops Room in the Airport Hotel, it became evident to the lads that they were not to have much time off. Mick Charles's logbook records that he was immediately off to Brunei for an area recce and then a trooplift demo before flying back to Labuan, all on the day of arrival.

Deep in the central highlands, thinly-spread units of the British Army were reliant on the support of the 103, 110 and Royal Navy helicopters for a full range of tasks, from routine trooping and re-supply, through specially-mounted hearts and minds exercises, to casevac missions.

The RAF Whirlwind squadron OCs had agreed the overall details with the Army. Five aircraft would be located at Brunei, two of them from dawn to dusk on fifteen minutes' notice to transport a 'standby platoon' of a dozen soldiers to any troublespot at the Army's command. The other three would be on ninety minutes standby but also available for routine tasking as required.

It was also agreed between them that 1st-line, day-to-day servicing would be carried out at Brunei by 110 Squadron, which had been there for some time and was well-established, and 2nd-line, routine maintenance by 103 at Labuan. It soon became clear that this arrangement did not in work. Pressure was on the ground crews through lack of spares and, in October, Whirlwind serviceability was down to just over twenty hours per aircraft per month. The squadrons reverted to independent maintenance units.

But aircraft and crews were effectively pooled and the 103 newcomers were able to pick the brains of the 110 guys. Even from the unsatisfactory maps they were handed, it was evident that the terrain was much more mountainous than in western Sarawak. Beyond the coastal plain rose the Mount Murud range on the Sabah-Sarawak border and above Jesselton, the principal town of Sabah, loomed the peaks of Kinabalu. The 110 pilots told them that they'd be operating routinely at altitudes up to 4,000 feet or more and that the country was considerably less populated and cultivated than around Kuching – mostly primary jungle. It was clear that the extent of the area for which they were responsible was massive – Brunei, most of the 4th and all of the 5th Divisions of Sarawak, and pretty much all of Sabah, a country of 28,000 square-miles. They could see that the distances from Labuan to the Kalimantan border areas were far greater than in Kuching – it was going to be something like an eighty-minute flight, one-way.

As well as the soldiers, the rotary men were going to be spread thin, and hard worked.

★ ★ ★ ★ ★

Labuan was to be Colin Ford's home base for the first two weeks of October 1963. He has a clear recollection of that first detachment on the island:

> Tasks were allocated by the Air Transport Operation Centre, the 'ATOC' at Brunei. But often, on arrival at the army base, it had all been changed and we carried out what the army commander required in the circumstances. So you had to be flexible and self-sufficient. Our squadron ethos helped. It was generally based on the surmise that if you treat a twenty-two-year-old pilot as an adult, he'll probably behave like one.
>
> We had to rely at first on the dodgy maps of Sabah and the border areas in north-east Sarawak but we very soon built a mental picture of the terrain – high ground, river junctions and villages. We'd make notes of the landmarks on our maps – little drawings of prominent limestone outcrops, particular longhouses and unusual trees. The ones with red fruit, or the dead ones with white or no leaves stood out well against the surrounding jungle green.
>
> The Sabah mountains were dangerous. Long Pa Sia – a new and dusty dirt strip at three thousand feet and just eight miles from the border – sat in a forested sandstone bowl.[7] If the cloud was lowish, the surrounding saddles presented 'sucker holes' which could close very quickly. If you were crossing the bowl en-route Pensiangan – which took several minutes – you had to be sure you could get clear across it and not become trapped

Dirt strip at Long Pa Sia in challenging cloud conditions: two AAC Scouts on bamboo landing-pads as RAF Whirlwind makes delivery. (John Dicksee)

Welcoming pipe band at Bario. (Colin Ford)

if the cloud base reduced suddenly. We'd say, 'If it looks iffy, it probably is.' Then it was better to turn around and try again later.

Bario, in Sarawak's Fourth Division was a forty-five minute trip from the coast, and also sat at three thousand feet. My first time up there was something I'll never forget – a dramatic ride over the mountain ridges. I went as a pair with Bill Oliver – in the days when we had just the short-range radios we flew as pairs whenever we had the aircraft available. When we got there, we were amazed to be greeted by a pipe band – several dozen kids from the village school, all lined up and blowing an enthusiastic welcome on their bamboo pipes. I remember we got fresh spring onions to eat, and compo cheese out of tins!

The long channel of Trusan Gorge up in the mountains was a good route home from those LPs in the interior – Bario, Ba Kelalan and Long Semado. It signposted the way down to the coastal plain, Brunei town, and home to Labuan.

Mick Charles picks up the story:

During my time on detachments to Labuan we operated along the whole length of the border from Kapit in Sarawak – well south of Long Semado – right up to Pensiangan in Sabah. We went east of that too, into 'The Gap'. That was an area of primary jungle, almost uninhabited – we only went there when we were inserting or recovering SAS patrols. In the early days we didn't go as far east as Tawau, but we'd go a long way down the coastline, to the south – on a medevac, as far as Bintulu and the hospital.

There was a lot of action up on the border. We carried a .38 revolver on a webbing belt and were also issued with a Sterling sub-machine gun and a couple of magazines. I carried other personal items in a rucksack and took a camp bed and mosquito net. And, of course, we carried a SARBE rescue beacon. I always had a supply of the compulsory paludrine tablets against malaria and, when I remembered, I took the salt tablets they issued to help with dehydration.

We were solo most of the time. They usually said something like, 'There's your aircraft – it's just had a fifty-hour check. Your first destination is Long Semado', or somewhere such. 'Off you go and make sure you come back before you run out of hours.'

In the early years of Confrontation, RAF helicopter air-loadmasters didn't exist. But if we were off for a mission from a forward base, one of the airframe or engine ground crew came with us to look after the aircraft. He was not a crewman as such – we'd offload him at the forward unit until we returned from the sortie.

Colin Ford awaits passengers at Ba Kelalan. The border ridge rises behind the aircraft to the frontier at the top. Note the very infrequently used ladder and seats, and the state of cleanliness of the aircraft – it was a VIP trip. (Colin Ford)

This was not a problem when we carried troops – they knew where they were going and would get off at the appropriate stop. Freight was more difficult because we were often carrying items for several different units. The soldiers would off-load everything if you weren't careful! With rotors still turning, we'd lean out of the cockpit and hammer the fuselage to get their attention. One of them would then climb up to the cockpit window where we could make each other heard and once we'd sorted things out, they'd off-load only the stuff that was down to them. Then they'd have to reload anything unloaded 'in error', before we flew on to the next location. That's how it went – we didn't need to leave the seat, unless to refuel, or take a toilet break. We had a funnel and tube in the cockpit, but that was a damned awkward business.

Where a second pair of hands was needed, such as lifting fuel drums lost off-target in an airdrop, we pilots would act as crewman for each other. One of us would fly the Whirlwind while the other got down into the cabin. Using the intercom and a 'monkey harness', we could lean out of the door and 'con' us into position.

Right from the start, we did a good deal of hearts and minds work – Ba Kelalan, south of Long Semado, stands out. This village was very close to the border and thought to be vulnerable so it was decided to move the whole issue to a safer area. We loaded everything and everyone, including the chickens and pigs, and ferried them down to Long Semado. It went on for some time, and became known as Op 'Pork Chopper'.

★ ★ ★ ★ ★

Ian Morgan was a Borneo Boy who never set foot on the *Albion*, but he was detached from Seletar to Labuan any number of times:

My abiding memory of my first trip out there is of an extremely early-morning journey to Changi followed by several hours in the back of a very noisy and slow Hastings. The Argosy would have been preferable in some ways, though I seem to recall that it was fitted with paratroop seats which weren't at all comfortable.

That must have been on October seventh 1963 – my logbook shows that I flew to Brunei and back on the eighth for local area orientation. The squadron had a small base there, just a tin shed and *attap*-palm huts. I then got to work further and further inland as the days went by.

Operations in this new area involved long periods of flying the single-engine Whirlwind over primary jungle – usually out of radio contact once you were twenty minutes out of Brunei. I always carried a bergen in the back, with a sleeping bag, a bottle of water and basic survival kit.

On October seventeenth I was in Brunei again and this time night-stopped, ready to fly to the so-called 'Relief of Bario'. It seemed that HQ had lost radio contact with the Green Jackets up there and had decided to task two Whirlwinds to take off at dawn and have a look, carrying six lightly-equipped soldiers in each, just in case. Fog and low cloud delayed us en-route at Long Semado, but when it lifted, we were able to get over the mountain ridges guarding this wide plateau known as the Plain of Bah. Bario was right in the middle, and only a dozen miles from the Indo border. We didn't know what we might find, so we made a somewhat nervous and circuitous approach. But there weren't any Indos to welcome us, just friendly Green Jackets. 'What's all the fuss about?' they said.

I stayed at Bario for a few days. It was a fast-developing military camp, but close to a totally unspoiled longhouse, a great one to visit. I flew support missions along the border, before carrying an urgent casevac to Brunei. Then it was back to Labuan, and a shower – a big plus for the Airport Hotel.

Two days later I had a fifty-five minute check ride with the infamous, moustachioed Squadron Leader 'Bushy' Clarke, the only rotary 'trapper' on the Transport Command Examining Unit at the time. They'd started to bring in Aircrew Categorization standards for RAF rotaries and had sent Bushy out to see what was happening and how the boys were doing. I suppose I did all right, as immediately after the trip Bushy went off into Victoria town saying he was going to meet up with some old mate, a captain on a merchant ship – and we had neither sight nor sound of the man again!

I remember vividly a casevac mission on October twenty-third to pick up a native woman, eight months pregnant with complications, at Long Lopeng. On the way back to Brunei and the hospital the baby was delivered – thankfully, mother and child did OK.[8]

Also memorable were trips from Bario to the Gurkha base at Pensiangan in Sabah. You routed through Long Semado, which sat in a forested valley at two thousand feet, then over the mountains to Long Pa Sia, at three thousand. From there you tracked across a high plateau to pick up a feature you couldn't miss, the river that took you down to Pensiangan.

Route to Pensiangan before...   *(Colin Ford)*

... plunge to village in river gorge...   (Mick Charles)

... and into Gurkha base with fuel dump and Officers' Mess.   (Colin Ford)

The village lay at the bottom of a deep bowl where a tributary joined the river – all highly scenic and dramatic. You'd land on the village volley-ball court and the local people would come out to meet you. To get out, you needed to climb at thirty to forty knots, so as to get an angle steep enough to clear the mountains.

I remained out on detachment for three weeks, flying casevac missions on the last few days – two to Long Banga[9] and one over the Murud range to Sepulot. That was just under two hours going out from Brunei, and a full two coming directly back to Labuan. And I remember that the weather was particularly bad that last week – heavy rain most of the time.

The North-East Monsoon had again arrived on schedule, challenging the pilots and crew as they picked their way through the mountain valleys.

★ ★ ★ ★ ★

The method of rotation of 103 Squadron pilots at Labuan was by roster, with the lads coming and going individually from Singapore. At the end of two weeks on the first detachment, Colin Ford took the Hastings shuttle back to Singapore for a spot of leave. Ian Morgan followed him a week later:

I'd racked up thirty-seven hours in the Whirlwind on that first detachment and was ready for a rest. But we needed the time at Seletar for night and instrument practice and of course we were also rostered for SAR – dawn-to-dusk one-hour standby – and VIP pilot duties. And very soon – after a session of night-flying the previous evening – it was another dawn call for the bone-rattling Hastings shuttle to Labuan. Then, straight after landing on November twenty-ninth, I was ferrying a Whirlwind to Brunei for ops.

On the ninth of December I managed over six hours in the air, troop-lifting between Brunei and Bario – seventy-five minutes one way. The next day, I put in some four-and-a-half hours between Pensiangan and Sepulot inserting the Leicestershire Regiment to counter a major Indo incursion.

On the way back from that op to Brunei I had Sergeant Mike Williams with me as co-pilot. It started to heave down with rain and we had to land at Limbang, short of Brunei. In the downpour, we were surprised to be met at the airstrip by an English school teacher who kindly offered us beds for the night. It was fortunate that we were well rested because after take-off the next morning, we were really put to the test. Cruising along on the short hop to Brunei, our Whirlwind suddenly and quite unexpectedly suffered a total failure of its two hydraulic control systems.

At Tern Hill we'd been told that the aircraft had been fitted with dual systems because without hydraulic assistance it would be uncontrollable. Well, they were right – the controls became absolutely rigid! Fortunately we were straight and level at the time, which gave us time to think what to do next.

Sergeant Williams was a muscular fellow, and the two of us managed by hauling on our two sets of controls to get the machine pointing roughly at Brunei runway in the distance. We sent out an emergency call, and set about trying to lower the collective levers to get the aircraft to descend. Mike was so strong that I became concerned his lever was going to snap off in his hands, which would have led to certain death. Mercifully, the mechanism stood up to our efforts and eventually the levers went down – but agonisingly slowly. Again mercifully, the runway at Brunei was long enough to give us a much-needed margin of error, and we succeeded in dropping the Whirlwind somewhere in the middle. Massive relief!

The ground crew quickly identified the problem as being water in the electrical control actuators and got them dried out. Then, with some trepidation, we flew the aircraft back to Labuan. All in a day's work.

That same month, December 1963, the Whirlwind squadrons adopted the policy of keeping aircraft permanently attached to army units in the field, to ensure the fastest possible reaction time. They would remain there unless unserviceability or fifty-hour inspections required a return to base. At the same time the 110 detachment at Brunei moved up to Labuan – the aircraft of both squadrons could now be serviced centrally, leading to an encouraging increase in availability. The 103 Squadron crews managed over 174 hours in the month, a large number of those now being in the escalating action at the port of Tawau.

The border up there was so close that it ran along the Serudong estuary off Tawau town, neatly bisecting the sizeable island of Sebatik which lay midstream. Sixty per cent of the inhabitants of the Tawau area were Indonesian immigrants making it a natural entry point for incursions. Prosperous from logging, tea plantations and coastal trade, it was a magnet for Sukarno's forces. Five companies of Indonesian Marines, the KKO, were reported as being in the border camps. The British base, at the time run by the Royal Navy, was garrisoned by 1/10th Gurkha Rifles, supported by the Whirlwinds of both 845 NAS and 110 Squadron RAF.

In November 110 had, for the first time, sent a detachment over there and within the month it had managed to mount 301 sorties and to carry 558 troops together with 37,700lb of freight. Tension in the area continued to rise and in December the 110 Squadron aircraft were joined by two from 103, just in time to support their RAF and Royal Navy colleagues in defending against a major Indonesian attack.

Just before Christmas a force of over 170 guerrillas struck at the two battalions of relatively inexperienced soldiers of the Royal Malay Regiment based at Kalabakan, a logging station forty miles up-river north-west of Tawau. The invaders, led by a renegade Dutchman, one Colonel Hendricks, killed eight Malay soldiers and badly wounded nine before a swift, helicopter-borne counter-attack by the Gurkhas relieved the town and put the raiders to flight.

Between 17 and 30 December, a Flying Officer Reynell of 110 flew forty-four sorties in twenty hours of Tawau operations and the squadron detachment moved 156 troops and twenty-two Malay Police, while flying ten casevac missions which included four dead. In the action, three Whirlwinds were damaged by automatic-rifle fire, suffering strikes in fuel tank and rotors – one bullet came so close as to lodge in a soldier's map-case. As a result, Peter Davis's request was approved – US standard-issue flak jackets were made available to the Whirlwind crews. These received a mixed welcome. In the words of Mick Charles:

> We couldn't decide whether to wear them or sit on them. They were too hot and sticky for routine ops, so we wore them when it was reckoned there was a distinct risk of ground-fire. Later on we'd wear one and sit on another.

Bren-gun mountings were fitted in the cabin, one in the door to starboard and another by the port window. In addition 'Full Precautions' flying was instigated for missions considered to be at a greater than usual risk of groundfire. These entailed two pilots up, one, or sometimes two crewmen at the Brens, and flak jackets for all. A programme was started to instal Collins HF radios, but the steel helmets never arrived. By the end of December all but half a dozen of the Kalabakan insurgents had been killed or captured, although Colonel Hendricks was never found. The identification of twenty-one of the prisoners as regular KKO was an indication that the campaign was intensifying. But the fact that the population had not risen up in support of the insurgents showed that the British hearts and minds campaign was becoming effective even in this Indonesian-centric area. And the harsh treatment meted out to the local Malays had turned many against Sukarno's cause. In Sabah, as in Sarawak, it was no longer just Britain's war – Malaysian allies were now fully engaged in the escalating conflict.

* * * * *

In August 1963 the RAF transport fleet had been reinforced by a re-formed 215 Squadron, based at Changi with twelve Argosy tactical transports. They were called forward to Labuan at the end of October 1963 to assist in the airdrop task. In the tropical conditions the Beverleys were suffering from engine problems, with an average of one failure in every four take-offs.

As well as air-supply missions, the Argosies, together with the Hastings of 48 Squadron and the Bristol Freighters of 41 Squadron RNZAF, were flying a regular shuttle service to the Labuan base, a four-hour leg, and to Kuching, an hour less. They were now set up to carry battalions of troops forward to Borneo, together with thousands of tons of essential supplies and equipment. Following the attack at Kalabakan, five Hastings and four Argosies promptly flew reinforcements from Singapore to Labuan – 380 troops and their equipment – in just twelve hours. The men were fed in the RAF field kitchen and despatched to Tawau within three more hours in five Beverley sorties. The next day six Argosies and three Hastings arrived, similarly loaded, and seven Beverley sorties took them to Tawau. In all, 1,500 soldiers were carried the 1,300 miles to the front line in two days. The logistics train was working[10].

At the end of the year General Walker went up to Tawau to see for himself how things were going. Ian Morgan had reason to recall that visit:

> During my second detachment to Labuan, which lasted until Christmas Day, I was one of those sent forward to Tawau. While there I flew a VIP party of Admiral Begg, General Walker and General Lascelles around the area – remarkable for a pilot with only five hundred hours total flying and no Aircrew Category of any kind.

The Director of Operations would have seen that the line of supply was functioning, that his string of border forts was under advanced construction, and that there were by now some 10,000 troops in the field. He wrote at the end of 1963: 'A year which began with the end of a revolution ended with the beginning of an undeclared war.' But to continue fighting that war, and hold the border, his forces needed still more helicopters. They got some of them by year-end, when 225 Squadron RAF flew in with its Whirlwinds.

★ ★ ★ ★ ★

The squadron's transfer from Hampshire had been far from smooth. On 21 September a formation of five set out on a ten-leg transit to El Adem in North Africa (just outside Tobruk in Libya) to take part in a joint-service exercise called TRIPLEX WEST. That first leg, to RAF Manston in Kent, proved to be the start of two years of extraordinary adventures for the whole outfit.

The formation was dogged by atrocious flying weather and unserviceability. In France it ran into fog and made an emergency landing in a field, only to be confronted by a pistol-toting customs officer. By the end of the month the Whirlwinds had progressed no farther than Naples, where they became stuck.

Happily, four more of the squadron's aircraft had been flown into El Adem by Beverley, and were there for the start of the exercise. Despite the Detachment Commander contriving to break an ankle and being flown home, and sickness incapacitating his successor, they managed pretty much to complete the task.

The fly-out party finally caught up with their colleagues on the tenth of the month, in time for the final day of TRIPLEX WEST, just as the OC in Odiham, Squadron Leader Henry Price, was receiving short notice of a November move with ten Whirlwinds, together with air and ground crews, for a one-year unaccompanied tour in Kuching starting 12 December. In the dry words of the OC's report: 'The administrative task of collecting men and materials in Singapore for onward movement to Sarawak, was considerable.'

Squadron personnel were flown back by Beverley to Odiham for embarkation leave while the nine Whirlwinds remained at El Adem pending transport to the Far East on the *Albion*. Two pilots and a ground crew party returned to El Adem to babysit the aircraft, while a tenth Whirlwind was airlifted out to make up the required number. While there, one of the pilots flew to the aid of two women with babies stranded in an ambulance in the depths of the desert. Soon after, the remains of a crashed Belvedere were lifted in sections to a nearby road and, by these means, useful work had been done before the machines were flown onto *Albion*.

Leave at Odiham over, pre-deployment admin could be completed. This included dental checks, following which, as a precautionary measure, no fewer than 146 teeth were extracted from the travelling detail. Squadron Leader Price and his colleagues flew off to Singapore on 13 November. Reunited with their Whirlwinds at Seletar a week later, the aircrews carried out a crash three-week familiarization programme, managing 133 sorties over the Malayan jungle and swamps before, on 8 December, mounting a ten-aircraft flypast over Seletar and embarking *Albion* in the Straits of Johore, bound for Kuching.

In transit, *Albion* hosted a number of deck-landings for AAC and RAF fixed-wing aircraft – a 225 Whirlwind lifted off to fulfil the role of 'Plane Guard' while others watched the show from the flight-deck. After two nights' steaming, the spectacle was repeated at Labuan, after which the carrier turned about and headed for Sarawak. Two more nights on board (courtesy of a twelve-hour bad weather delay) saw them arriving off Tanjong Po on the morning of 12 December. After close on twelve weeks of alarums and excursions, 225 Squadron had managed to fly their ten aircraft into Kuching Airport exactly on schedule. When the squadron became operational, Whirlwinds in the Borneo front line numbered a fifty-strong force.

The accommodation allocated to the squadron at Kuching did not please the OC. An extensive military building programme was in progress but, for the meantime, all but six of his officers lodged with their Royal Marine colleagues of 40 Commando at Semengo Barracks, outside the base while an unlucky half-dozen were billeted in a bungalow at Kuching Mental Hospital. Seventy per cent of the airmen lived at Semengo and the rest in a house in Kuching town. Getting everyone in to work was a nightmare, particularly as the squadron transport was delayed en route from Libya and when it did arrive it appeared that desert conditions had rendered many of the vehicles unserviceable.

225 Squadron flying-suit arm badge. (John Davy)

The squadron's Operations Order, issued by Headquarters Western Brigade, allowed for a short theatre familiarization period before relieving 845 NAS and becoming operational in support of British and Malaysian forces in 1st and 2nd Divisions of Sarawak, targeted for 15 December. But true to form, exceptional circumstances arose.

225 Whirlwind approaches squadron dispersal and base at Kuching. (Rick Atkinson)

The day after arrival, 13 December, one of the squadron's aircraft ran into small arms fire near Biawak while on a border reconnaissance flight. Four .303 calibre bullets lodged in the rotor, the engine and fuel tanks, leading to an emergency landing. The action had begun for 225 Squadron two days early and the incident led to an instruction that pilots should avoid flying within five miles of the frontier except in the case of operational necessity.

Two days later, the handover from the Navy at Kuching was complete and the pilots began a daily round of missions in the border areas, in support of the ground troops in the 1st Division – 40 Commando and 5 Royal Malay Regiment. On the same day, two aircraft flew up to Simanggang, to take over the detachment there, supporting the 2/10th Gurkha Rifles covering 2nd Division.

The squadron was also tasked with maintaining two aircraft on dawn-to-dusk Kuching standby for emergency troop-lift and re-supply, and casualty evacuation. Casevac response was soon needed. On 18 December, an army

Simanggang base Officers' Mess. (Rick Atkinson)

Simanggang town on Lupar River. (Rick Atkinson)

Auster was shot down by hostile small arms near the same hot-spot of Biawak. The standby Whirlwind was scrambled to the crash site and brought out the pilot to Kuching hospital, but his passenger, an RAF padre, was mortally wounded and died at the scene of the incident.

The 225 aircrews were promptly issued with the nylon armoured-waistcoats that Peter Davis had initiated, and, not before time, the conspicuous day-glow red panels were removed from their Whirlwinds.

After 'a number of semi-operational tasks', including delivering Santa Claus and his bagful of gifts out of the skies to the Sarawak and Turf Clubs, 225 Squadron's 1963 closed without further untoward incident.

Chapter 6

Frontier in Flames

As the air and ground crews of 225 Squadron were getting to grips with Sarawak operations, the course of the Borneo Campaign was taking a further unexpected turn. The Brunei HQ had called in the Labuan rotary assets to support a fighting ten-man patrol of the Royal Leicesters in the mountains of Sabah. Following the trail of eighty IBTs the soldiers, led by a subaltern, had found, attacked and cleared an Indonesian jungle camp, killing seven and putting the rest to flight. But the Leicesters themselves had taken casualties. At the very time that the Whirlwinds were lifting the wounded men out of the forests and into the care of the nurses in Jesselton, news reached General Walker that President Sukarno was ready to agree to a ceasefire.

The countries of South East Asia had become increasingly concerned that the hostility between Malaysia and Indonesia might destabilize the whole area, and talks had been convened in neutral Tokyo under the sponsorship of the UN. A tentative armistice was brokered, scheduled to take effect on 25 January 1964. The newly established Royal Malaysian Air Force (RMAF) now had a permanent detachment of two Twin Pioneers at Labuan and, flying at treetop height over the border villages, they braved Indonesian machine guns to sell the ceasefire through loudspeakers to locals and guerrillas alike. But an outline agreement made in Tokyo had no hope of holding among Sukarno's firebrands on the Kalimantan frontier.

Press-ganged tribesmen, brandishing *parangs* and joined by committed Sarawak Communist Chinese with their shotguns, stepped up their incursions fivefold, supported in the rear by Indonesian regulars. In the 1st Division a group of insurgents was even persuaded to swarm over the frontier with instructions to dig in, make themselves a nuisance, and await supply by air. They were summarily chased out by the Gurkhas. The objective of these forays seemed to be to terrorize the native population – a plausible plan as the ferocity of Sukarno and his followers was well known from the jungle telegraph. In the post-war anti-Communist purges, they had instigated the massacre of over 300,000 Chinese.

Along the Sarawak/Kalimantan border each British battalion by now had a frontage of up to 200 miles. In response to the continuing Indonesian aggression, company bases were further strengthened with 81mm mortars and by outer picket lines of trip-wires, American Claymore mines and sharpened bamboo *panji* stakes. Any intruders who managed to evade those and get in close met heavy machine guns. In the 1st Division, the forts were set up at approximately six-mile intervals, and provided with sandbags, overhead cover, and protected sleeping accommodation.

The forts were bases for aggressive patrolling. Twelve-man platoons were supplemented by four-man surveillance groups, usually three Gurkha or British troops and one native Border Scout for intelligence gathering. All patrols would engage the enemy if seen and intruders were constantly harassed.

In the 1st and 2nd Divisions permanent helicopter LPs came under construction every 1,000 yards or so. In the more rugged terrain farther north and east, they were perforce fewer and farther apart but, nevertheless, infantry commanders, working day-by-day alongside the same helicopter pilots, forward-based with the soldiers, were able to evolve a push-button response to every alarm and emergency. Reinforcements had raised the number of

Sarawak hill fort, and...   *(Mike McKinley)*

... permanent forward LP.   (Mike McKinley)

battalions available to General Walker to six. He reckoned that, with helicopter support, the operational usefulness of that force was tripled.

Artillery was dispersed so that two batteries, each interlocked with the next base, might cover 100 miles of frontier when combined with mobile 105mm pack howitzers. These could be broken down into manageable sections, slung under helicopters and flown to hotspots as required. The Whirlwinds could, and often did, manage this in a series of lifts but here, the Belvederes of 66 Squadron (the natives came to call them 'Flying Longhouses') added a new dimension. One could carry a complete gun and another, the men of the detachment together with their kit and ammunition. The tactical mobility afforded by the helicopters made it appear to the Indonesians that guns were emplaced virtually everywhere along the frontier.

★　★　★　★　★

When the British Minister of Defence, Peter Thorneycroft, visited RAF Labuan in January 1964, he found twelve transports and a Shackleton operating from the airfield, together with half-a-dozen Hunter and Javelin fighters and fifteen helicopters. The number of men stationed on the base had risen to nearly 500 and although many were still housed in six-man tents, construction was well in train to provide more amenable *basha*-hut accommodation. Aircraft movements had dramatically increased, racking up to over 1,000 in the month, including 100 at night.

The daily workload of 103 and 110 Squadron Whirlwinds showed no sign of easing and it was pointed out to the Minister that the critical factor in improving aircraft availability and operational effectiveness was a rapid resolution of the spares problem. Ian Morgan remembers:

> The supply chain was quite unable to keep pace with the rate of operations with the result that one Whirlwind at Labuan was progressively robbed of parts to keep the others flying and quickly became a 'Christmas tree'. Eventually there was little of the aircraft remaining apart from the basic fuselage which had to be tethered to the ground to prevent it blowing away – a really sad sight. The rest of the aircraft was represented by a large boxful of AOG [Aircraft on Ground] vouchers for the outstanding parts. This scandalous situation was duly leaked to the *Daily Express*, drawing appropriate criticism, but no apparent results in the short term.

The Whirlwind squadrons' technical staff were perforce becoming masters in the art of 'make do and mend' – learning from the naval guys, who had been at the same game for over a year.

★ ★ ★ ★ ★

During January 110 Squadron transferred its home base down from Butterworth in the north to Seletar, leaving a three-Sycamore detachment to cover the Thai border. In Borneo, alongside 103, its Whirlwinds were now allocated to the infantry at a number of widespread locations: Brunei, Long Semado, Bario, Pensiangan, Meligan and Tawau.

At Brunei a permanent 103/110 commitment was a dawn-to-dusk immediate readiness pair, ready to go with a standby platoon of the King's Own Yorkshire Light Infantry as various hotpoints flared. In the remote, incident-prone mountainous area where the Sabah, Sarawak and Kalimantan borders met, the aircraft remained airborne throughout most daylight hours in support of patrolling Gurkhas and Green Jackets.

Outstanding reserves of courage and determination were needed to fly lengthy missions over awesome and mostly uninhabited mountain-ranges, often on their own in the cockpit of a vulnerable helicopter. In torrential downpours the Whirlwind's somewhat basic windscreen-wipers were totally inadequate. To have any chance of seeing where they were going as they bucketed through the hammering rain, pilots would slow down to a 20-knot crawl, cant the fuselage and skew the whole machine into a side-slip. That way, they could stick their head out of the side-window, and squint into the drenching slipstream for references – uncomfortable, relatively cold and very wet, but necessary.

The northern parts of Borneo were even less well surveyed than out of Kuching. Mick Charles has some comments on this:

> The standard charts we had were very basic, especially in the interior, and then over to the east. As we went on, we were able to fill in greater detail from our own observations as well as those plotted by army patrols which had walked the ground. We'd all got to know the terrain and the positions of the landing sites and we'd use hills and features for orientation. But this didn't work so well when the weather was bad. With a low cloud base, major features got hidden and the hillscape took on an altogether different appearance. Later, in the so-called dry season, the native farmers would slash and burn the jungle scrub, and visibility into sun might be well under half a mile. So we'd stick only to well-known routes, if we could.
>
> And we steered clear of short cuts. They could lead to blind valleys, where you could be trapped if the weather closed in behind you. There were times when I had to retrace my flight path until I could get a fix on a known feature, and then start again. Dead-reckoning[11] and flying blind were an absolutely last resort.
>
> It was all a bit of a challenge, but we managed. We had a well-used mantra drilled into us: 'Man is never lost – merely unsure of his position'!

Out of Kuching 225 Squadron were soon pitched into battling with the North-East Monsoon – it had been awaiting their arrival, striking down there much later than usual, in the middle of January. They were another unit to be hindered by lack of spares, in particular replacement rotor gear-boxes. The squadron was able to carry on only by robbing parts from aircraft undergoing routine maintenance, and wherever possible delaying that maintenance for the operational machines. Nevertheless, they not only coped with the relief of 40 Commando by 42 in 1st Division, and the needs of the 2/10th Gurkhas out of Simanggang in the 2nd, but also answered the call to fly a rare UK television camera crew, from ITV, around the hotspots.

They were helped in these efforts by the gradual fitting of Collins HF radios in all cockpits, which gave pilots a much more dependable lifeline to base. They opened up the possibility of making routine quarter-hourly 'Ops Normal' calls, which allowed missions to be tracked leg-by-leg, re-tasked in the air when necessary and provided with support if an aircraft or crew hit a snag en-route. However, they were not the complete answer. HF has by its nature short ground-wave and long sky-wave ranges – find yourself between the two, which was the case in much of Borneo, and there was no connection at all. On top of that, the set was noisy to monitor and in payload terms weighed about half a soldier. Perhaps its greatest benefit was to the Operations Staff, under instruction to control RAF assets right out to the front line.

It was perhaps inevitable that such control would increase in depth and breadth as the campaign progressed. In the early years the RAF rotary pilots, remote from the various levels of headquarters and Order Books in Singapore, enjoyed a level of freedom that was rare, if not unique in the Service. But then, as Kuching and Labuan, and eventually Tawau became established RAF bases they, too, issued Order Books.

Out in the field, taking their instructions from local army commanders, the Whirlwind pilots usually 'just got on with the job', tasks mostly demanding enough in themselves without worrying too much about RAF procedures. In February 1964 missions in support of 1/6th Gurkha Rifles out of Lundu, a forward base to the west of Kuching, required the Whirlwinds to operate for long hours in the 5,000-foot Pueh border range. Here, as elsewhere, the heavy cloud base prevented the morning mist from burning off and for whole days it was a challenge to make out treetops from mountain crags.

Of further concern to the Whirlwind pilots were the efforts of the Indonesians to shoot them down. At all points on the frontier, increasing numbers of Indonesian medium machine-gun emplacements were being reported, and flying low and slow the rotaries made tempting targets. On 10 March in the area of Long Semado, the gunners hit their mark when a 110 Squadron Whirlwind came under fire. Rounds landed in the radio compartment and one bullet penetrated as far as the pilot's seat. The pilot completed his mission, doubtless grateful for the quarter-inch armour-plating recently installed in that vital area.[12]

The Air Task Force Commander issued an instruction that whenever tasked to fly within two nautical miles of the border, or where the area was 'hot', the aircraft were to operate under Full Precautions. For 225 Squadron in 1st and 2nd Divisions that in effect meant a large number of their missions and in the face of operational necessity the order was widely ignored.

In March, 225 lost an aircraft in a crash south of Kuching and that, together with worsening serviceability problems, forced the squadron to withdraw from Simanggang for lack of operational aircraft. Once again the Navy, 845 NAS with their Wessex, were called in to fill the gap. Heroic work by 225's technical staff managed, through a hectic month of operations against mounting incursions, to keep the Whirlwinds in business out of Kuching and Lundu but the CO was concerned that if the spares situation didn't improved, and fast, his squadron would cease to operate within four more weeks.

★ ★ ★ ★ ★

In the previous November there had been nine reported Indonesian Air Force incursions into Malaysian airspace. In the first months of 1964 Sukarno's air forces continued to join in the harassment of British and Malaysian forces. Even as cease-fire talks were in progress in Tokyo, Indonesian fighters and bombers intensified their buzzing of Sarawak towns. Four were B-25 Mitchell bombers escorted by P-51 Mustangs. Then on 2 February an Indonesian TU-16 Badger bomber flew at 1,000 feet over Labuan, Brunei, and Sabah, followed by another later in the month. In another incident, over in Tawau, Colin Ford was centre-stage:

> I was on a low-level, 'treetop' recce trip west along the border from Wallace Bay on Sebatik Island. When I got back to base, the guys told me they'd watched me disappear over the horizon, and minutes later seen an Indonesian Mustang swoop up from the south. It turned to port, and did a wing-over right along my track. Fifteen minutes later, they were very relieved to see me appear again. I was never sure whether the Indo saw me but chose to do nothing, or whether he just didn't see me. One thing's for certain – I never saw him.
>
> There was another thing about that trip. Because the maps were so bad, we had been asked to offer any assistance we could in improving them. So, back at Labuan, I reported to Ops that I reckoned the position on the map for the Wallace Bay settlement was a couple of miles out. The Ops guy replied, 'Actually, the settlement's geographic reference is known to be correct – it's the whole island that's in the wrong place!'

In response to the airborne incursions, Brunei HQ issued an order for an Air Defence Identification Zone to be set up over the whole of Malaysian Borneo, out to three miles offshore. The ADIZ was enforced by the four Hunters of 20 Squadron RAF in Labuan and the four in Kuching, together with the two 60 Squadron Javelins in each.

★ ★ ★ ★ ★

As the first Tern Hill tyros were nearing completion of six months' campaigning in Borneo, a further stream of young men was entering the pipeline to join them. One was John Davy.

He was born in the summer of 1944 in Nottingham where his father, a wholesale grocer by trade, was for the duration serving as a corporal in RAF pay accounts. At around the age of ten, his father paid a princely sum for a trip in an Auster on Southport sands – the flying trap was set. John attended Grammar School in Nottingham where he gained five O-level passes. But his main interests, apart from rowing, were aeromodelling and airshows. At one of the latter he picked up a black and white brochure promoting Direct Entry aircrew commissions in the RAF, filled in the application form on the back page and sent it in.

He was called for aptitude tests at RAF Biggin Hill, and Officer Selection at Cranwell. He passed both with flying colours, but on the basis that the Cranwell course would have eaten up three years of his young life, he signed up for the Direct Entry route. He had to wait a bit until he reached eighteen, so he buckled down to get A-level Maths Pure and Applied, together with Physics. A careers meeting with the headmaster was short and sweet – John Davy had made his own life decisions.

In July 1962 he left school and embarked on a thirty-five hour Special Flying Award, the equivalent of a Flying Scholarship but aimed at those who had not been in the ATC or CCF. In September he reported to South Cerney for IOT, and spent 1963 completing flying training at Leeming on the Jet Provost. He won all the flying prizes and as a result was given his choice of postings. He opted right away for helicopters, knowing they would get him to the front line, possibly in Borneo. At the end of January 1964 John reported to Tern Hill for training on the Sycamore and the Whirlwind 10, on course to becoming the youngest Borneo Boy yet.

One month after John were Dave Reid and Fraser Skea. Dave was born in Radlett, Hertfordshire in April 1943. The family home was in Colindale, where the sight and sound of gleaming aeroplanes operating from Hendon airbase inspired him to dreams of captaining a BOAC Comet. At Grammar school in Edgware, he joined the Air Training Corps and flew in Chipmunks, Ansons and Varsities and was the first cadet ever to fly solo in a winch-launched glider at Hendon – but his first attempts at starting a career in aviation proved nevertheless somewhat obstacle-strewn.

In the sixth form, aged just sixteen, Dave made an application for the RAF College at Cranwell doing well in the flying aptitude tests but not passing the officer selection procedures. Meanwhile, his elder brother had chosen to try for the AAC as a trainee pilot and Dave thought he'd try for the Army as well – but again, no joy. Leaving school, he took up a succession of more-or-less mundane employments in London. One of these went pretty well – work as a sound engineer at the Olympic Studios, where he played a part in launching Mike Sarne's *Come Outside* to Number One in the charts.

During all these difficulties his ATC successes continued, including the award of a Chipmunk Flying Scholarship. Passing the aptitude tests gave him the confidence to apply once more to the RAF and his persistence was rewarded, with the offer of a twelve-year Short Service Commission. He opted out of the Flying Scholarship and, as soon as he could, joined up at South Cerney – in October 1962, alongside Fraser Skea.

Fraser was born in April 1941 and educated at the Royal Grammar School in Worcester. In the CCF he won a Flying Scholarship at Halfpenny Green, where he had the distinction of joining the elite bunch who have managed to crash a Tiger Moth. On his final solo cross-country he decided to show off to his chums with a low-level pass over their favourite recreation ground. Disastrously, he lost speed in the turn and spun into a wood, finishing up ignominiously nose-down in a stream. The marshy ground saved him, for the Gypsy engine ploughed through the fuselage but was slowed by the mud and came to rest just before it got to Fraser in the rear seat. With an engine by his ankles and his face in the instrument panel, he sat suspended in his straps, concussed and abashed, but in one piece. The Flying Scholarship was no more and at the subsequent trial, Fraser was found guilty of dangerous flying and fined £25.

Despite all that, he graduated at the University of Edinburgh, applied to the RAF and joined up with Dave Reid at South Cerney. The Tern Hill production line then set to in turning them both into rotary pilots.

Chapter 7

RAF Navigator on Naval Base

In March 1964 Flying Officer Geoff Walker, a youthful 215 Argosy Squadron navigator on his first operational tour, was told to pack his combat kit and prepare to leave Changi for a four-week stint as Officer Commanding a Mobile Air Operations Team (MAOT) at Tawau airfield, at that time the home of 846 NAS with their Whirlwind 7s.

This was the first deployment of a MAOT on the base, and Geoff found himself, at the age of twenty-three and with little or no briefing, in charge of an RAF corporal, an SAC wireless operator, two Royal Marine signallers, one Land Rover and an HF/UHF mobile radio installation. He was billeted on his own in an eight-man tent, the other seven beds being made available for visiting aircrew. As he remembers it from a gap of nearly fifty years:

> The MAOT operated seven days a week from another eight-man tent, out by the runway. It was our job to act as communications post between the sector HQ at Labuan, the 846 NAS guys, and Headquarters East Brigade at Tawau, where my boss sat. He was also an RAF nav, but a Squadron Leader.
>
> The runway was a coral-shale affair of only a thousand yards or so, with a definite slope down to the sea. The navy fliers had their base right by it. We knew when they were off on a mission all right – their Whirlwind 7s had a single Alvis Leonides radial piston-engine, which was started with a cartridge gun, and made a racket like a threshing machine.
>
> They were enterprising guys. They'd somehow got hold of a job lot of Citroen 2CVs which they used for buzzing around dispersal and down to Tawau town.
>
> The MAOT was not active in tasking their squadron – we simply passed on HF messages from and to Labuan, reporting activity and

weather three times daily. And we acted as a listening post for the aircraft when they were on ops.

I flew with the Junglies many times – I remember two casevac missions especially. In the first, one Whirlwind in a two-ship in action over Sebatik Island was shot up and had to ditch – the crew got out OK but sadly, a Gurkha on board had drowned by the time he got pulled out. In the second, I was press-ganged into navigating a casevac Whirlwind all the way up to Sandakan on the NE coast.

Sandakan, the third town of Sabah, had a sad wartime history. It was the place where hundreds of prisoners-of-war died in early 1945 when the Japanese, anticipating an Allied landing on the Borneo east coast, forced their charges out of the camp and on to the infamous Ranau Death March. Those that were left at Sandakan died of malnutrition and disease, or were killed by their captors.

During Confrontation the port was a vital refuelling station for Far East Fleet ships patrolling the seas off Kalimantan. Geoff had never been there before:

We made it – by map-reading and dead-reckoning, judging drift by the movement of treetops. It was about one hundred miles one way, and with the heat limiting its range, the poor old Whirlwind 7 had to make two refuelling stops on the way – but we got the casualty back to hospital in Tawau all right.

In all, I made half-a-dozen sorties in the navy Whirlwinds, some nine hours in total. As a 'crab', I was viewed with some suspicion at first, but after the casevacs I get on well with the Fleet Air Arm guys and their boss, Lieutenant Commander Stewart-Jarvis, asks me along one evening to their Mess – a bungalow on stilts.

In the wardroom bar, the 'Queen's Issue' alcohol ration's available – as apparently it is on all active service. In Borneo, that's usually two cans of *Tiger* a day – the Gurkhas get rum. Anyway, I have a few, and get on a chair to sing them 'Cock Robin', with all the gestures. I'm immediately christened 'Tweetie-Pie' and welcomed as one of them.

I get on well with the Army, too and go on a recce sortie in an AAC Auster – acting as official photographer. The pilot's a jumbo-sized Captain from the Duke of Wellington's Regiment who takes up most of the space in the cockpit. In what remains, I have to haul this chest-mounted camera into a position where I can capture images of the Indo landing-craft reported to be on the south side of Sebatik. I've just managed that when I spot white puffs of smoke – on enquiry, I'm calmly informed we're being shot at! We get the pictures, nonetheless.

Other MAOT duties included bidding for fixed-wing aircraft as required, and receiving the transports when they arrived – Argosies, Beverleys, and VIP Valettas from Butterworth. And we kept in radio contact with the Shackletons of 205 Squadron as they patrolled the Sabah coastline. I put that to good use early on. I'd forgotten my laundry back at Labuan and put in a quick call. So the next morning a Shack roars down the runway at fifty feet, and delivers the laundry through the depth-charge 'chute.

Geoff gave his team an exercise in mobility, moving the HF in the MAOT Land Rover up to a jungle clearing. All concerned reckoned it was a useful experiment but he was torn off a strip for his trouble by the Squadron Leader, for leaving his MAOT post on the airfield. Thereafter, he used the Land Rover only as transport into Tawau town for drinking parties, and their social life took off.

He enjoyed a friendly relationship with Lieutenant Colonel Burnett and the 1/10th Gurkhas:

With them on one side and the SBS [Special Boat Squadron] on the other, I felt safe at night in my tent, apart from the rats. I found they couldn't reach me in my bed, which was on stilts, but they made a mess of my soap. We were also protected by the RAF Regiment, and by a screen of barbed wire. But it wasn't all stand easy.

The Indos persisted in their guerrilla raids over the border, just a mile or two away across the harbour, and the RAF Regiment Flight Sergeant re-armed me with the standard-issue FLN. Sure enough, one night the alarm-bells go off and the Gurkha Sergeant Major stands me to for action. So, clad in Y-fronts and a jungle-hat, and gripping my webbing belt of ammo and brand-new weapon, I jump into the MAOT slit-trench. It's empty of MAOT team members but half-full of water. Anyhow, I cover my arc-of-fire as briefed with bullets whistling around at the end of the runway, down by the sea. Next comes the command, 'Fix bayonets!' and then, 'Guns are open!' It all got fairly hairy – but mercifully, down at the bottom of my soggy trench I didn't get to see any of the real action.

However, after a further incident Flying Officer Walker found a bullet hole in the MAOT tent. He sent a message back to Changi on an Argosy saying that he expected to get shot at in the air but not, please, on the ground. He said goodbye to his navy and Gurkha friends (and the MAOT guys, who carried on under another officer) and was extracted by a Borneo Airways Dakota to Sandakan and onwards to Jesselton. He arrived safely back at Changi, none the worse for the challenging experience and in possession of Honorary Membership of 846 NAS for life. Having survived the slit-trenches of Tawau and the hazards of Borneo supply-dropping Geoff had a full and distinguished RAF career, including a full tour on helicopters with the Queen's Flight out of RAF Benson. He retired as a Squadron Leader to the Thames Valley.[13]

The month after Geoff left Tawau, 846 were also relieved. The *Albion* had departed for East Africa but the *Bulwark* – known from the state of her paintwork as the 'Rusty B' – sailed in to replace her. She rounded the Sabah coast to anchor off Tawau, and the Whirlwind 7s clattered away in formation to join her. The ground and support crews were extracted in an Argosy, which gave them a lap of honour above the town and a farewell-salute pass over the runway at fifty feet.

A detachment of 103 Squadron RAF Whirlwinds replaced the Fleet Air Arm men, and, by June 1964, Tawau was officially declared an RAF station.

Chapter 8

At Full Throttle

By the end of March 1964 the January ceasefire was long dead but the South East Asia Treaty Organization (SEATO) nations kept up the diplomatic pressure on President Sukarno to withdraw his troops from Malaysian territories, where their presence was now increasingly obvious. For the longer-serving of General Walker's forces, full-scale raids by strong forces of Indonesian regulars – professional, skilled, and tenacious – made the conflict reminiscent of the Second World War jungle campaign fought by the British and their Allies against the Japanese in Burma. Now, as then, in defence against a determined hidden enemy, mobility became the watchword.

Inevitably there were never enough helicopters to satisfy every requirement and the Brunei HQ staff responded by implementing more heavily centralized, and consequently more convoluted, authorisation procedures. For both rotary pilots and fighting soldiers this led only to frustration as it became more difficult to respond immediately to the needs of field commanders. For the RAF aircrews, the situation was made all the more galling by the Navy's apparent continuing ability, initiated by *Albion*'s Captain Madden during the Brunei Rebellion, to go gung-ho into the fray at the request of the Army and deal with procedure later – if necessary.

But, in the interior, the 103 and 110 Squadron pilots operating out of Labuan and Brunei were seldom within reach of the enforcers back at base, and there was still a frequent requirement for self-authorisation. Ian Morgan gives an example:

> We were often detached with our aircraft in ones and twos for weeks on end – left on your own at a remote location with only the Army for company you had to have plenty of self-reliance.
>
> At Bario I was asked by the soldiers to take a number of *Kelabit* tribesmen from A to B. 'Hey,' I thought, 'what do I recall the procedures men saying about this? Casual civilian rides need Station Commander's approval or some such. Hmm, bit difficult here in Bario.' In the event, I

had once more to take my own decisions and make up the rules as I went along. Naturally, I gave 'em all a lift back home.[14]

Colin Ford has another:

> When I was up at Bario, at the end of one day's tasking the army commander asked me if I could return one of the *Kelabit* trackers to his longhouse, and save him a long day's walk. I didn't even think about it – I said OK.
>
> But I'd no idea where the longhouse was and my blank map was of absolutely no help. However, the army blokes were sure he would know the way. So I strapped the chap in the left-hand seat and took off.
>
> He seemed totally at ease with the whole affair and calmly directed me with hand-signals. He seemed to be able to recognize the ground below him from his many years trekking in the jungle hills and about ten minutes later, we successfully arrived at his longhouse. As I returned to Bario, I wondered whether I would ever fly with a navigator like him again!

The *Kelabit* tribe was one of an estimated twenty-eight ethnic groups forming around half the population of Malaysian Borneo. In the towns the majority of the inhabitants were Malays and Chinese, originally immigrants who had brought their culture with them. The indigenous groups in the harsh environment of swamp and jungle had, over the centuries, developed their own ways of flourishing. In the coastal areas of Sarawak, Sea *Dayaks*, a branch of the dominant *Iban* tribe, lived and fished in the *kelongs*, while the *Kenyah* and *Kayan* of the great rivers built longhouses, slashed and burned both primary and secondary jungle to cultivate their crops, and moved around in dug-out boats and canoes. In the remote highlands nomadic *Punan* gathered fruit and edible plants, and for meat hunted monkeys and birds with blowpipes.

But up on the Plain of Bah and its surrounding hills and mountains the *Kelabit* ranged their territories on foot, growing tall and muscular. They produced and traded salt obtained from upland springs and by mastering irrigation had developed a rice-culture second to none in the whole of Borneo. They and the *Muruts*, their rice-cultivating neighbours beyond Mount Murud to the north and east, had been the people who hosted Tom Harrisson and his fellow parachutists in 1944. They were the first recruits to his swarming *semut* who so terrorized the Japanese. For a *Kelabit*, navigating a Whirlwind back to his longhouse would have been a breeze.

★ ★ ★ ★ ★

Whirlwind 10 delivers radar equipment at 8,000 feet (max operating height 10,000 feet) up on slopes of …

… Mount Kinabalu.   (pictures Paul Logan)

As well as continuing missions in support of ground troops, there were other tasks requiring the services of the Labuan Whirlwinds. Military engineers had taken on the considerable challenge of siting a radar station some two-thirds of the way up the precipitous, wooded and rocky slopes of Mount Kinabalu. The 110/103 detachment got the job of lifting the first-stage equipment up from the road-head, at 6,800 feet and sixty minutes' flight from Labuan, to the radar site at 8,000. The aircraft and crews were up to the job – they would manage to complete the entire lift by the end of July.

In May the same Royal Engineers initiated a complete aerial survey of the Borneo peaks. In support, the Whirlwinds first roped teams of *parang*-wielding *Iban* Border Scouts down onto the mountain tops where they would hack out an LP. The surveyors and their kit could then be landed-on to do their work.

Such jobs, although high priority, put Whirlwind availability under strain. As well as 225 down in Kuching, the Labuan squadrons had also run into a period of poor serviceability, down to 50 per cent, much of that caused by shortage of spares and a spate of engine troubles. The harshness of operating conditions was taking its toll on turbine blades. Assistance came from the AAC who stationed Scout helicopters at Long Pa Sia.

But in April things improved dramatically. Spares arrived, the techies worked their wonders and 103 Squadron managed 345 flying hours, a record month. This achievement was bettered in May when, for the first time since the re-establishment of the squadron in the Far East, the monthly target of 426 hours was achieved. Both squadrons had combined to mount a detachment at Long Semado, working with both 2/7th Gurkha Rifles and the Argyll and Sutherland Highlanders in direct response to Indonesian insurgencies. Accommodation in this remote base was improved when the Gurkhas, assisted by large numbers of locally-employed civilians, in double-quick time knocked together two *bashas* for RAF use.

Meanwhile, in western Sarawak, the 225 Squadron Commander's prayers had also been answered, for, in April and May, the much-needed spares began to arrive in Kuching, too. Three more Whirlwinds were shipped in from the UK, these fitted out to carry the Nord SS11 wire-guided missile, and the rejuvenated fleet was able to cope with a busy period of trooping, re-supply to Gurkhas on ten-day patrols, and night casevacs. They also moved back into Simanggang, working alongside the Navy to support the 2/2nd Gurkhas operating in the dense jungle of the border hills. There was a spate of insurgencies in both Divisions. An attack near Biawak resulted in three Indonesian deaths and four wounded, for the loss of two Gurkhas killed.

In May, the squadron flew 400 operational hours for the first time and morale was further improved when quarters on Kuching base became available, and the tented administrative buildings on the airfield were exchanged for new-built *bashas*, with the added luxury of an air-conditioned Crew Room.

★　★　★　★　★

By this time, after ten months on active service, the 103 Squadron Tern Hill Tyros, with close on a dozen Borneo detachments apiece, were not only becoming battle-hardened, but their appearance had changed. The supply chain had come up with an answer to the flying-suit issue by acquiring a job lot of Australian lightweight models in jungle-green. Colin Ford has an angle on that development:

> It is universal for servicemen to reckon that some of 'the other bloke's kit' is better than his own. That certainly applied to flying-suits. The RAF-issue suit was too heavy and hot for our type of operation. The Aussie model was a significant improvement as it was very light and dried very quickly. However, after the constant cycle of soaking and drying, the material became rotten and fragile – it was prone to rip, often across the back.
>
> If that happened when you were away from Labuan, you just had to live with it until it could be replaced – I remember flying in one that had the entire lower-left leg missing. At refuelling stops, we'd sometimes take

the suit off and hang it out to dry over the undercarriage leg – or, later, when we got them, over the wire of the HF aerial. Then we'd carry on refuelling in shorts and suède desert boots.

The lads were also becoming more and more at one with Borneo life. It wasn't just the exotica of the jungle and the scantily-clad native girls that got to them – the culture of longhouse, village and town was imprinting itself on their young, open minds. Ian Morgan was one of those who had even picked up some knowledge of the Malay language, and he says that that came in useful when he was detached to Tawau:

> We had two Whirlwinds based over there, and the two pilots lodged in a comfortable two-star hotel just minutes from the base, where after a long day's work, there was chilled *Tiger* to be had.
>
> After one morning briefing at the Malay Regiment's HQ, I was tipped off that the next day was National Language Day, and the briefing, normally conducted in English, was to be given in Malay. So that evening I sat down with my Malay dictionary and rehearsed a few words which I dutifully delivered the following day without a problem. However, the newly-arrived captain of the Malaysian Navy patrol boat we were to work with was an Indian, who'd had a British public school education and spoke impeccable English. But, it seemed he'd little or no Malay at all – a bit embarrassing, for all of us.

As the campaign developed, the longhouse culture was becoming increasingly opened up to outsiders, not the least through development of existing airstrips. Those in service at the start of the campaign had been built by missionaries, logging companies and the Japanese. Usually of turf, they were often laid on a foundation of logs. These, through flooding and the attack of voracious soldier ants tended to rot, much to the distress of light-aircraft pilots under whom they would on occasion collapse. The engineers moved in, supported by airdrop and the rotaries.

At Long Pa Sia the job had been completed and, to lift out the earth-working machines, a pair of Whirlwinds was sent in. Flying one of them was Colin Ford:

> A bulldozer had been airdropped up there to open up the old Japanese airstrip – the tractor by Beverley and the blade by Argosy. The construction work was finished and two of us had been tasked to lift what we could of the dismantled machine. We had to return the kit over a three-thousand foot ridge to Brunei about forty-five minutes away. To maximize the lift capacity this would have to be a solo-pilot operation.

So, apart from at the very beginning and the very end of the lift, we had no sight of our load at all, and could only 'feel' the additional weight.

I successfully completed a round-trip but then as I stood on the pan at Brunei while my aircraft was being refuelled, I saw the other Whirlwind approaching. I could see that his hook was empty. Apparently, he had successfully lifted the load – I think it was the engine – but somewhere during the transit it had come off the hook and plummeted straight down into the ulu. Most likely still there! Even now, I wonder just how important was it to recover bits of the vehicle anyway?

On detachment at Labuan, Colin was witness to an incident up-country at Ba Kelalan which came close to disaster for an AAC Scout and its pilot:

My Flight Commander, Dave Todd, and I were at Ba Kelalan right on the border, on medevac standby for an operation which had started at dawn. It had rained during the night and the usual morning mist, the 'jungle cotton wool' was hanging around in the treetops, yet another hazard for flyers.

An army Scout was up, spotting for the pack howitzer when the sun got up and the mist began to rise and thicken, filling the valley with continuous stratus cloud. We got the Scout on the radio and warned him of the deteriorating conditions. He was 'on top' and running out of options – soon all he could see was the tops of the hills.

We then had to tell him that we had gone out in fog and, well before the sun began to burn the lot off, he ran low on fuel. As there was no diversion he had no alternative but to descend blind. We could hear him very carefully creeping about in the fogged-in valleys – like a fly in a bottle – trying to find his way back to Ba Kelalan. There was nothing we could do but wait and everyone, especially the Scout pilot I suspect, was pretty relieved when he finally appeared out of the fog and landed, safe and sound.[15]

At about this time John Richards, an army Sergeant, was being processed for Scout aircrew at the AAC flying-training base, Middle Wallop. Born in Frimley, he went to school in Farnborough where his interest in aviation was sparked by the Royal Aircraft Establishment (RAE) flying displays overhead, as well as by a joint share with other airminded pals in a Tiger Moth. At the age of fifteen he opted out of grammar school and A-levels and instead, took up an engineering apprenticeship at the Army College, Arborfield. This surprised his parents but caused no great ructions as his grandfather had had a career in the Royal Engineers and his father in the Royal Signals, serving in the Eighth Army.

He had a comfortable time at Arborfield – board and lodging, army pay, and much-needed discipline – and he got his A-levels in any case. He joined the REME and was a full sergeant by the age of twenty-one. In 1962 he was transferred to the AAC and, becoming increasingly interested in flying the aircraft he was working on, he applied for aircrew and passed the aptitude tests at RAF Biggin Hill. He gained his Army Flying Badge in 1964 and was selected for rotaries – on course for service in Borneo.

★ ★ ★ ★ ★

The men of 225 Squadron, being wholly based at Kuching, were able to immerse themselves in the Borneo experience and way of life. For their Whirlwind colleagues on 103 and 110, there were spells out in the heady atmosphere of front-line operations interspersed with periods in the tighter military environment of Seletar base. Not that the flying in Singapore or the Malay Peninsula was much less exciting. For a start, there were the SAR missions. One evening earlier, in 1964, Colin Ford was requested by the Rescue Co-ordination Centre (RCC) to ferry a specialist doctor from the British Military Hospital (BMH) in Singapore to the one at Kluang where a woman was experiencing childbirth complications. The one-hour-thirty-minutes round-trip in squally torrential rain, resulted in the increase of Colin's helicopter first-pilot night experience to a total of just under six hours.

At the end of May 1964, again back at Seletar, Colin was grabbed for an unusual supplementary duty. More recruits were needed to swell the ranks of RAF aircrew and space had been acquired in the British press for a major advertising campaign, contracted out to the Clifford Bloxham agency. Borneo was where the drama was, and the admen had scoped out a half-page spread on three men in the front line – a fighter pilot, a transport co-pilot and, naturally, a young Whirlwind man. Colin was the one they chose (he thinks they liked the look of the girlfriend and the car) and for a few days, he was immersed in the public relations business.

The copy writers worked up a story which took him from Labuan into the Borneo interior, through Brunei for ops with the SAS and back to Seletar and SAR duties. The resulting *A week in the life of Colin Ford* featured no fewer than eight pictures, ranging in subject from time-off in the Seletar 50-metre swimming-pool to a smiling Colin at a longhouse surrounded by *Murut* hunter-gatherers. Sub-titled, *Could this be the life for you?* the ad ran in most British newspapers and magazines. Whether or not it effected an increase in recruits is not known but it certainly attracted more than a few ribald comments from the rest of the Whirlwind guys.

★ ★ ★ ★ ★

The running of that advert was a rare reference to the Borneo Campaign in the British media. Confrontation was kept in low profile by both sides, for their own reasons. Sukarno could not afford to let Indonesian aggression become evident to the world – he wanted his people to appear the victims of British colonial bullying. The British needed to hold back any outcry against its increasing military response while its diplomats worked tirelessly, and with slowly-increasing success, in seeking UN and US support behind the scenes.

Meantime, the fighting escalated as border incursions increased. In June, the Labuan Whirlwinds were in action with the 1/10th Gurkha Rifles and the SAS at Long Lutok, near Lawas. A fierce firefight developed in an area where the position of the frontier was particularly disputed and both sides took casualties.

This was the month when, in an apparent attempt to wrong-foot the British diplomats, Sukarno again deemed it opportune to go back to the Tokyo conference table. But these talks, too, broke down almost as soon as they started and President Sukarno publicly vowed to crush Malaysia – '*Ganjang Malaysia*'. What is more, he gave his full commitment to achieving that by the end of the year.

As a consequence, in July 1964 his regular troops launched thirty-four forays across the border. The 1/6th Gurkha Rifles suffered a severe reversal at Rasau in Sarawak – five killed and five wounded – in what was a professional attack. In the second fortnight of the month the Gurkhas fought a running battle with the hundred-strong forces of a determined and persistent Indonesian commander near Kabu, up in the hills above Pensiangan, on the western edge of a forty-mile unmapped stretch of the border known as 'The Gap'. In most of these incidents the insurgents suffered badly, against minimal casualties among the defenders, but General Walker's resources were becoming stretched.

British infantry companies continued to operate from their permanent, heavily-defended bases, with full artillery and air support. The four-man patrols stayed on the border, gathering intelligence, and incursions were met with well-targeted cut-off squads, whistled up by helicopter.

But the enemy was becoming more organized, and his troops could strike at will from their own secure bases. It was a precarious situation. General Walker and his staff knew that several mass attacks at one time might seriously threaten to overwhelm the defenders. More troops were needed. Reinforcements were on their way and would before long bring the numbers up to a level requiring a full divisional organization under a Land Forces Commander, reporting direct to the Director of Operations. The snag was that, with the exception of replacement SAS and Commando units, the new men were unused to jungle fighting. It was generally reckoned that it took a three-month tour at the very least to acclimatize and become truly effective in Borneo.

The Gurkhas were something else. Each of the eight Gurkha battalions now serving were on a rota of six-month stints in the Borneo territories and these tough little Nepalese had had long experience from Malaya and were skilled in setting ambushes, tracking and all other essentials of jungle fighting. They knew not to use scented hair oil, to smoke or talk above a whisper – all likely to give away their position. They had total and constant awareness of their immediate surroundings, and could deliver fast and accurate fire when needed. At the same time, they were superb in the use of cover in more open ground and had the almost superhuman endurance of high-mountain men.

General Walker was looking to all his units to dominate their section of the frontier as the Gurkhas did. He wrote:

> The troops had to become so well-trained that they were able to fight the guerrillas both in the jungle and out of it, and to kill and harry them until they were utterly exhausted…The type of fighting, the type of country and the type of climate called for individual stamina and fortitude, stout legs, stout hearts, fertile brains, and the acceptance of battlefield conditions almost unimaginable in their demands on human endurance.

The General and his staff worked hard to obtain the equipment the troops sorely needed to ease their task. Their personal weapons had been designed for Western Europe and turned out to be unsuitable for jungle fighting. The standard rifle, the SLR, weighed in at a shoulder-aching 11lb – Armalites had been requested but were proving slow in coming. Another weapon, the heavy General Purpose Machine Gun (GPMG) was effective but a burden to hump on patrol – the soldiers preferred the more manageable and proven Bren Light Machine Gun (LMG). Obsolescent and unreliable radios were another liability. In the middle of 1964 the right sort of kit seemed to be months away.

The helicopters too, were increasingly hard-pressed. The 66 Squadron Belvederes were much in demand out of Kuching and fortunately were enjoying much-improved serviceability. They had also by now extended their crewing, signallers having been seconded to crewman duties – they were not very happy about it, but they got on with the job. That job, in the absence of a winch, included being key man in the drill for hauling survivors out of the jungle – 'manpower, with rope'. In March a Belvedere had lifted a 225 Squadron force-landed Whirlwind out of the scrub just south of Kuching Airfield and, in May, another brought back to Nanga Gaat a Royal Navy Wessex that had crashed near Long Jawi. That same month, the squadron carried out the relief of 42 Commando by the Green Jackets, in the 1st Division. The big lifters had become crucial to the gunners in West Sarawak, continually hauling 105mm howitzers from point to point to keep the insurgents within range of their devastating fire.

A new technical hitch hit 225 Squadron in June. Engines were becoming scarce – there were now more Whirlwinds than there were Gnomes. The gap was filled by transferring engines from airframes on scheduled maintenance, until the setting up of an engine bay and the flying-in of a manufacturer's specialist turned the situation around.

The same month, with the collapse of the Tokyo talks, came a spate of Indonesian night attacks on defenceless native longhouses in western Sarawak, and 225 had its busiest month yet. These forays, clearly designed to terrorize the local population, had the opposite result – an even greater motivation in the *Iban* and *Dayak* peoples to support the security forces. At Lundu, a determined attack by regular Indonesian troops was more successful, resulting in the Gurkhas losing five dead and suffering five wounded, the Whirlwinds bringing the bodies and casualties down out of the hills to Kuching. At Batu Lintang, out of Simanggang, the outcome was reversed, with the enemy losing ten killed – again the helicopters were called in on hearse duty.

In July Squadron Leader Davis shoe-horned a 103 Squadron Whirlwind into the tightest of clearings south of Long Pa Sia, to extricate the body of a staff sergeant. This was one of the sadder incidents of a month in which each serviceable aircraft on the squadron clocked up its targeted forty hours. Two more pilots had joined, bringing the unit up to its establishment of sixteen.

This was the moment when, with their operations at full throttle, the bosses at Brunei HQ decided the time was right once again to split the two Labuan squadrons, each with its own aircraft, Engineering Officer and 1st and 2nd-line servicing. The plan was for Central Brigade to have two sub-divisions, with one squadron allocated to each: 110 was to take on all tasks from Long Semado, south-west to Long Pa Sia, with a forward base at Bario; 103 was to turn its eyes eastwards to Sepulot, where the RAF Regiment was reconstructing and reinforcing the camp in preparation for the Whirlwinds, and right over to RAF Tawau on the coast.

In Kuching officers and men of 66 Squadron were relieved to leave Semengo Camp and move into new quarters on base. In the air, they continued their sterling work in moving guns around the border forts. Hostile anti-aircraft fire was reported more than once, leading to approval for the squadron's silver Belvederes to be repainted in jungle camouflage.

Ian Morgan has an illuminating story about Indonesian anti-aircraft fire:

When I was newly detached to Simmangang, I was being shown around the area by Sam Smith who told me as we were flying along the border, to look out for the tracer ammo coming from the Indon 12.7-millimetre ack-ack gun at a known location. Sam assured me that we were well out of range as you could always see the tracer falling short.

As we passed the said location, I watched avidly for the tracer of which there was no sign. We landed and shut down at the next position and Sam said to the officer in charge that we were surprised and disappointed not to have seen any tracer from the 12.7 gun. The reply was that we would surely have known that it had been replaced by a much bigger 20-millimetre weapon which only had ball ammo, and ball ammo has no tracer. We would have been well within range of that – so we'd probably had a very lucky escape!

Those guns were to be reckoned with and, when two supply-dropping Hastings transports were hit near the frontier, the Belvederes were called on to fly supplies into the riskier DZs – at treetop height.

General Walker continued to press for more helicopters and it was decided that 225 Squadron was needed for a further year in Kuching. As the planned one-year unaccompanied tourists would be coming up for repatriation all at the same time, a phased changeover was started. The programme for the ground crew was soon in full spate and went well – sufficient new men were coming in to maintain numbers. The same was not the case with pilots – there were not enough in the pipeline in the short term. The solution was to transfer a number of unmarried pilots from the other two Whirlwind squadrons and, in August, three bachelor pilots on 110, and four on 103, were given notice of a move to 225.

But before that could happen, in August and September there was an immediate shortage of pilots in Kuching for what turned out to be 225's busiest two months of the campaign thus far. This was partly through both Belvederes and AAC Scouts again suffering technical glitches but also because the entire length of the border was 'hot'. Javelin as well as Scout pilots and even Air Traffic Control officers were persuaded to go along on 225 Squadron missions in the left-hand seat – they at least provided another pair of eyes and perhaps had a chance of keeping the Whirlwind straight, fairly level and on a rough course for base in the event the pilot was hit by Indonesian sharp-shooters. The squadron somehow met its task.

★ ★ ★ ★ ★

While the action was hot in Borneo, the Whirlwind squadron base units at Seletar also had their hands full, as the air and ground crews found on roulement from Borneo detachment. As well as continuation training, Search and Rescue needed constant attention. In July 1964 Colin Ford was at the forefront of a desparate search for an aircraft that had simply disappeared in the jungles of Johore:

I'd returned from Labuan on the Thursday and gone straight onto the SAR roster the next day. I was immediately involved in the ongoing search for an AAC Scout which had disappeared on the Tuesday. The crew of two had put out a 'Mayday' call about six minutes into a low level navex out of Kluang.

The RCC controller immediately organized a search. He had to fix as many variables as possible. He knew the time of the crash, which was six minutes after lift-off from Kluang, and the Scout's planned heading and cruising speed. Using a ten per cent error factor, he worked out the 'area of probability' for the initial search, an area of primary jungle. It yielded nothing. The next step was to target an 'area of possibility' – a circle centred on the airfield, of radius six minutes of flight at maximum speed. This greatly expanded area was searched for two days but again nothing was found. It was decided to reassess the whole operation at midday on Friday.

103 Squadron Search and Rescue Whirlwind at Seletar. (Colin Ford)

I arrived at Kluang early on the Friday morning in the yellow SAR Whirlwind with Ken Coles as navigator and Dickie Bowler as winchman. The search team had expanded to a Navy Wessex, AAC Scouts and Austers, a PR Canberra and us. We would all be on the same radio frequency. I would carry the leader and a couple of others from the FEAF Jungle Rescue Team and the rest of the team would be in the Wessex. With the Canberra as top cover we would each search an area of one by three thousand yards, flying a co-ordinated 'creeping line ahead' pattern at a slow crawl just above the treetops.

Suddenly, there was a yell over the radio: 'Got it – but can't hold it!' It was an Auster – against all the odds, in a steep turn he'd seen his wing tip pass right over the crash site. I could see that he was in the grid pattern next to me so I raced across, calling him to keep above me and direct me to the site. I also asked for another aircraft to go high and fix our position.

With the help of the Auster in a tight orbit above us, we found the site in deep jungle. The Scout was barely visible and the tree tops bore no sign of the entry trajectory. I came to the hover over the crash, but then somehow drifted off by no more than a few feet and we lost visual contact. Very, very carefully we crept slowly back over the trees and found it again. It was so well concealed that it could only be seen from within a very small arc. I asked Dickie to open my survival bergen rucksack, take out my red para hammock and drop it to mark the site.

The Jungle Rescue Team leader wanted me to put him into the treetop to abseil down – at least one hundred and fifty feet. I said, no. Sadly, we could see that the crew were still in the cockpit and as the crash had occurred three days before, the conclusion was obvious. The task now was one of recovery not rescue and no risk taking was warranted.

So we looked for somewhere nearby to land and found a jungle track with a natural clearing. But it was like a chimney, very small and at least a hundred-and-twenty-feet deep – too tight. So we found a slightly bigger clearing and I was about to start my approach when the nav said that the Wessex had just gone into the first clearing! I thought, 'He's bigger than me – if he can get in so can I.' So when he climbed out, I made my approach and entered the chimney – it really was very tight, but we made it.

Now all safely on the ground, the Jungle Rescue Team made their way to the crash site on foot. I returned to Kluang for fuel and saw the Wessex which by now had shut down. I walked across the grass and asked the pilot how he managed to get a Wessex into such a tight clearing. He simply pointed to his main rotor – all his blades had been 'tipped' by the branches.

The bodies of the Scout crew were recovered to Kluang where the RCC controller asked me, as the SAR captain, to carry them to BMH Singapore. It had been three days since the crash so, to increase ventilation in the cabin, we removed the emergency windows and Dickie the winchman sat on the sill with the door all but closed behind him. It was a long trip home.

I couldn't help but think, what would our chances be should that happen to us, in Sabah for example? The Sepulot-Tawau leg was forty-five minutes over completely uninhabited primary jungle. Even if we survived a crash, we would simply disappear for ever.[16]

By this time, the SAR standby (daylight hours only) had been reduced from one hour to fifteen minutes. In September 1964 there were five more scrambles, one of them to go to the aid of a Hunter that had plummeted into the sea off the Johore coast. In October it was the crew of a 110 Squadron Whirlwind that had ditched at Batu Pahat on the east coast that needed rescuing. Then two navy Buccaneers making emergency landings at Changi required a Whirlwind standing by, and this was followed by a search for an RAF Canberra that had disappeared over the China Rock firing range off Pulau Tioman. The Canberra pilot and crew were sadly lost.

★ ★ ★ ★ ★

Helicopters were in greater and greater demand but it was clear that factory deliveries of reliable Whirlwinds were never to be the critical path – that was shared by the supply of spares to maintain them, and the pilots to fly them.

The Tern Hill production line was in top gear. By July 1964 John Davy had completed the Sycamore and Whirlwind course and was posted to Odiham. He never got there. The demand for pilots in Borneo was so urgent that he was siphoned off the mainstream and sent straight to 103 Squadron at Seletar, aged nineteen years eleven months. The British Eagle airline now had a trooping contract and John arrived by Britannia at Paya Lebar, at the time Singapore's international civil airport, on 26 August, and was up and reporting for work early the next morning.

Operational conversion followed, mostly dual in the local area but with some jungle work up-country. It was on one of these missions that he witnessed one of the events that marked a watershed in Confrontation:

> We were flying merrily along at dusk over the jungle in the area of Kota Tinggi in central Johore, when we saw these parachutes coming down – scores of them. We got on the radio and tried to raise the alarm at Singapore Centre, but it seemed that they only worked nine to five.

What John and his fellow pilot had seen was the latest twist in Sukarno's strategy for Confrontation. He had carried the conflict to peninsular Malaya.

This had started in the early hours of 17 August 1964 when boats loaded with a hundred-strong force of Indonesian commandos and Chinese Communists landed on a beach in West Johore. Obviously expecting the inhabitants to rise up in their support, they did little to conceal their movements – Malayan police and troops rounded them up in double-quick time.

The paratroop attack fared not much better. Four Indonesian C-130 transports had loaded 200 men at their base in Sumatra, aiming to drop them near Labis, 100 miles north of Singapore, astride the railway line to Kuala Lumpur and in an area where Communist activity had been among the heaviest in the emergency of the 1950s. But only three aircraft actually took off, and one of them crashed en-route while making a low-level approach to avoid radar detection. The remaining pair ran into an electric storm and scattered their paratroops way off-target.

Despite the lack of response of Singapore Centre to John Davy's alert, retaliation was swift. The insurgents' ill fortune continued when they ran into the battle-hardened 1/10th Gurkha Rifles, resting and retraining before returning to Borneo. The Gurkhas were ferried around by the Wessex helicopters of 845 NAS off HMS *Bulwark*, and supported by air strikes from the Hunters of 20 Squadron RAF. The Seletar and Butterworth Whirlwinds were also brought into the action – the tyro John Davy logging five hours and forty minutes in the air pulling Indonesian bodies out of the paddy-fields. Again, the Malaysians failed to rally to Sukarno's cause and the raid was a complete failure.

Nonetheless, the President persisted in his efforts to stir up trouble on the other side of the Malacca Straits, encouraged by signs of internal Malaysian political unrest, in particular in Singapore. In August racial tensions there reached breaking point and exploded into violent riots.

Sukarno saw his moment to raise the stakes. A flotilla bombarded an Esso bunkering station in the Singapore Straits, as well as the Malaysian patrol craft that came to its defence. Indonesian anti-aircraft guns started firing from the Riau Islands off-shore from RAF Changi, twice hitting an RAF Hastings on the approach – needless to say, air-traffic patterns were hastily altered.

On 3 September, the Malaysian Government declared a State of Emergency. Military installations in Singapore were sandbagged, slit trenches were dug and aircraft dispersed. Nightly curfews were imposed and local civilians were kept off military bases. Guns were deployed and all leave was cancelled. RAAF Sabre jet fighters arrived in Singapore from Butterworth together with FAA Buccaneer bombers off HMS *Victorious*. Aircrew officers and airmen not on Borneo detachment or standby were ordered to report to RAF Regiment field squadrons for duties in crowd control.

The turmoil back at base put further pressure on Walker's forces in the front line, not only by diverting resources away from Borneo but by damaging the morale of those with loved ones in Singapore. During the unrest, life was far from comfortable for servicemen's families in any event and now they saw some of their menfolk armed and facing angry mobs. There was also danger from fifth-column Indonesian bombs, exploding at military establishments and in the streets.

The unrest in Singapore had spread into Sarawak and on 18 August, there were riots in Sibu, Communist sympathizers swarming into the streets vowing to make an end to British and Malayan power in the land. The mayhem rumbled on into September, the month when a 225 Squadron RAF Whirlwind detachment flew in to relieve 845 NAS and their Wessex – just as, in the slightly barbed words of the Junglies, 'the fighting was virtually over'.

Tempers were cooled in Sibu by the unusually early arrival of monsoon rains, but the frontier remained 'hot'. 225 Squadron Whirlwinds were kept busy by continuing Indonesian attacks on native *kampongs*, Sukarno's B-25s and B-26s making frequent strafing runs. Up at Pa Umor near Bario, 110 supported a fierce action in which the Argyll and Sutherland Highlanders claimed six Indonesian dead. Both squadrons reported a new Indonesian tactic, the laying of hand-grenade and other booby-traps on border LPs.[17]

On 9 September the Tunku appealed to the UN Security Council, and a resolution was moved requiring Indonesia to end its aggression. This was vetoed by the Soviets. After close on two years of Confrontation, Britain's and Malaysia's resolve was still strong but their resources were becoming stretched.

The total number of soldiers under Walker's command in Borneo had risen to little more than 10,000 men. West Brigade with a front of 620 miles had just five battalions, one British, three Gurkha and one Malaysian, supported by no more than twenty-five troop-carrying helicopters. Central, with 270 miles had two Gurkha battalions and twelve helicopters, and East with eighty-one miles had one Commando and one infantry battalion forward, one Malaysian in depth and no helicopters at all.

General Walker pressed for reinforcements – they could not come too soon.

Chapter 9

Transfer to 225

The strain on 225 Squadron was eased somewhat in October 1964. It was a quiet month for operations and the transferred pilots started to arrive. From 103 Squadron came Flying Officers Mick Charles, Ian Morgan and Sam Smith. Mick has clear memories of their arrival:

Sam and I found ourselves on a wonderful squadron with a whole bunch of young pilots who were by then very experienced in theatre. Our average age was about twenty-three, even including the QHI.

Our Flight Commander at first was Tim Hannay but after a short while, he was repatriated and the legendary Flight Lieutenant 'Chunky' Lord took over, transferred from 110. His nickname says it all about his appearance and he was quite a laid-back character, one of the lads. He'd flown Vampires in Hong Kong and had a reputation for being a bit of a rebel, but he was highly dependable and professional in the air and inspiring as a leader. He led us all on a pretty long leash – he showed his confidence in us and we responded with responsibility.

There was a very lively Officers' Mess in Kuching. I can remember one of our favourite records was 'Swinging Safari' and after a few *Tigers* we'd start to bounce up and down on the springy floor in time to the beat. Once, in our enthusiasm, we broke some of the joists. We used to go downtown in the evenings about twice a week for a good feed at the open market – you had to get the hang of the chopsticks pretty damn quick or you'd not get anything to eat!

Many of the men had pets. Chunky kept a Malay civet-cat – the locals called it a musang, we called it 'Shitty Death', for obvious reasons. Bren Spikins had one as well – that was known as 'BO'. I have a memory of a toucan at Lundu that had an RAF roundel transfer on either side of its bill.[18]

It was all pretty relaxed at base but the flying was something else again – ground fire on the frontier, and the monsoon in full spate. However, the charts were very much better – proper contours and rivers marked in so that you could actually map-read!

At the end of that same month Squadron Leader Henry Price handed over command, proud of the achievements of 225 in its first year. The Whirlwinds had flown more than 4,000 operational hours, transporting over 20,000 troops and passengers, and carrying 1.5 million-plus pounds of freight. His successor was Squadron Leader Pete Bulford who was, at the time, the only married man on the squadron.

Ian Morgan made the transfer to 225 on 30 October:

Mick, Sam and I were back in Kuching where we'd started in Borneo some fourteen months before. 225 Squadron must have been a very trusting bunch as I had no squadron acceptance of any kind, and on the fourth of November was flying as first pilot around the First Division of Sarawak!

In November a squad of new Borneo Boys, a substantial proportion of the recently graduating Tern Hill course, was flown in to join 225 Squadron on a one-year unaccompanied tour. Among them were Pilot Officers Dave Reid and Fraser Skea.

Dave, who at the time was just twenty-one years and six months old, can still recall the journey:

We went out on a British Eagle Britannia. It was a thirty-hour trip, with stop-offs in Istanbul, Bombay, and Colombo. We landed at RAF Changi and stayed there a few days, bedding in. We had lodgings at the Changi Creek transit hotel, and spent time acclimatizing by the pool at the Officers' Club. We got kitted out with tropical kit in Changi Village, and then boarded the dawn Argosy for Kuching.

We younger pilots were part of a deliberate policy. Up to then a lot of the rotary guys were ex-Single and Twin Pioneer men, the 'Old and Bold' of the Short Range Transport force.

Fraser adds:

It had always been reckoned that you needed a good deal of fixed-wing experience before tackling the mysteries of helicopters. We'd had no more than two hundred hours in training, on fixed and rotary both but after about forty-five hours theatre conversion we were set free to operate in support of the Army all on our own. That was unless a task was considered particularly hazardous when two were detailed for the mission. It was an unheard of free rein for first-tourists.

And we started off in the monsoon period and in 'eighty, eighty, eighty' conditions – that's degrees Fahrenheit, per cent humidity and

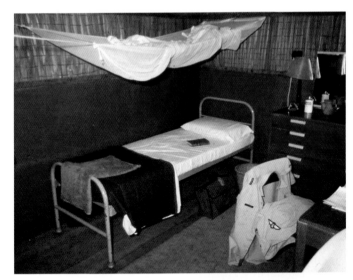

RAF Kuching Officers'
Mess room...
(Rick Atkinson)

...and amah.
(Martin Mayer)

monthly inches of rain.[19] But squadron morale was high, and the risk of enemy action made the flying exciting. We minimized that threat by keeping low along the border, behind the cover of hills and trees.

And, of course, we had a comfortable Mess to go back to at Kuching. The new buildings were all wooden-framed, with *attap*-palm partitioning, but light and airy. Unfortunately, they suffered from the presence of *attap* beetles – and their droppings. At least those were dry, but they rained down in spades and you needed to set up a returned-

91

unserviceable 'chute to catch them. As we brought those back in the Whirlwinds we had access to a ready supply.

Dave continues:

Our rooms were small and basic, but clean – they suited us fine. There was shiny green packing paper fixed to half-way up the walls – we could pin pictures and such onto that. You could hear the beetles scratching away behind it, though.

The Squadron base was on the other, west side of the runway, and the Land Rover would pick us up in the morning and deposit us back in the evening. We were issued with the Oz-pattern lightweight flying-suits, together with jungle boots and flak vests, and got going on ops right away. Early on, I went in the left-hand seat with Chunky Lord on a hearts and minds casevac mission – down to one of our bases right on the border.

It turns out it's the son of a *Dayak*. He's fallen out of a tree and got himself impaled on some panji stakes set up around a military base. Not

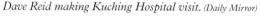

Dave Reid making Kuching Hospital visit. (Daily Mirror)

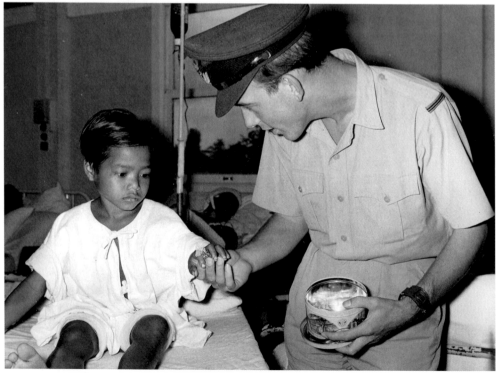

one of ours though – one over the border in Indonesia! The boy's dad has hauled him off the stakes – one of them's gone right through both of his thighs – and rather than take him to the Indons for treatment, he's carried him six miles over to our side. That says a lot. Anyway, we've no crewman so Chunky tells me to sit in the back, holding the lad, while he flies the Whirlwind back to the hospital in Kuching. The boy holds on to me for grim death and by the time we get to Kuching, he's delirious and I'm covered in his blood – seems he'd lost at least three pints. But the lad recovered, and I got my picture in the *Daily Mirror*!

But that apart, I didn't have a very happy first few weeks. I'd suffered from heat cramps right from arrival at Changi on the way out – I learned to put those right with salt tablets, which I took in Coke. But nobody told me what the equatorial sun could do to a light skin like mine – even through the overcast, after one too many sessions at the new swimming-pool downtown, I'm burnt to a frazzle. I'm confined to my room for days, while one of the local *dhobi* girls anoints my blistered back with calamine lotion – a remarkably soothing experience.

Soon after that, I find out that the mozzies like my fair complexion and I go down with an attack of dengue fever. It came on all at once. Ten minutes out on a mission, my teeth begin to chatter so much they can be heard on the intercom, through my throat mike. Then my back starts to ache and I have to unstrap, grab hold of the cockpit roof members and arch my spine to get any sort of relief. Fortunately, we were two up so the other guy flew us back to base. They had to carry me out of the aircraft, and then into hospital with a soaring temperature. I was there for a couple of weeks.

I'm glad to say I was right as rain, and back on ops, by Christmas.

During all those comings and goings in Kuching the Indonesians had made further landings in the Malay Peninsula. In October 1964 twenty-nine Indonesian insurgents landed by sea at Kesang intending to work their way inland, but the soldiers of 28 Brigade, supported by the helicopters of 103 Squadron, had them all in the bag within forty-eight hours. On 8 November, in the teeth of the monsoon, a landing was made at the scenic tourist beach of Jason's Bay, on the east Malayan coast, followed up in December by a further incursion at Pontian Kechil. These incidents gave 103 and 110 Squadron pilots the opportunity for continuation training on actual operations, including rescue sorties, many lifts at tight LPs, and long night cross-countries. A beneficiary of these sorties was John Davy who, within three weeks of his arrival, had completed his theatre conversion:

I was single-pilot operational on 103 Squadron by the seventeenth of September, just two years and three weeks since joining the RAF and just a fortnight past my twentieth birthday. Before the end of the month I was at Labuan, operating mostly in the area out to Sepulot and Pensiangan.

After receiving a tasking signal, we'd fly from Labuan, over the sea and then the mangrove swamps, and follow the single-track railway up the valley and over the bridge and the ridges to Sepulot with its Twin-Pin earth strip.

I learned straight away that you sat the troops forward in the cabin for centre of gravity optimisation. And it was immediately obvious that the available maps, mostly white with some rivers marked, often inaccurately, were little help – I'd have to rely on terrain recognition.

Sometimes, weather necessitated a landing on a dried-up river bed or shingle bank, which would give Ops at Labuan a headache as our shortwave signals were usually blocked by the hills and mountains. It was simply a case of waiting patiently for base to come into range. And we, as well as the Ops Controllers, were frequently put out by the morning mist and fog, which delayed lift-off on morning missions.

A further operational hazard was that spilled rice grains got stuck between the metal plates of the Whirlwinds and in the heat and humidity,

Near miss on AAC Scouts and cookhouse at Long Pa Sia. (Mick Charles)

94

they'd rapidly germinate and grow like wildfire. If they weren't caught early, they'd push the plates apart.

And another danger we had to watch out for, particularly at Sepulot, was from the Beverley and Argosy airdrops.

During one of those drops, Ian Morgan had a near-death experience:

I spent quite a lengthy period at Long Semado airstrip, where the Gurkhas in residence relied entirely on air-resupply for their food, rations, ammunition and defence stores. One day, whilst a drop was in progress, the Company Commander and I were quietly having lunch in the Officers' Mess *basha* under the jungle canopy alongside the runway when there was a huge bang – a veritable explosion from very close quarters and a cloud of dust.

As the air cleared, we saw that following a parachute malfunction a consignment of six-foot steel picket posts had speared through the jungle, embedding themselves in the ground immediately alongside our table. A very narrow escape! From then on, everyone was ordered onto the strip during airdrops so that they could watch and if necessary dodge the descending loads.[20]

John Davy has offered a tribute to the air-supply tactical transports:

Today, airdrops in valleys as confined as Sepulot, Pensiangan and Ba Kelalan would be a Special Forces task in powerful C-130s and C-17s. To suggest it was hairy in a Valetta, Beverley, Hastings or Argosy in the 1960s might be the understatement of the century!

In early December, John became another nominee for transfer to Kuching:

I wasn't at first slated for 225 but swapped with Colin Ford, who wanted to stay based at Seletar to be near the girlfriend who was now to be his future bride.[21] When I got to Kuching, I was checked out by Chunky Lord, and was straight off into battle.

That battle was raging – on all fronts.

Chapter 10

Over the Border

The insurgencies launched by the Indonesians in Malaya and Singapore had proved to be something of a diversionary nuisance, but in military terms they were insignificant. On the other hand, in deciding the outcome of Confrontation, they constituted a watershed. The cat was out of the bag. Indonesia had overtly invaded a sovereign nation and in doing so had provided ammunition for British and Malaysian diplomats, lobbying the UN and the USA in New York and Washington. The raids had also given General Walker additional firepower in his campaign for reinforcements.

In the new situation Walker not only got the promise from Whitehall of three more battalions but also received the commitment of Australia and New Zealand to bring their troops into the conflict. They had hitherto been cautious. Indonesia was a vital trading partner and, with a population of some 85 million, an overwhelmingly large and powerful next-door neighbour, with whom the Australians shared a long land border in New Guinea. But Commonweath air forces were already operating behind the front, and units of the Royal Australian Regiment and Royal New Zealand Infantry Regiment, based in Malaya as part of 28 (Commonweath) Brigade in the Far East Strategic Reserve, had seen action against the Indonesian landings on the peninsula. Now, the evidence of Sukarno's true aggressive intentions gave their governments the political cover to be able to send their soldiers to Borneo. They would be operational from the year-end.

At the same time 230 Squadron, detached with their dozen Whirlwinds at RAF Gütersloh in West Germany and in Cyprus, was put on short notice for service in Borneo. With them at the time was a first-tour Flying Officer, Ron Hepburn. Ron had joined the RAF direct from high school in Glasgow:

I was never an air cadet but years of aircraft spotting at Prestwick had set me on trying for a pilot. I passed the aptitude tests at Hornchurch but as for a commission – it was all-officer entry for aircrew at the time – it was 'thanks, but no thanks'. So I was called up for National Service, as an airman GCA-radar tracker in a hut by the runway – they said if I wanted to be a pilot then university would probably be my best route.

So in 1957, aged twenty-two, I got into Glasgow University, joined the UAS and after going solo in the Chipmunk in seven hours, gained my PPL. This confirmed my credentials and when I applied a second time to the RAF, they offered me a five-year Short Service Commission. I got swept up in the call for younger rotary pilots and after getting my Wings in March '62, it was the Sycamore at Tern Hill. I managed that all right, after I'd learnt that the trick was not to fight the controls, and then found the Whirlwind 10 much more straightforward – the fuel-flow computer was a boon.

I'd married Elspeth, a medical graduate, while on training and as soon as I got to my posting to 230 Squadron, we found we were off to Germany. It was all quite difficult as I was under the magic age of twenty-five when you qualify for full marriage allowance and all that. It didn't become any easier when, after making it through the '62–'63 snowstorms in a six-ship to RAF Gütersloh, I was sent on a two-month detachment to Cyprus. It became even more unsettling when, on leave in Glasgow at the end of November '64, prior to an expected squadron relocation to South Cerney, I received a telegram informing me that the squadron was instead slated for an unaccompanied detachment to Labuan in Borneo and that I was required immediately in Gütersloh to lead a section of four back to Odiham.

So Christmas 1964 found Ron Hepburn and his three charges over Belgium, battling against a 45-knot headwind. Their slow rate of progress (near Ostende they were overtaken by a tram rattling along below them) led to an unscheduled refuelling stop at a handy coastal airfield before tackling the Channel crossing. None of the Whirlwinds had the mandatory Schermuly flares on board, necessary at night to illuminate any forced landing, but Ron and the formation pressed on in the failing light to customs clearance at Manston, eventually touching down in the pitch black at Odiham. There to meet them was the Station Commander. Ron, expecting a rocket, was surprised and relieved to receive nothing but a hearty 'Well done!' to them all.

A newcomer to Ron's squadron was another Tern Hill tyro, Pete Chadwick. A Lancashire lad, Pete had his interest in flying kindled at the age of ten when a grammar school chum suggested they vary their trainspotting with aeroplanes – which they did, at Speke Airport. He joined the local ATC branch and went flying in the Chipmunk, which he loved, as he did the gliding. He completed a Flying Scholarship, passed the two A-levels he needed to qualify for RAF aircrew training and applied:

I was awarded a Direct Entry Commission – with a 38/16 option which earned me an extra pound a week – and inducted at South Cerney in

January '63, aged just eighteen years and two months. I then became another young recruit to rotaries – up to then the preserve of what we called, irreverently, the 'Knackered Old Shits'. I don't know of any particular criteria for this, except perhaps that it was obvious that in fixed-wing training on the Jet Provost I'd not been what you might call a gung-ho pilot – I'd do a loop if they absolutely insisted – but I was a very organized person. I was happy with the thought of helicopters and had a hankering for the up-front world of Search and Rescue.

I got my Wings in June '64 and reported to Tern Hill, where I passed my Final Handling Test early in December '64. When I got to 230 Squadron it was only to find that the whole outfit of nineteen officers and a hundred and eighteen men had been put on notice of relocation for a one-year unaccompanied tour in Labuan.

Pete was to be a Borneo Boy

* * * * *

Largely in response to Indonesian sallies on the Malay Penisula, the 'cavalry' was now on its way. Equally importantly, Sukarno's change of tactic had triggered the Malaysian government into clearing the way for General Walker's troops to cross the Kalimantan border. The Director of Operations had long been pressing the British government for this. SAS and SBS patrols were already operating in Indonesian territory, seeking out the enemy and harassing his operations, but border penetration by other British and Malaysian troops had been thus far strictly prohibited. Despite intense provocation, there had been no hot pursuit. Now that Malaysia was facing Confrontation on two fronts – an insurgency in top gear in Borneo and attacks in the rear in Malaya – Walker saw his moment, and won his case with the Tunku as well as with Whitehall.

A Labour government had been elected in Britain in October 1964, led by Harold Wilson, and Walker found his cross-border proposals supported wholeheartedly by his Secretary of State for Defence, Denis Healey. Healey had served as a major in the beach landings at Anzio in the Second World War, winning the MC. As well as having an understanding of military matters, he was up to date with the campaign, having very recently visited Borneo as Shadow Minister to see for himself what was going on. Accordingly, clearance was given in November 1964 to escalate the SAS patrols into a procedure for authorized operations into Kalimantan, under the codename of CLARET.

They had to be completely clandestine, limited to 2,000 yards' penetration and carried out on a non-attributable and deniable basis – no leeway could be given for Sukarno to claim that British imperialists and their Malay lackeys were the real aggressors. Every patrol was to be authorized by the Director of

Operations and carried out by elite jungle fighters – the SAS and Gurkhas. The sole aim was to inflict sufficient damage on the enemy to limit his capacity to mount incursions. The Indonesian president, as a result of his raids on the Malay homeland, had given Walker the means to go on the offensive.

But CLARET operations were not to be mounted in retaliation and civilian casualties were to be avoided. In addition, each raid had to be self-contained because no close air-support was authorized except in dire emergency – an aircraft brought down while flying over the border would not only be a military and human disaster but would present the Indonesians with a priceless propaganda coup.

So had Sukarno made a colossal strategic error? Had effort and resources been focused on the over-stretched defences in East Malaysia, might the Indonesians have carried the day? As it was, the diversion to West Malaysia had put the British and their allies onto the front foot in Borneo.

The President had publicly vowed to crush Malaysia by the end of 1964 but, as the days advanced through December, he had less and less time in which to do it. Following the first Indonesian landing in West Malaysia, the British air commanders had extended the ADIZ to cover Malaya, right up to the Thailand border. That had the required effect of limiting forays by Sukarno's air forces but in Sarawak, Indonesian troops were reported to be massing along the frontier. Tasking for the rotaries was heavy as West Brigade troops were constantly ferried from strongpoint to strongpoint and delivered to LPs (often simple pads of bamboo and clay) right on the cusp of the border ridge and as near as possible to their objectives. CLARET raids had begun.

To maintain the cloak of utmost secrecy, aircrews were kept in the dark about CLARET operations but 110 Squadron records show that their first involvement in the action was to launch a cross-border mission for 2/6th Gurkha Rifles out of Bario. The pilots must have been aware that they were delivering their passengers mighty close to the frontier. Denis Healey had allowed the limit of penetration to be extended to 5,000 yards, and the Gurkha raiding party was able to advance far enough into the jungle to set up an ambush on a track identified by the SAS as being regularly used by Indonesian troops.

All along the Sarawak border, small clearings were being hacked and blasted out, mostly by Gurkhas with *kukri* and hand-grenade, making room for landing-pads to be built. The pilots' restricted-area landing and lift-off skills were put regularly to the test, as was their appreciation of low-level cover afforded by hillock and crag. It was a time of all-out effort from the rotary men.

Efforts were also being made to reduce pressure on the helicopters wherever possible. The scarce roads were being improved and more built, and full use was made of rivers. Waterborne transport had always been the quietest and stealthiest way for a soldier to to get about in the jungle and wherever a longboat or Royal Marine canoe could do the job they were pressed into service. But that December, the monsoon rains in West Sarawak were even heavier than usual and rivers turned into lakes, and streams into torrents – even canoes were unable to make it through. And all roads, including a new one being built to Lundu, were impassable.

The result was that by the year-end 225 Squadron, now up to its full establishment of pilots, had once more broken the monthly flying record, pushing the total up to 435 hours, flown in no fewer than 2,186 sorties. For the year, the total of freight carried had risen to 2.2 million pounds and the number of troops moved totalled over 45,000. Casevac missions now topped 750.

General Walker's pleas for more helicopters and additional troops were by stages being answered. Not only were the Whirlwinds of 230 Squadron on their way but, also, the Belvederes had been reinforced with four aircraft and crews transferred from 26 Squadron in the Middle East. With one further machine being shipped in from the UK, there were now eleven aircraft on the 66 Squadron strength and, in consequence, the tonnage of stores and equipment moved in December was a unit record. With the arrival of Australian and New Zealand troops at month-end, the rotaries would now be supporting ten battalions as they held the line in Borneo.

On 23rd December 1964 President Sukarno made a desparate bid to make good his promise to his people. He sent a 740-strong force of Indonesian regulars to launch a further seaborne attack on the west coast of Malaya. Like all previous assaults, it failed. Three hundred were repulsed before they landed and, of the remainder, over a hundred were killed and most of the others captured. Again, there was no support from the local people.[22]

It was still a close-run thing but, as 1964 led into 1965, the peoples of South East Asia could see that despite Sukarno's rantings, Malaysia remained, as yet, uncrushed.

Chapter 11

Conversions to Rotaries

As part of the late-1964 reinforcement to the RAF's air assets in the Borneo Campaign, six maritime-reconnaissance Shackletons of 203 Squadron flew in from Northern Ireland. Captaining one of them was the twenty-six-year-old Flight Lieutenant Keith Harding, and he has a story to tell:

In August 1964, rumours spread at RAF Ballykelly that the station would be required to send a number of aircraft out to Changi, to reinforce the resident Shackleton squadron, 205. I lost no time in convincing my crew that we should volunteer on the basis that we would be home for Christmas, whereas the crews who were sent out in due course to replace us, would not.

On September the eleventh, we and five other Shacks departed for Singapore, looking forward to a spell away from the watchful eyes of station and squadron commanders, and to sampling the delights of life in the Far East, plus the chance of being involved in a shooting war. That was how it turned out – well, almost.

First, it took four days and forty-one flying hours to reach Singapore, an epic for my crew most of whom were even younger than me – many of them had never been outside the North Atlantic area of Coastal Command. The 205 Squadron guys were surprised to see us – nobody apparently had told them we were coming – but they were not slow to take advantage of our arrival, many promptly going on leave. It wasn't long before we found ourselves up at Labuan on our own.

Labuan impressed me as the sort of Second World War operational base I had read about in books. Living conditions were basic. A mixture of aircraft, from small Single Pioneers through howling Javelin fighters to the largest transports, arrived and left in what appeared to be a completely random manner. On one occasion an Army Air Corps light aircraft took off across the main dispersal almost under the nose of my aircraft while I was starting engines.

And then there were the helicopters. As far as I remember I had never seen a helicopter before. When I finished flying training no one on my course was posted to helicopters. Helicopters, we understood, were the preserve of very experienced Master Pilots and war-time Flight Lieutenants who had spent years learning dark arts that had nothing to do with normal healthy aviation and who, to a man, suffered an incurable death wish. They spoke a different language and there were dark rumours of crashed helicopters with their crews found in deep holes in the ground having suffered from an awful disease called 'vortex ring'.[23] It was enough to make your hair stand on end. It never occurred to me to think of flying a helicopter.

But it turned out that Shackleton operations in Borneo were not the most exciting in the world. We flew mainly at night searching for large canoes with multiple very powerful outboard engines smuggling arms from Indonesia to Borneo. To do this we depended on radar. On an average night we would illuminate with flares twenty or thirty radar contacts all of which would turn out to be floating palm tree trunks. On returning to our tents in the early hours we would have a beer or two and then retire only to be woken an hour later by the morning Beverley flight running up its engines and threatening to blow our tents away. Any attempt to sleep after that was futile as the temperature in the tent began to soar with the rising sun, so it was back to the beer and hope that there would be no call out that day.

There were compensations. Seen from over the sea at night the display of flickering lightning in the solid wall of cloud along the coastline was reminiscent of a stage curtain lit from behind by a mad electrician. It was hugely impressive. Flying in a four-engine aircraft not known for its manoeuvrability up steep-sided river valleys at low level in the hope of seeing bare-breasted *Dayak* maidens was certainly not boring. Unfortunately that had to stop when after one such escapade I was reported by at least seven police posts as an enemy aircraft.

Then I met Bill Oliver in the Officers' Mess. We had been on the same IOT course but whereas I was a cadet he was an officer 're-badging' from the Army, where he'd served in the Korean War. But I'd not seen him since and was surprised to find that he had escaped from, I believe, Transport Command and was now flying helicopters on 103 Squadron. Somewhere in the back of my mind I remembered reading that an RAF helicopter pilot in Borneo had been awarded a Distinguished Flying Cross so during the casual banter I asked jokingly if he had got his DFC yet. I was somewhat embarrassed when he said 'Yes'.[24]

Over the next glass or two of *Tiger*, Bill explained what the helicopters did in Borneo. I was intrigued. A pilot and perhaps one or two ground crew disappeared into the jungle for several days at a time, supporting an army unit and having virtually no communication with base. Landing near, or if you got it wrong, over the border meant a fair chance of being shot at. In the Shacks, I'd been in the front line of the Cold War but this was something else. Then, to show me, Bill took me flying.

With no more preparation than a Spitfire pilot in the Battle of Britain we strapped in and were away. Bill found a football pitch in a cleared area of jungle where he hovered near the centre and then gave me control. I had had no briefing whatsoever and had only the vaguest idea of what the controls did. For the next few minutes I charged around the pitch like an enraged bull, bellying up at the trees at either end and rigid with terror. Bill meanwhile laughed extravagantly and I thought rather unnecessarily at my performance and showed absolutely no sign of concern – definitely DFC material.

I came back from that flight convinced that the Support Helicopter role, as it became known, was for me. It had everything that appealed including a good chance of another Far East tour. Never mind the fact that I was well established in Coastal Command and a role change at that point would probably not help my career. In the bar of the Membedai Club I asked myself – what career? Bill had got me hooked.

The very next day a signal came from the Air Secretary telling me that I was posted to Malta on a ground tour and was to report in four weeks' time. This news was disappointing but it spurred me into making that application for helicopters. It took three years, but I made it. I had some fascinating and rewarding flying in Northern Ireland, Belize and Norway as well as on exercises all over the UK and Germany.

My life would have been very different had I not volunteered my long suffering crew for the Borneo detachment – and met Bill Oliver in Labuan.

★ ★ ★ ★ ★

Events at the turn of the year 1965 resulted in two more unexpected conversions to rotaries. Serious metal fatigue had been discovered in the wingspars of V-Force Valiant bombers and the entire fleet was scrapped almost overnight. All six squadrons were disbanded and on one was a young co-pilot, Bob Turner.

Bob was born in 1942 in Clevedon when bombs on the Filton aircraft factories, where his father worked, had driven the family to the Bristol Channel. At school in Weston-Super-Mare, he was an enthusiastic member of the ATC but his urge to fly dates from when he was seven years old and the Bristol Brabazon roared over his home, blotting out the sky.

After gliding training and then a PPL on Tiger Moths through the Flying Scholarship scheme, he joined the RAF at the tender age of seventeen, training on the Piston Provost and Vampire. He joined 18 Squadron Valiants at Finningley and for one year, operated in the Electronic Counter Measures role (the fuselage was stuffed with Second World War-vintage equipment). The duties mainly involved training fighter pilots and GCI (Ground-Controlled Interception) stations. This was repetitive but led to many an enjoyable overseas visit to, among others, Singapore, Malta and Cyprus. His colleagues helped him celebrate his twenty-first birthday by escorting him on a visit to the infamous drinking-den of 'The Gut' in Luqa.

In contrast, when on detachment to El Adem in Libya, he met Carole, a teacher in Tobruk. Despite the restrictions imposed in the RAF on a married officer under twenty-five years, Bob and Carole became husband and wife.

After Finningley it was RAF Marham – here, when on fifteen-minute Quick Reaction Alert, the Valiants were loaded with live nuclear bombs. But Bob found the long hours of high-level straight-line flying tedious in the extreme and he was considering his options for a way out of the V-Force when fate took a hand. In February 1965 he and a batch of ex-Valiant co-pilots reported for helicopter conversion at Tern Hill.

The batch included Dave Lanigan. Born a few months before Bob, in 1941, his was another family relocated by the Luftwaffe – out of Southampton and into Dorset. Moved back home after the war, aged twelve he and a school chum set off by bike to explore nearby Hamble Airfield, aiming to get closer to the fascinating aircraft that flew over their houses.

They managed, against all the odds, to talk their way through main-gate security and into the control tower where they asked the Chief Instructor of the Air Service Training Flying School if they could go flying. He responded to their cheek and obvious enthusiam by agreeing that they could. Later that same day, having got their mothers to sign indemnity forms, they were both in the air, grinning widely in the back-seats of Austers and Airspeed Oxfords.

After further air experience with Southampton's ATC Squadron, Dave applied to the RAF at the tender age of fifteen, and again his pluckiness paid off, for in due course he was he was awarded a Flying Scholarship at Hamble and a full Air Force Scholarship – £2 weekly to his mum to ensure he went on to A-levels – before going up to Cranwell in September 1959.

Following fast-jet training at Valley, in 1963 he was posted to the V-Force and settled down to what he expected to be a long career on the Valiant. Then he, too, became one of many young co-pilots at Tern Hill, converting to rotaries.

Chapter 12

Holding the Line

In January 1965 the Federation of Malaysia was elected to the UN Security Council, whereupon an indignant Indonesian delegation stalked out of the Congress chamber. Unfazed by his failure to deliver on his promise of *Ganjang Malaysia*, President Sukarno ordered an increase in the tempo of *Konfrontasi*. General Walker's intelligence network reported enemy troops massing at points along the border and that made for a month in which all the rotary squadrons were more than ordinarily busy.

225 Squadron Whirlwinds worked with 2/10th Gurkha Rifles and the SAS out of Lundu in reinforcing a new patrol base at 5,000 feet in the Pueh Range

Gurkha base in Pueh Range. (Colin Ford)

while, from Simanggang, which had become a further Brigade HQ, the Mid-West, they flew 2/2nd Gurkhas out and a refreshed 1/10th in. The unit establishment, now up to fourteen Whirlwinds, in 1253 missions flew 454 hours in the month. That was still well below the target of forty hours per aircraft – but the OC, Squadron Leader Bulford, reckoned that sixty hours should be possible, if the shortage of spares could be fixed.

Also out of Kuching, in January the Belvederes of 66 Squadron put in 163 operational hours in troop reliefs in 1st Division and in repositioning 105mm guns in the 2nd. In North-East Borneo, 103 and 110 were hampered by the monsoon – the 103 Detachment at Sepulot was cut off for fixed-wing operations for six days, the ridges being hidden under stubborn low cloud and blinding rain. But the Whirlwinds managed to carry out all but a couple of tasks, and lifted Intelligence staff to the border daily to pick up the latest from local informants.

Before the end of the month, HMS *Bulwark* carried the Wessex Mk 1s of 845 NAS down from a period of maintenance in Hong Kong, to join the Whirlwinds of 846 at Sibu, where the squadrons were divided, half afloat and half ashore. The half ashore was further split between Sibu and Nanga Gaat. Those who remained at Sibu spent their time mainly flying resupply shuttles to 'the Gaat', a forward base still right in the thick of the action and hungry for weaponry as much as rations.

★ ★ ★ ★ ★

For the 103 men operating out of Labuan a further move was now on the horizon. It was no secret that 230 Squadron was on its way to the island, and that the 103 Detachment was slated to retrace its steps to Kuching. Colin Ford, for one, would leave North-East Borneo not without some regret:

At Labuan, there was a really friendly relationship between all the crews – helicopter, transport, maritime and fighter. We'd meet them in the bar and in the Ops Room. The next day's tasking would come in from Brunei at around nineteen-hundred hours and we'd all be there, waiting to hear what lay in store for us. We'd meet them in the air, too. When on task, the occasional 'buzz' by a Hunter or a Javelin was not unknown – accompanied by a 'Good morning choppers' on the common UHF frequency.

The transports would tend to return to Labuan at about the same time in the late morning and the practice of mixed-bag formations developed whereby they would 'meet up unofficially' over the sea for a run-in and break. The first formation that I can recall was a Twin Pioneer and a Single Pioneer of 209 Squadron, in echelon. The practice grew and spread across the types – a Beverley with a Twin Pin, two Bevs

48 Squadron Hastings and 52 Squadron Valetta in normal working environment, abnormally in 'mixed bag' formation. (Mike McKinley)

with Twin or Single Pins – and so on. I think my favourite was two Shackletons, somewhat nose down, and two Hunters, somewhat nose up, in echelon.

Hunters and Javelins were now ubiquitous throughout Malaysian Borneo. Based at Kuching and Labuan, they mounted regular sweeps over a huge area, some 1,000 miles in length, enforcing the ADIZ. They maintained a constant readiness to scramble at fifteen minutes' notice to intercept any 'bandits'. They never caught any – by the time the troops on the ground had radioed in, and the fighters had got there, the birds had flown – but they certainly had a deterrent effect on the Indonesian Mustangs. And their low-level passes kept insurgents' heads down and boosted the morale of defenders and locals alike.

Colin believes that the Station Commander, a Wing Commander, may have been a fighter man at some stage:

It wasn't long before he called a halt to mixed bags. He appeared to me to have little time for young heli pilots, who I suspect he regarded as 'tearaways' operating with very little supervision and having, in my case, a slightly cavalier approach to dress regulations. One day as I crossed the pan in flying gear, he hauled me over and barked that I was dressed like a 'bloody beatnik' – perhaps it was the sunglasses and suède chukkas.

But he seemed to love his fighters. When the Javelins first appeared, he stood beaming on the apron as the pair taxied in. I confess to a wry smile when, as they turned onto their parking slots, they opened up the taps a little and appeared to successfully sandblast one side of the Station Commander's car which had been imprudently parked on the dispersals.

Colin has many unforgettable memories of Northern Borneo operations, some hairy and some inspiring:

When our dispersal area was being extended in January, old Japanese munitions were uncovered and I was tasked to lift these – inside the aircraft! – and dump them in the sea. I was not particularly keen as the ammo – it looked like clumps of .5 machine-gun rounds that had fused together – looked a bit dodgy to me. But nothing untoward happened, thankfully.

I can clearly remember one particular mission that turned out to be a salutary lesson. The steep-sided Trusan gorge was 'route one' out of the interior especially in poor weather when the high ground and passes were in cloud. It could be transited in just a few minutes at normal speed and, having made a 90 degree right turn at its end the valley widened and fell comfortably away to the coastal plain. But it could be yet another 'trap for young players' as I found out late one afternoon.

Creeping along just above the treetops in heavy rain and low cloud, I made the decision that I could reach the right hand turn and so I pressed on, while retaining the mental option of turning back. Shortly after entering the gorge the weather turned even worse – the rain was by now torrential – and I was being forced to fly even lower and even slower. So, I decided to turn back. Unfortunately, my escape route had closed completely and, with nowhere to land, I simply had to press on and make the right hand bend. Very wet, pretty scared and at little more than walking pace, I did reach the corner – and gratefully descended to the coastal plain.

Then, on the transit over the sea to Labuan, I was rewarded with one of the best of the stunning sunsets, and a sighting of veritable squadrons of manta rays gently swimming just below the surface, effortlessly flexing their white-tipped wings.

* * * * *

Colin's ex-colleagues, down at Kuching, were now fully paid-up members of 225 Squadron, and its ethos. At the time of the order to all the 103 and 110 single guys to transfer to the permanently Sarawak-based Whirlwinds, Ian Morgan and others protested at the heavy-handiness of this decision:

> We managed to make a bargain with the Senior Personnel Officer at FEAF that, in return for us going, our cars would be transported to Sarawak. This resulted in me motoring happily around Kuching in my MG roadster, and although there was a high tempo of operations – six days on, one off if you were lucky – the car made sure I made the most of scarce leisure time. I even managed to win the affections of the pretty and exotic Lettie, the Kuching Airport ground hostess, despite my being rostered for regular duty at the forward bases.
>
> I did time at both Lundu and Simanggang. At Lundu, in February and March 1965, the key jobs involved carrying hundreds of 2/10th Gurkhas to within striking distance of the border for what I now know were CLARET operations. The Gurkhas, the more senior among them being veterans of the Second World War, were noted for their courage, cunning and tenacity which went a long way towards ensuring success against the Indonesians. And their battalions had the manpower strength – one thousand of them as opposed to maximum seven hundred in the British – to allow them to maintain a high rate of activity.
>
> The relaxed atmosphere on 225 was unique in my experience. We felt special as we were the only rotary squadron wholly based in Kuching, four hundred miles from Seletar.

The squadron had for some months been short of a Training Officer. The gap was filled in January 1965 by the arrival of Flying Officer Hugh Lake. He was one of the older Borneo Boys, having reached the age of thirty. His father and uncle had flown as Royal Flying Corps pilot in the Great War and then with 100 Squadron in the new RAF, so Hugh was an aeroplane enthusiast from an early age.

At school in Charlbury, Oxfordshire, he joined the ATC squadron and soloed on gliders at Weston-on-the-Green. After a five-year apprenticeship with Gloster Aircraft, he progressed to reading Aircraft Design at Cranfield, where, as part of the syllabus, he achieved a Private Pilot's Licence.

Instead of deferred National Service, he went for and got a three-year Short Service commission in the RAF as a pilot and, aged twenty-four, reported to South Cerney for IOT, where he won the Best Cadet award. He trained on the Jet Provost at Syerston and the Vampire at Swinderby before choosing helicopters, deciding that they were the only remaining examples of 'real flying', operating as they were in Malaya, Cyprus, Aden, Germany and Ireland.

Hugh did two years on the Sycamore in Aden, before qualifying as a QHI at Tern Hill. Then came the demand for a Training Officer on 225 Squadron. Hugh was a replacement for the original selection, a Cranwell Sword-of-Honour man who had refused to go because 'it was not his promised career profile'. He went off to prison and Hugh took the Comet to Singapore, en route to Kuching.

Hugh was a candidate for the job partly because it was to be a one-year unaccompanied tour and he was single, but things changed during his embarkation leave:

> Over the Christmas holiday I married my long-time girlfriend, whom I'd met in Aden and therefore, rather to the RAF's surprise, became the third married officer on the squadron. The others were the Squadron Commander Peter Bulford and the Navigation Officer Jack Canham. All the other pilots were single, had an average age of twenty-one and were a simply amazing bunch. They all seemed to have been out in Borneo forever.
>
> The bosses followed the principle, which I have held to ever since, that if you do not tell young people that something is difficult, then they will simply go and do it. I, however, being old and wise, realized just what was being asked of us. I had no 'theatre orientation' and we were simply too busy for me to go on a jungle survival course. I had never in my life seen a two-hundred-foot tree or fifty-foot bamboo, endless jungle or weather like this.
>
> Chunky Lord, the Flight Commander, treated me at first with deep suspicion. He made it clear that 'training' was not to interfere with operations. He put no pressure at all on any of us to conform. I could do exactly as I wished – as long as I did not get in the way and did my bit of tasking. His only criterion of judgement of anyone returning from a sortie was 'Did you get the job – as set out on the tasking sheet or as asked by the local army commander – done?' Only after that would he listen to complaints against his men or by his men against anyone in the field.
>
> Jack Canham had actually been a navigator on 225 Squadron in North Africa in the Second World War, operating Lysanders. He had a tricky job as Navigation Officer. What to teach? The state of the maps meant that finding your way around was mostly down to landscape recognition and there were no navaids save the compass. Jack spent most of his time inventing useful things.

One of Jack Canham's inventions became known as the 'multi-lift hoist' system. In May 1964 he and his colleagues had become frustrated with the limitations of the sixty feet of winch cable on the Whirlwind, critical in operations amongst the 200-foot trees of Borneo. His solution was to provide a 200-foot nylon webbing line organized with loops every fifty feet to match the reach of the Whirlwind's winch. It was operated by moving the hook back up and attaching to a further loop each time. It worked, albeit the chap on the end of the strop had to make sure he unhooked the right loop and had a hair-raising trip dangling on the end. Also, it could take twenty minutes for the whole procedure to be completed for one man, and it required the pilot to maintain an accurate hover at up to 200 feet with almost full left rudder, probably uncomfortably close to trees. But there was nothing better on offer and a requirement was tabled for an official development of the system, together with a more reliable winch and hoist.

Hugh got down to learning the ways of jungle flying on the job:

I will admit to being more or less completely lost during my entire year in Borneo. I was simply amazed at how the pilots, to whom I was meant to act as 'Training Officer', could find their way around with no maps, in all kinds of weather and over country they had never flown before. It has to be remembered that I had spent all my low level flying time in the desert and mountains of Aden – with twenty-mile vis, apart from the occasional sandstorm – or over Shropshire.

Once, early on, accepting a short-notice recovery task, I was given specific navigation instructions by a colleague to 'Go up the river, turn left past a big rock, due north up a valley for ten miles – that's ten minutes in the fog – until you see a green tree' – this over solid jungle – 'and the LZ's in a small cutting on the right.' It worked – navigation was mostly done like that.

I was at once most impressed with the SAS patrols we inserted high up on the border ridge. They would go into the jungle very overweight and carrying just the one week's food and after a fortnight come out thin – looking cheerful but smelling quite horrible.[25] I knew I was in 'new experience' territory when, on an early mission to recover a native Border Scout patrol after dark, a report came up from the cabin below that the sack they had loaded on board at the LZ contained human heads.

Hugh started work straight away on categorizing the nineteen pilots on strength. Of these, five were B Cat, five D, and the rest 'Cat-expired'. With the heavy operational workload, few airborne hours could be allocated to training, so Hugh would fly on tasking sorties. Formal night and instrument flying and engine-off landings were somehow shoe-horned into the busy schedules. In his whole time on the squadron, just the one new pilot had to be sent home, judged unready to take on the role demanded of every pilot in theatre.

John Davy working with SAS... (John Davy)

Problems with serviceability didn't help the training schedule. The Whirlwinds were suffering from increasing rotor and compressor-blade erosion – for the latter, action was in place to develop and instal an air-intake filter on the nose cowling, but that would take a while to implement.[26]

With his Cranfield knowledge and experience, Hugh soon saw a major culprit for the engine erosion besides the sand:

> It was clear that one of the problems was the way the aircraft were being used. It was very difficult to calculate the safe performance at any given time. The trouble was that, while the engine could give all the power you needed, the gearbox could just not take it all.
>
> With no torquemeter, fuel flow was used to monitor engine power. But the power for a given amount of fuel varied with air and engine temperature, and altitude. The various limits were marked by three little red strips pasted to the dial of the fuel-flow gauge, indicating the limit at sea level, five and ten thousand feet – not always easy to see when you were hovering among waving branches, in bright sunlight, in pouring rain or under fire. The gearboxes were being regularly over-torqued.
>
> Added to that, when hovering hot, high and heavy, the left yaw pedal was constantly flat on its stop – meaning that the tail rotor systems were also at full stretch.
>
> I could see the problem – a solution was another matter. There was no torquemeter in sight and the Whirwinds continued to be caned to get their job done – operational necessity and all that.

... and their token of appreciation. (John Davy)

Rotor blade maintenance was also a constant problem, as Mick Charles explains:

> The main rotor blades had a D-section main spar at the leading edge, and the trailing edge, formed in a series of sections, like pockets, was bonded to the rear of that. The flexing of the blades in flight put a strain on these pockets, particularly the twelfth pocket along. We'd check the security of the bond by tapping the pocket with a coin and if it was particularly clunky, we'd get the blade changed. They could be swapped out individually on the Whirlwind, unlike the Sycamore where they came as a balanced set.
>
> Anyway, to strengthen the bonds, two turns of black masking tape would be wound around the blade, with the tape starting and finishing at the rear. This worked well but the heavy rain – and there was a lot of that in Borneo – would drill through the tape at the leading edge and then roll it back in a kind of sausage. This set up a once a revolution vibration. It was, 'wump, wump, wump, wump', a couple of hundred times a minute – infuriating.

For one day in February 1965 Sam Smith was the talk of 225 Squadron. He and his winchman rescued a trio of Gurkhas who had got into difficulties while taking a cooling swim in waters that turned out to be not as inviting as they looked. Throughout the month visitors continued to impose a strain on Sarawak squadrons' daily tasking load, headed by HRH Prince Philip, Duke of Edinburgh, accompanied by Lord Louis Mountbatten on a tour of the border posts. Hugh Lake has a story about that:

We had many visitors to Kuching – most were judged to be of dubious quality, a waste of space, but some were good value. 'Cyclops' Brown, the one-eyed, one-armed Air Marshal, he was great. He immediately followed up the Engineering Officer's complaint that FEAF was stealing our spares, intercepting them on-route from the UK. And Prince Philip was also good news.

The decree came down from Caesar Augustus – 224 Group – that HRH was to visit. Attached was a note that he had specifically instructed that no special arrangements should be made for his visit. Good enough for loyal subjects like 225 Squadron!

It was a Sunday. On Sunday our Pakistani cook, 'Pop', always brewed up a lethal curry mixture in a huge saucepan, which he served with slabs of naan bread and sliced fruit. The Squadron invited guests of various colours, creeds, denominations and genders. A good time was had by all but the Duty Crew, who could not drink the *Tiger* beer on offer.

On this Sunday the guests were swept away at the early hour of two o'clock and the Prince duly turned up at two-thirty. He had his Winco aide, with a line of assorted senior officers making up a long tail. We pilots, all Flying and Pilot Officers, lined up. Philip did not flinch as each man breathed fire all over him. Nor did he even raise an eyebrow at the squadron dress code of the day – no one had on the same uniform. As was our wont, some were in shorts, some in long tropical slacks, and some in jungle green. Some wore shirts, tropical or green, some tropical jackets. Some wore berets and some normal blue peaked hats.

Our Flight Commander, Chunky Lord, was leading our parade – short and round, he'd been out in the Far East a very long time. His clothes were clean but certainly old. His RAF flat hat was very old and literally green with age. It had spent so long in the tropics, and a good part of that time stuffed down the back of the seat in the cockpit, that its peak had worn right through. On special occasions Chunky used to keep this in place by pressing the top and bottom material hard against the central cardboard, depending on the high natural humidity to glue the peak together. On this Sunday however the sun and the wait in the line conspired against his sartorial adjustments. The brim dried out. As

Philip shook his hand vigorously, Chunky's cap-peak split open and the lower material fell down over his face – almost touching his very impressive moustache. Not a flicker from Philip but horror from the entourage and barely suppressed mirth from the line.

Philip addressed each one of us. He knew all about the squadron – that the average age of the pilots was about twenty-one and that only three were married. He also knew all about one-year unaccompanied tours for single men and the problems of the 'Dear John' letters which inevitably resulted.

At the end of the line he got to Corporal Pierce of the RAF Regiment. 'This is our armourer,' says the OC. 'And what do you do?' asked the Prince. 'I look after all the guns and the missiles we have mounted on that standby aircraft over there,' replies Pierce. 'This I must see,' says Philip, setting forth at a brisk pace across the dispersal with the Corporal, followed by the entourage in close order. Philip turns his head and, with a glance, freezes his aide dead in his tracks. The Seniors behind him however, are not trained to expect this non-verbal Halt! command, and finish up in a disorderly heap in the middle of the dispersal pan.

The Duke completes his tour and departs with his thanks and our admiration. The only setback in the whole visit is that, despite manful attempts, he gets no information at all from Pop about the contents of the curry cauldron – the poor man is so overawed he can hardly speak.

Next day we get two messages. The first is from Prince Philip with further thanks for the interesting visit and expressions of admiration for the work the squadron is doing. The second is from 38 Group which begins, 'When an order is sent that no special arrangements are to be made for royalty, what is really meant is …'

Hugh has a postscript to this story:

The standby SS11 missile-carrier was there in case the Indons decided to attack in earnest, with vehicles and heavy guns. The aircraft was rotated, but often one would not be used for a couple of weeks. All the aircraft had a ply covering on the floor to protect from damage by the cargo. In this particular aircraft a previous cargo had clearly been rice because, when we went to close the cabin door after the visit, we found a healthy rice crop about six-inches high sprouting out of all the joints in the plywood, nurtured by the damp, the dark and the high enclosed-cabin temperature. Just as well the entourage was stopped in its tracks by HRH!

* * * * *

There were fewer VIP duties at the more distant Labuan but in February 1965 base facilities were busy with preparations to absorb the arrival of 230 Squadron with its Whirlwinds. Seventy-five per cent of the squadron, commanded by a former wartime fighter pilot, Squadron Leader Doug Thomas, were married, and the prospect of a year unaccompanied in the Far East was met with very mixed feelings. The move was accomplished in two waves. A quartet of bachelors accompanied the twelve Whirlwinds on the maintenance carrier HMS *Triumph* while all other air and ground crew flew to Singapore on a Caledonian Airways DC-7C via Istanbul, the Arabian Gulf and Bombay, arriving on 20 February 1965. On that flight were Ron Hepburn and, as Officer-in-Charge of Troops, Pete Chadwick:

> I was dicked for the job – keeping the younger non-coms in order – as I was the junior guy. The up-side was that we officers were in the First-Class compartment at the back and the crew plied me with gin-and-tonic all the way, in the hope I'd write a good report. The aeroplane ran out of beer before the Gulf – don't ask me where, I was well-gone by then!
>
> So by the end of February 1965, less than two years after joining up, I found myself enjoying the tropical delights of Seletar.

Before the *Triumph* arrived with the squadron's Whirlwinds there was time for a session of jungle survival, most of which was spent wading through Singapore's Mandai swamp, as well as a visit to the Frazer Neaves factory downtown, the home of *Tiger* Beer. Pete fills in the detail:

> The 230 Squadron badge, conceived in the Far East in Sunderland flying-boat days, was based on the *Tiger* beer logo of a tiger and a palm tree, and it was this that got us the visit. But as it was on a Sunday, the factory itself was closed – so the MD happily took us off to the bar, where our boss presented him with a badge and one of our number beat the record for downing a yard of the famous brew.
>
> In due course, the aircraft were craned off *Triumph* in Singapore docks, and reassembled and airtested at Seletar. Two weeks of theatre orientation operations followed, which included getting used to leeches on the instrument panel on a wet morning. After that, the Whirlwinds were duly flown onto *Bulwark* for ferrying to Labuan, where we flew them off on the eighth of March, to what turned out to be a new PSP dispersal down at the southern end of the runway, opposite side to the control tower and the Airport Hotel, which had been taken over as the Officers' Mess. There was no aircon there, but there was in the more comfortable annexe, the Shell Membedai Club down by the beach.

Within two weeks, the Boss had selflessly got himself elected as PMC, whereupon his first action was to engineer the transfer of us all down to the Membedai.

We were operational by the tenth, flying hours-long missions over Brunei Bay and the mountains to Sepulot and Tawau. I was twenty years and four months of age – say no more.

Pete Chadwick and 230 Squadron badge at Labuan HQ: Malay motto Kita Chari Jauh translates as 'We Search Far'. (Pete Chadwick)

From their Labuan base 230 Squadron's operational area stretched from the Borneo coast over to Tawau in the east of Sabah and down along the Sarawak border to a point just before Ba Kelalan. In Tawau the squadron based a single Whirlwind, tasked with positioning and re-supplying the Royal Engineers' survey teams and with working alongside four Alouette helicopters of the RMAF, which had the job of supporting 42 Royal Marine Commando patrols along a forty-mile frontage with Kalimantan. Two 230 Whirlwinds were detached forward at Sepulot where the crews were pleased to find new longhouse accommodation nearing completion. Built by the Gurkhas, with single and double rooms, and bunkbeds on the sidewalls, it was a surprisingly substantial affair. Here, the Whirlwinds worked with the 2/7th Gurkha Rifles along eighty miles of the Sabah/Sarawak front.

Shell Membedai Club, Labuan. (Paul Logan)

Mess basha, Sepulot. (Colin Ford)

At the end the first month of Borneo operations, Doug Thomas declared himself satisfied with the squadron's performance, having achieved over 78 per cent of the monthly task in just twenty-one days, in unfamiliar terrain and weather, and with four of his pilots straight from Tern Hill. In his first report he noted the restrictions on efficiency imposed by the limited refuelling facility available in the field, observing that at many of the LZs no Avtur stocks were available. That meant extra needed to be carried in the Whirlwind's tanks, further limiting payload.

The viewpoint of a first-tourist pilot comes from Pete Chadwick:

We were taking over from a detachment of 103 Squadron, but there was no babysitting by them – after they'd given us the grand tour of the area, we were on our own. The first two weeks were spent getting to know the local area, two-up in the cockpit. My first nav trip was to Tenom on the fifteenth of March, and soon after, staging through Jesselton, I had to find my way as far as Tawau and Sandakan on the east coast. I made my first operational trooping flight a week later, out of the Gurkha base in Brunei to Lawas, with a further lift back to Labuan.

The drill at Labuan was to hover-taxi from the PSP dispersal to the taxiway alongside the runway, and from there we'd do a vertical lift-off. We rarely needed a running take-off from Labuan as we'd usually set off lightly loaded, picking up our payload from over on the mainland. And up-country we'd mostly lift-off too – all the so-called runways were grass strips and very lumpy. The Whirlwind's two small castoring nosewheels didn't cope very well with potholes. In a clearing, if there was room, we'd use a technique of overpitching the rotor to accelerate as quickly as possible followed by a zoom climb to gain height. But in tall trees there was nothing for it but straight up.

At the end of that first month, March, the Flight Commander came up to me and said 'Right young Chadwick, pack a bag, you're off to the Sepulot detachment'. That was a long haul, across to Long Semado, and on over the hills. I took along a crewman on that trip, a techie corporal trained on the squadron, but on all trooping flights we flew alone, to maximize the payload. We did our own refuelling, using the wobble pump, and routine maintenance. I was at Sepulot until the sixth of April, and then went on direct to Tawau for a further three weeks – and still just five months out of training!

I had to learn the tricks of the trade fast, in challenging terrain and weather that was changeable, to put it mildly. The majority of the work was in support of SAS and Gurkhas. The Gurkhas were very smart. I'd give them a fingers-up signal for the number to be carried but they'd be out of my line-of-sight from the cockpit when boarding, and the patrol leader would be responsible for strapping the blokes in and closing the sliding door, when we had one fitted. On occasion, he'd slip in an extra man, and I'd only realize it when the Whirlwind needed just that bit more power to get airborne.

Up on the border, I was aware of Indonesians running all over the place, but I was lucky and never suffered any hits from groundfire – the enemy didn't seem very proficient in that department.

Ron Hepburn was also sent forward to Sepulot, from as early as 4 March for three weeks, flying forty hours of general army support, and then on to Tawau until mid-April for more of the same. Despite his time in Germany, he too was on a steep learning curve:

At Seletar, I'd got my operational ticket after just ten minutes under two hours in the air. But Borneo was all a lot different from the neat fields of northern Europe and the barren slopes of Cyprus. From the air, the jungle with its one to two hundred-foot trees had the appearance of a vast field of green broccoli – somewhat daunting. I was pleased the pilots of 103 were there long enough to show us the way.

Ron Hepburn, operational on 230 Squadron Whirlwinds. (Ron Hepburn)

And, after daily dramas in the rain up on the border, it was good, at both Sepulot and Tawau, after the usual can of *Tiger*, to stroll down to the Ops Tent in the evening and get the next day's tasking. Strangely enough, these were always sent through from Labuan by HF, 'in clear'. I wonder whether the Indos had as much trouble with Borneo telephone lines as we did.

★ ★ ★ ★ ★

In January and February 1965, operating in the 5th Division of Sarawak out of Brunei, 110 Squadron had found the border ominously quiet. Nevertheless, they were busy with routine re-supply and sent two aircraft forward to Long Pa Sia where the army Scouts were suffering prolonged unserviceability. At the same time, they were also involved in the Royal Engineers' survey, which gave their pilots the task of checking the height of likely-looking hills in the area. In the words of the Operational Report:

This calls for an accurate hover over very high ground whilst a rope of predetermined length is lowered through the trees to the ground. In this way a rough estimate of the height of the ground is obtained. Once a hill has been selected, a ground party is, if possible, lowered onto the hill or a place nearby from which they can reach the hill by foot. Once there, they will cut a hole so that heavy tree-felling equipment can be lowered to them, another task for helicopters.

A straightforward task in the detached tones of a Monthly Report but the effort and time needed to carry it out at altitude and in the teeth of a monsoon wind can only be imagined. The same 110 Squadron report writer summarized a further unglamorous but valuable service provided by the helicopters:

Among the many tasks that the squadron is called upon to undertake is the carriage of mail on an ad-hoc basis to troops out on patrol. Mail flown from Labuan and Brunei in fixed-wing aircraft is sorted at Battalion Tactical Headquarters at Bario and the next Whirlwind flight out carries it to the patrols on the border, in fact, almost to the hand of the addressee.

These background tasks – as well as hosting the likes of HRH Prince Philip and the 'Top Brass' – were undertaken while shuttling Gurkhas and Paras in and out of Bario on front-line CLARET missions.

★ ★ ★ ★ ★

Kuching Airport from south-west, 1965: 225 Base in foreground; Army Scouts, RAF Belvederes and Dakota beyond; Javelins on QRA at threshold; Beverley and Argosy transports together with PR Canberra on airport apron. (Colin Ford)

At the beginning of March 1965 the Squadron Commander of 103 Squadron at Labuan said to Colin Ford, 'I've got a job for you. Go down to Kuching and set up our new Detachment HQ.' This was being constructed at the other end of the runway from the old one and was to be shared with the Belvederes. A few days before the majority of the squadron came down courtesy of the Royal Navy, Colin made the trip on a scheduled flight and set to work. He found there was a problem with drainage in the dispersals, which, built between a series of dykes, became virtual paddy-fields when it rained. Colin had to deal with the Base Commander, Wing Commander 'Bluey' Atherton, RAF. Bluey was a bluff Tasmanian who had somehow found his way from Singapore to Australia when the Japanese invaded in 1942, and a somewhat intimidating man, especially to a mere Flying Officer. When shown the problem, Bluey's advice was to 'dig the bloody drains out', which Colin got done – and it worked. He remained in Kuching until his colleagues from Labuan arrived, and was not detached to Labuan again on his FEAF tour.

The Seletar-based Whirlwinds of 103 Squadron spent much of March rounding up Indonesian invaders in Malaya – under interrogation they admitted that they were confused and demoralized by the constant racket of helicopters overhead. Up at Sepulot, the four detached Whirlwinds were flown onto the *Bulwark* on the 10th for ferrying down to Kuching and six days later the three at Labuan flew to join them there. The eighty-one ground crew took over the now-splendid technical accommodation and aircraft and aircrew – thirteen officers, eight Masters and three airmen – were fully operational in 1st Division by the end of the month, alongside 225.

* * * * *

For Chunky Lord's men, the highlight of February 1965 was a dramatic casevac mission late in the month, tasked with locating two British soldiers wounded in an Indonesian ambush. Flying on the Whirlwind crew was Hugh Lake:

We had to fly two-up when close to the border, so Flying Officer Collinson[27] was the pilot, and I was there to do the navigation – SAC Dyet, of the RAF Regiment, was detailed as the crewman. The basics were that there were five SAS men running from the furious Indo response to having one of their senior officers and many more slaughtered in their rivercraft – and a couple of the SAS were shot up.

We were scrambled in the afternoon from Kuching, and flew down to the border. We'd been told that the injured man had a SARBE beacon, and sure enough, when we got to the area, I picked up a signal. When I triangulated it and fixed its position as being over the border, I radioed back to the Lieutenant Colonel in command of the op, and he ordered us to go in and rescue. But the beacon suddenly went silent.

We continued to search until the light gave out, but no joy. However, our fixing of the SARBE's signal had given a steer to the ground party, who found one of the men. It was a tricky winching through tall trees – Collinson had to back the tail rotor into a gap – and the SAS sergeant said we were under fire. But we got the guy into the cabin and flew him back, in the dark and skirting a line of thunderstorms, to Kuching hospital. He was all right.

At first light next morning we went back to try again and there was the signal, loud and clear and on our side of the border – just. We couldn't land – the trees were over a hundred feet high – so we threaded the new two-hundred-foot abseil tape[28] through the branches. The soldier just managed to sit in the strop and we flew him back into the clear where we could land. The poor guy was swinging like a conker on a string, the tape resonating like a piano wire. We dropped him as gently as we could onto the ground, then landed next to him. He had a badly

The abseil tape. (Colin Ford)

wounded leg and had done well to drag himself back over the border in the night. We put him on a stretcher and flew him to hospital.

He came through all right. Funnily enough, I met him years later at the SAS base in Malvern.

For that mission Collinson was awarded the DFC and Dyet and Lake were Mentioned in Despatches.

March 1965 was the busiest month for 225 Squadron since its arrival in Borneo. Troop movements were intensive – 3rd Royal Australian Regiment relieving 1/7th Gurkha Rifles, and 2 Para into the new strongpoint of Balai Ringin. The men of 3 RAR immediately ran into trouble – once into an Indonesian booby trap and once when two of the Australian patrols disastrously mistook each other for the enemy. Fortunately, in each incident, casualties were light. The Lundu Detachment extracted the 1st Argyll and Sutherland Highlanders and inserted the 2/10th Gurkhas, which involved an extensive lift of 150 men from Melanu Beach to a new position some twenty miles into the interior. Despite heavy rain damage to rotors and blade tips, the 225 Whirlwinds achieved the long-awaited forty hours per aircraft in the month.

That required the best of fuel management. Hugh Lake has a further story about that:

The Whirlwind 10 was a thirsty beast. Its Gnome engine had the advantage of using not petrol, which was liable to explode in a crash, but Avtur. Mind you, it used a lot of it. The principle in war is to try and avoid transporting fuel by air. You tend to use most of the fuel you ship out just getting the transporting helicopter back to base, leaving you not much better off than when you started.

In West Brigade there was increasingly good road and usually good river communications so fuel could be shipped in bulk to the forward LZs, usually in 42-gallon drums but to the more remote areas, in jerry cans.

In the heat, water used to condense inside the cans and a slug of it would stop the engine dead – not a good idea. So when we needed the fuel, we had to let it settle for about half an hour and then take a water sample. Then, we'd leave the bottom ten per cent in the container, which we used to give to the locals. But Shell complained that we were killing their trade, and after that we had to tip it away. There were instances of pilots having to hold off the *Ibans* with a pistol while this was done – they thought, quite rightly, this was a criminal waste of a valuable resource.

One day, in the forty-hour frenzy, one of our pilots was pre-positioned with his aircraft at a remote army base for the day. The CO invited him to a fierce curry lunch, and asked him if he would take back a load of jerry cans, as the base had been under sporadic attack for a week and had not managed to get them off the site. This was agreed and the lunch proceeded until mid-afternoon.

The cargo was about a hundred-and-fifty cans, neatly stacked on the floor of the cabin and standing not more than three feet high – a modest cargo. The pilot checked that they were secure, slammed the cabin door shut and bade farewell to his generous hosts.

This army site was cut out of the pinnacle of a hill. The landing pad was right on top and just big enough for the Whirlwinds wheels to fit. So, when – after the lunch! – the pilot climbed aboard, fired up the motor, and whirled the blades, he had nothing in his way. Raising the collective lever, he leapt into the air at full power and tipped forward over the edge of the pad. With an appropriate flourish, he was away.

At once he knew he was in real trouble. The blades were making a terrible noise and the vibration was severe. He could only just maintain height. There was no question of making it back to the pad on the peak. He crept home very carefully, back to the main base about forty miles down the valley. As he approached he radioed ahead that all was not well – but the detachment had already been alerted by the loud banging noises which preceded him.

He daren't come to the hover, so he did a run-on landing, and shut down. On investigation it was found that nothing was wrong with the blades or the rigging. It was the cargo. The jerry cans each had, as regulations required, about ten pounds of fuel in them. That is fifteen hundred pounds, on top of their own weight. The helicopter was about twenty per cent overloaded. Much maintenance activity ensued.

★ ★ ★ ★ ★

In March 1965 an important step was taken in the RAF Support Helicopter (SH) world. From 1953, when the Whirlwind first entered RAF service, it became evident that, as its passenger compartment was separate from the pilot, a crewman was essential to take charge of emplaning and deplaning of troops, winching, and manning the machine gun.

In the Far East, in the Malayan Emergency and then in Borneo the need became urgent and, in the front line, crewmen were press-ganged from the RAF Regiment. But power considerations often prevented them from being carried on the final stages of operational sorties and, away from base, the technical function, for in-the-field maintenance and running repair, was considered of prime importance. So crewmen were detailed from ground crew NCO technicians. But the need for a professional crewman was acknowledged and at the end of March a retrained Flight Engineer, Flight Sergeant Hammond, arrived on 110 Squadron in Labuan to take up post as one of the first Senior NCO aircrew crewmen. It was expected to take another six months for the Borneo squadrons to be brought up to full crewman establishment, but Flight Sergeant Hammond was a start – the start of a line that was to continue to RAF helicopter operations of the present day.

Chapter 13

Showdown at Plaman Mapu

The new crewman was quickly into action. By April 1965 the defensive posture of the security forces had almost totally morphed into a series of aggressive CLARET patrols over the frontier. The limit of penetration had been extended to 10,000 yards and patrols were now being inserted high on Sarawak and Sabah slopes of the border ridges, so that they could advance immediately into the Kalimantan side. These operations gave the crewmen many an opportunity to man the winch and the Bren gun.

Out of Bario 110 was working closely with the Australian SAS and 2/6th Gurkhas, into and out of tight LPs that tested the pilots' skills, not just in helicopter-handling but also in giving and receiving hand-signals. Where an LP proved to be unapproachable the gestures became more and more frenetic both ways.

CLARET patrols were continually covered by repositioned 105mm howitzers and, when a Belvedere was not available, the job was carried out by a Whirlwind. Ian Morgan explains how it was done:

> It had to be planned in some detail. The 105-millimetre pack howitzer was like a kit gun – it broke down into several pieces. Arriving on site with just sufficient fuel for the event, one would start by lifting some ammo together with a few of the gunners to the new LZ, ready to receive the gun. Then the remaining items were attached in increasing order of heaviness to the under-slung hook and shuttled to the new position – first the wheels and chassis, then the armour-plated shield, and finally, with absolutely minimal fuel, the very heavy barrel in an under-slung load net. Then it was off to refuel before returning to lift the remainder of the men and, again in nets, the ammo.[29] It showed what could be done with ingenuity and planning!

Ian's point is borne out by the fact that, in April, 110 Squadron demonstrated their operational *nous* by managing to move an entire gun from Bario to Pa Main as an internal load. Another exceptional lift was made in the same month by a 230 Squadron Whirlwind, tasked with an unusual casevac mission. Two civilians were reported badly injured in a fall from the 13,455-foot summit of Mount Kinabalu. Their colleagues set to at humping them down the mountain to a ledge known to be at 8,300 feet, where a helicopter rescue might just be possible. In heavy rain the Squadron QHI, Flight Lieutenant McEachern, edged his Whirlwind alongside the crags and right up to the ledge, where he succeeded in making a safe landing, aided by directions from his crewman, Sergeant Ashall. There the two men spent an uncomfortable and damp nine hours clinging to the mountain before the climbing-party managed to stagger across the crag with their awkward load. In torrential rain and fading light, McEachern and Ashall flew off their perilous perch to carry their charges the thousands of feet down to the coast, and the comforting safety of Jesselton Hospital.

★ ★ ★ ★ ★

In Kuching the endless stream of visitors to Sarawak continued. The authorities had decided that the General Service Medal (GSM), with Borneo clasp, was to be awarded for active service in the campaign, backdated to December 1962. This might very well have encouraged more staff and ground-tour people, understandably keen to tot up their thirty days' qualifying time at the sharper end of affairs, to take the Changi to Kuching morning shuttle.

On 225 Squadron, recovered from his earlier ailments, Dave Reid had been sent forward to Simanggang for a three-month stint, which he very much enjoyed:

> We were originally housed on the army camp but later moved into a concrete bungalow on stilts which belonged to the local doctor – and that was much more comfortable. And it was separate from the base, nearer the village where the girls were always pleased to see us – a couple of them extremely so.
>
> We relished our independence in that bungalow, and the freedom we were given to do our job – flying three Whirlwinds in support of the 2/2nd Gurkhas under Lieutenant Colonel Hamish Grey. But don't think that we were slap-happy in the air.
>
> Of course, there were those who took risks – right to the limits, too close for my liking. I was once paired at Lundu with a chap who took the radios out of his Whirlwind to save weight. We were tasked to lift a company of Gurkhas off a village *padang* to a forward location, operating with a 66 Squadron Belvedere alongside. With minimum fuel, and using a running take-off, this bloke managed to lift more than the

Belvedere could manage. Of course, our turn-round time was less than theirs but I reckon he took about sixteen in one go.

He argued that he was not overweight as he was carrying so little fuel, but many of the men were not strapped in – there weren't enough belts. Questions were asked, but Pete Bulford decided that the chap was only doing his best to maximize load and cut down the hours flown. In any event, I'd learnt a good rule of procedure – I looked at how many he was carrying, and then took two fewer.

But early in that Simanggang det, I took a risk too. I was called in to carry out a ground-run engine test. When I got to the strip, I could see only two aircraft where there should have been three – the other turned out to be hidden down over the far side of the runway, which was raised up quite high for better drainage. The crew chief shamefacedly confessed that during refuelling, the man on the brakes had not done his job properly and the Whirlwind had run away, ending up tilted backwards off the strip, bending the strut that we called the 'hockey stick', mounted under the tail-boom to dampen any rough landing.

The crew had been digging for some time and had got the machine level but you could only just see the rotor. They asked could I possibly fly it back up to the runway for them? This I did. But, before long the OC's asking 'What's all this about a hockey stick reorder?' I manage not to give the game away and I'm a hero to the crew from then on.

Wherever they went on their missions the Whirlwind pilots were always looking for opportunities to further the hearts and minds campaign. Hugh Lake found that rewarding in more than one way:

Flying with Dave Collinson you always found yourself playing football – whenever we landed in a *kampong*, he'd produce a ball. The local kids loved him. From this contact with the locals I found out a gruesome piece of Intelligence. When the Indons raided a village, the first two people they killed were the headman and the schoolteacher – without leadership and school-learning, the *Dayaks* were wide open to terrorist propaganda.

The football helped me in a bit of hearts and mind campaigning too. While flying in Aden I had worked as head of Drama and Talks on the Forces Radio station and I used this experience to put together some schools broadcasting in Kuching. Flying into the remote areas I could, thanks to Dave's football, find out from the kids just how effective any particular programme was. This I fed back to the US Peace Corps writers, who could then change the texts and style to fit the youngsters' understanding.

At Simanggang, as well as supporting CLARET raids, and flying almost daily casevac missions, the detachment had a major task lifting supplies to the new hilltop base the Gurkhas were constructing at Jambu. Over on the western border at Lundu, further base-building materials were being shifted, 10 per cent of them as USLs.

Permission had been granted for Continuation Training to be carried out in the field and Hugh Lake had started to make inroads into the Pilot Categorization backlog – Ian Morgan retained his C, and Dave Reid, Fraser Skea and John Davy joined him at the same level. Squadron Leader Bulford reported that, for the first time, he had more pilots than he had serviceable aircraft – more Borneo Boys had arrived. Pilot Officer Brian Skillicorn had been, as a sergeant, on the same Tern Hill course as Dave and Fraser, but had gone off for commissioning before going out to Kuching[30]. Twenty-four-year-old Flying Officer Mike McKinley had taken a rather more tortuous route to 225.

His grandfather had served as a pilot in the RFC in 1918 before transferring to the new RAF for a full career, and his father and three of his uncles were following in his footsteps. Mike was born in October 1941 in Dumfries, where his father was operating Sunderlands. The eldest of three brothers, Mike set out to add his name to the family RAF list. After schooling, and the CCF at St Edward's in Oxford, he took the aptitude and selection tests and won a place in 1959 on 81 Entry at the RAF College, Cranwell. To maintain the McKinley family's fine service record, his middle brother went into the Army and the youngest into the Royal Navy.

Mike graduated, with Wings in July 1962. During Advanced Flying Training on the Gnat at Valley he was already looking for something at the sharp end and applied to serve in the Sultan of Oman's Air Force on the Caribou but had no success. The RAF Establishment wanted him on the V-Force, as a co-pilot on the Vulcan. After twelve months of 'sitting at the end of the runway waiting to annihilate the Soviet Union', he engineered a transfer to helicopters. At Tern Hill he had no difficulty with the transition from fixed-wing to rotors, likening it to 'moving from car to motor-bike – same element, different mechanics'. He arrived at 225 Squadron in Kuching on 10 April and found himself in just the environment he was looking for, the *laissez-faire* and challenging regime of Pete Bulford and Chunky Lord.

There was no opportunity for dedicated training hours, so Chunky Lord sent him out on operational sorties for conversion. In his first letter home Mike wrote:

The Kuching base has grown to vast proportions and has started to accumulate the usual lists of orders and restrictions, and the little private empires that build up on full-size stations. But 225 seems to enjoy something of a unique position here. There are parts of all sorts of squadrons operating from the airfield – Hunters, Javelins, Pioneers, Hastings, Valettas, Belvederes and other Whirlwinds – but ours is the only self-sufficient and permanently resident unit.

It is also quite the youngest squadron that I have come across so far. I'd always understood that helicopter units consisted of ageing Flight Lieutenants and Master Pilots, but on 225 the only two Flight Louie pilots are the Flight Commander and the chap who's i/c our largest Detachment. The rest, almost twenty in all, are Pilot or Flying Officers. In fact, it would really have blown the system if I had passed my promotion exams!

The result of all this is that nobody minds taking orders from those qualified to give them, no matter what their rank might be, and no one is furiously fighting to impress anyone else – altogether a most happy state of affairs. All on the squadron, including my cynical self, take it for granted that there is no better outfit in the Service. But the rest of the station regards us, perhaps with a tinge of envy, as a disgusting bunch of rowdies!

For a Cranwell graduate who'd escaped from the rigid and unrewarding world of the V-Force, the shorts, shirt and jungle-boot rig, continuing round of front-line self-reliant tasking and squadron camaraderie must have been a revelation and a great release. Mike was one of the few Cranwell-trained officers to find their way to Borneo rotaries.

Two weeks after his arrival in Kuching, following involvement in an action at the Paras' border strongpoint of Plaman Mapu, he wrote another letter home:

On Tuesday morning, the twenty-seventh of April, we were all pulled out of bed at 6.30am with the news that the Indons had attacked a hilltop Para position on the border, killing one and seriously wounding two as well as inflicting various minor injuries. We were to ferry 2/2nd Gurkhas along likely withdrawal routes and later into the strongpoint itself.

We flew off in three Whirlwinds to the Gurkhas' Company HQ at Balai Ringin and had a very full and exciting day collecting and delivering troops and supplies – operating together as a squadron. It was all very satisfying.

In the afternoon we had real drama when we were tasked to go right onto the border to drop off a platoon of belligerent Gurkhas to cut off the Indonesians' retreat. I was sitting at number four when Chunky Lord went off in the lead Whirlwind with machine guns fitted in the doorway. He went in to see if the landing-site was clear and collected two bullet-holes in his aircraft for his trouble.

He came back beaming from ear-to-ear – his crewmen had emptied three Bren magazines into the jungle around the landing-site, and he'd fired all the rounds in his pistol. Obviously, the place was heavily ambushed and it was decided we couldn't go in. Unfortunately, the Army couldn't get accurate fire down on the position so the chances are most of the enemy will have got away. But we're still looking for them.

In this action Fraser Skea flew seven hours in the one day. He was at Plaman Mapu too, as first pilot in the lead aircraft:

With Chunky Lord in the left-hand seat, I made a Full Precautions approach to this dodgy LZ. Over the radio, the Paras advised opening fire on approach – I remember the 'pop, pop, pop' from our Bren gunners downstairs being answered immediately with a much more powerful 'brrr, brrr, brrr' from the Indo machine guns. We scarpered with two bullets in the airframe – one hit the tail boom and another ploughed into the cabin bulkhead, not more than an inch from our gunner's nose.

Intelligence staff concluded that the cross-border raids of the British and their allies were causing the Indonesians considerable trouble and the Plaman Mapu attack was by way of a counter-punch. It was carried out by crack Javanese troops, on a pitch-black night, in pouring rain – 120 of them against a post manned by forty.

The next day Mike McKinley wrote home that he'd seen his first dead body:

It was one of the Indonesians. He must have been a very brave man – he had a great wound in his leg and a tourniquet above it. He had apparently been wounded quite badly in the first attack, had applied the tourniquet himself and then led the second. He'd got through two lots of barbed wire and into the mortar pit inside the camp before the Para Sergeant Major shot him. I hope we can assume that most of their troops are not of that calibre.

But many of them were, and they were nothing if not persistent. In mid-May another group, apparently from the same force, tried again. As Mike wrote:

The day before yesterday, things started to build up again near the scene of the earlier drama, and the Paras were again on the receiving end. This time, there was said to be an even larger party of Indons sculling around in the area, but they were discovered before they could mount a real attack. Even so, one Para was killed when a foot patrol ran into his party.

It was decided that this time they should be taught a real lesson – artillery first, then the Hunters would go in, for the first time out here! Then, after they'd been softened up there would be a grand helicopter-borne attack.

The Hunters had indeed been given clearance to use their firepower in support of the Paras, but on the Sarawak side of the border, in concert with the howitzers at Mongkus, Mujat and Gunong Gajak. The pilots and gunners had come to action stations and were raring to go. But it was not to be. The whole thing was foiled when a gigantic thunderstorm stationed itself over the entire area and stayed there until it was too late in the day to trigger the action.

But within the week there was more excitement for Mike:

We were called out to sort out yet another incursion aimed at the 2nd Paras. We took four aircraft to Balai Ringin and stayed there for a couple of days and had some superb and varied flying in and out of all sorts of strange landing sites. We got plenty of practice of our technique for going into potentially dangerous clearings. First, they're softened up by concentrated fire from 105-millimetre howitzers, directed from the air by an AAC Sioux.[31] and then the Whirlwinds go in, Brens and Sterlings firing furiously. Then, if all is quiet, we land.

One of the patrols we put in had a shock. They – about eight of them – ran into a party of some thirty Indons, who believe it or not, ran up to them, waving, laughing and shouting! They looked to be either drunk or drugged. The Paras were so astounded that they held their fire to see what was going on – and then opened fire at six yards' range. They killed five, and injured fifteen, before beating a hasty retreat.

★ ★ ★ ★ ★

May 1965 was a full month for the Kuching Whirlwind squadrons. For 225, apart from the business in the Plaman Mapu area, there was a casevac call-out when two Australian troopers stepped on American-manufactured jumping anti-personnel mines. In the continuing shortage of serviceable Belvederes the Simanggang detachment flew 180 hours hauling 400,000lb of stores to the Jambu construction site, and, at Lundu, the 1st Battalion Royal New Zealand Infantry Regiment were moved in as the 1/10th Gurkhas moved out. The squadron reported 544 hours in the month, forty-six per aircraft, and Pete Bulford wrote: 'There was not a great deal of hours spare for training at dets but the new guys gained a high level of experience in successful joint ops with the Army.'

103 also found the action in May intensive, flying a series of cut-off and medevac missions with 2 Para. The squadron's tasking rota was beginning to feel the strain as tour-end repatriations by the end of the month brought the complement of pilots down to thirteen, out of an establishment of sixteen.

Up in Labuan and Brunei 110 and 230 Squadrons reported that although the tasking was heavy (230 had flown 1,510 hours in its first eleven-and-a-half weeks) the border had quietened down. CLARET missions were beginning to achieve their purpose.

On the last day of the month 110 Squadron Whirlwinds at Seletar were called into action to counter a further Indonesian landing in Southern Johore. Some twenty-five Indonesians landed at Penggarang and were swiftly rounded up by helicopter-borne troops – this was to prove to be the final Indonesian incursion in Western Malaysia

Chapter 14

Counter-Punch

From the first quarter of 1965 the battalions under General Walker's command were able to muster some 14,000 men, supported by sixty troop-carrying helicopters. But Sukarno must have been aware that this force, in an area the size of England and Scotland combined, was still spread so thinly that there was always the possibility of success with a sudden mass attack. He could make a move either through Tawau, down the rivers to Brunei, or across the lowlands to Kuching. He might even deploy his massive air force in support.

To discourage any such plans General Walker increased the power of his counter-punching. RAF Victor and Vulcan bombers flew in as a deterrent to air action. The limit of CLARET penetration was extended to 20,000 yards and a fourth British battalion was moved into the Kuching area.

The British intelligence network went into overdrive. As well as the admirable SAS, Gurkhas, *Iban* Border Scouts and trackers, there were codebreakers who untangled Indonesian military and diplomatic ciphers, and a Government Communications Headquarters listening post in Singapore. Together they gained information vital to the planning of CLARET raids as well as providing prior warning of Indonesian troop concentrations.

In support the helicopter effort continued at full throttle.

★ ★ ★ ★ ★

In June 230 Squadron Whirlwinds at Tawau flew a number of CLARET insertions and casevacs at night. One of the four-man SAS patrols had the ill fortune to run into a rogue elephant, an encounter in which one man was seriously injured. They were out of SARBE range, so three of the men took the beacon and, leaving their immobile colleague, went off to raise the alarm. This they did but, by the time the rescue party got back to find him, the injured man was dead. On the 29th of the month, a beacon signal was again triangulated as being over the border and a Whirlwind was cleared for a night-rescue flight over Indonesian territory. Fortunately for the crew the two distressed soldiers made it to a border LZ after all.

On a round-trip to the Plain of Bah Ron Hepburn found that, at Bario, a written-off Twin Pioneer fuselage had been creatively inverted to form an extra classroom for the local children. He reports that he was delayed up there, dangerously, by an army officer's dalliance with the headman's daughter. He was back at Sepulot until 6 June, where, after flying 152 hours in three months, he made his final sortie in theatre.

En route to Labuan in February 1965 Ron had had just the single week at Seletar and not seen much of Singapore town. On the way home five months later he did manage an outing or two but, after the picturesque unspoiled country and *kampongs* of Borneo and the military order of Seletar, he was not the first to find it somewhat disappointing – perhaps it was the town's extraordinarily pungent smell.

Back in the UK, and reunited with his young wife, the commercial helicopter world beckoned and at the end of his short service commission in September, Ron found himself on a contract to train AAC pilots on the Hiller at Middle Wallop.

★ ★ ★ ★ ★

The roulement of pilots of 103 Squadron aircrews at Kuching meant that a deal of their time was spent on dedicated SAR duty at Seletar, operating with two yellow-painted Whirlwinds, trained navigators and winchmen. Missions in June 1965 ranged from escorting a Beverley on two engines in over the Indian Ocean, through pulling transport aircrews out of the South China Sea on 'Changi Splash' parachute training, to investigating a torpedo floating in the Straits of Johore that turned out to be an old fire extinguisher. Towards the end of the month there was a pre-dawn call out for Colin Ford:

> I'd been downtown with my fiancée and got back to my room at around one in the morning to find a note pinned to my door – 'Call the RCC', the Regional Control Centre in Singapore. They told me there'd been an incident during the evening when a Royal Navy ship had intercepted an Indonesian *kumpit*, a large wooden boat, in the Straits south of Singapore Island. It seems a naval officer had boarded the boat, whereupon it promptly blew up. The officer was still missing.
>
> I was to start a search at dawn and as we were authorized to overfly Indonesian waters, a 60 Squadron Javelin was to provide top cover in case of interference from Sumatra. I made arrangements with my crew and then grabbed a couple of hours sleep.
>
> We were airborne before dawn, made radio contact with the Javelin over St John's Light and started our low level search. Then, out of the gloom I saw a warship, gently easing through the water without lights

and approaching head on. For a split second I thought, Oops! But it turned out to be friendly – probably on the same search.

Sadly, although we stayed out there a long time we found no sign of the naval officer.[32]

The same month, out in Sarawak, there were three more incursions in the 2 Para area, during one of which a 103 Squadron Whirlwind acted as air observation post for the army howitzers and in another a patrol was winched out under fire. June 1965 was also the month when Peter Davis was awarded the DFC for his successful command of 103 Squadron in Borneo. And it marked the introduction of a new system for guiding down helicopters at night

This, designed by Wing Commander Dowling, OC Helicopter Wing Seletar, and a doyen of the rotary world, comprised five torches (two red and three white) held by five brave men placed so as to give the approaching pilot a sense of perspective. As long as he kept the red lights (held low in the front rank) below and within the three whites (held high in the rear) he'd be safe. The system was christened Seletar Helicopter Night Approach Pattern, or SHNAP for short. It was simple and it worked – so long as those brave men stood their ground in the downdraught and din below a descending helicopter, in the dark …

For 225 Squadron the month saw a new record of 885 flying hours. FEAF had made a case to the newly-established Ministry of Defence that a further helicopter squadron was needed in Kuching to support West Brigade. There was no slack, they said, to respond if the Indons really attacked in force. The result was that HM Treasury had insisted on a 'stress test' to see how a squadron might manage in a surge situation, and 225 were chosen. They were set a target of sixty hours per aircraft, and for this they were given preferential tasking over 103 and 66 Squadrons. Hugh Lake picks up the story:

> It has to be remembered that 225 was not a FEAF squadron. It was detached by 38 Group from Odiham to support the Confrontation operation and they thought themselves pretty special. So when the Boss, Peter Bulford, came into the Crew Room and announced that, for the next month, we were to be offered all the tasking in West Brigade, others only flying those missions we could not manage, the challenge was on. We wanted to show FEAF that 225 could cope with any surge.
>
> The ground crew were put on full alert – virtually banned from leaving the base. Arrangements were put in place which allowed us to steal spare parts and whole engines from other squadrons. Priority supplies from the UK came direct to 225 without passing through the thieving hands of 224 Group in Singapore. All training was stopped and going anywhere away from the squadron was only allowed if the Duty Officer knew where to get hold of you.

We flew our little socks off. All missions were one pilot up and some of us flew every day that month. We flew from dawn to dusk and into the night. We were re-tasked while airborne and away from base. We over-nighted in remote locations to limit nugatory positioning flights and, best of all, we smugly sat down to late meals in the Mess alongside pilots from the other squadrons who had not flown for a week!

Of course we showed how much spare capacity the 'part timers' actually had in hand. No new squadron was deployed. Once again 225 was not flavour of the month in FEAF HQ!

During the trial, missions came thick and fast. Four aircraft were despatched to Gunang Gajak, where a hard core of Indonesian insurgents, plus a group from the CCO, attacked at the eighteen-mile post on the Serian Road. SAS missions were flown from Kuching to the border and the 2/2nd King Edward's Own Gurkha Rifles were flown in to replace not only the Argyll and Sutherland Highlanders but unfortunately also their two Sioux light helicopters, which had proved so useful for reconnaissance and the ranging of howitzers. A seemingly endless stream of corrugated iron was hoisted from the Lundu detachment to the new camp at Jambu. At the end of the month a patrol of the Royal New Zealand Infantry was ambushed in the jungle, and a 225 crew had the grim task of bringing out a wounded man alongside three bodies.

In addition the squadron flew hearts and minds missions to remote longhouses and gave lessons in trooping and stretcher winching to the Medical Officer of the New Zealand Infantry and his team. In just a month, 225 broke the sixty-hour barrier by four hours per aircraft, carrying 1Mlb-plus of freight and 8,478 troops. On top of all that Hugh Lake found time to award Sam Smith a B Category, and Her Majesty the Queen gave Chunky Lord her Commendation for Valuable Services (QCVS) in the Air.

★ ★ ★ ★ ★

In the midst of this whirl of activity, posted into Kuching in June for a one-year unaccompanied tour on 225 Squadron was the twenty-three-year-old Flying Officer Bob Turner – graduated from Tern Hill and by now the father of a one-year-old son. He found himself plunged into a 'most extraordinary experience':

The squadron had fifteen aircraft, and twenty pilots, of whom sixteen were first-tourist pilot officers. My arrival raised the number of married officers to three. The nature of the operations granted a much greater degree of autonomy and responsibility for such junior pilots than in almost all other RAF roles. However, although the mountainous jungle

138

terrain made the flying extremely challenging, it was extraordinarily rewarding.

The squadron spirit on 225 was very strong and despite the busy daytime role, frequent evening visits were made by most of the aircrew to downtown Kuching to eat at Ah Tek's 'restaurant' – transported in a motley collection of old bangers and the odd Vespa-type scooter!

Hugh Lake, as Training Officer, was the one to introduce Bob to the area and mode of operations. Hugh paints the picture:

First, there was transit flying. A lot of the time, that meant skimming the treetops just below the cloudbase. Here and there, extra-tall trees, exposed above the main canopy, had been struck by lightning and died. This made them excellent way-markers in good visibility but very much of a hazard in pouring rain and in the dark. Frequent flying through clouds of fruit bats at night was disconcerting, but the creatures' radar enabled them to avoid all collisions, which was just as well as the Whirlwind canopies were made of two-mil plastic, and they were very big bats.

Radio contact was difficult, given the terrain and the limited radio kit we carried. On occasion it was possible to relay through another aircraft. Once, when we were at treetop height below a particularly violent storm, we got a message through to a Javelin sitting at fifty-five thousand feet, on top of the same cloud. Using HF it was sometimes only possible to contact base by relaying a message through a helpful American patrol three thousand miles away in Vietnam – a simple 'Mission two two five – Ops normal – Leg five' for example, would tell Kuching where we were.

Our Whirlwinds were stripped down to save weight and maximize payload – still never much more than five soldiers. But even so, flying up to the top of a ridge in filthy weather was difficult – although no one had told the young pilots that it was difficult, so they just did it! If you were in formation in thick fog the trick was to make a slow forward climb alongside the slope, with each pilot taking the lead in turn, calling the next one in as he left an agreed way-point.

Pilots had their choice of weapons – 9-millimetre Browning pistol, Sterling sub machine gun or SLR rifle. A GPMG was mounted in the aircraft for missions at special risk from enemy fire. The Indons were known to lie in wait at remote, unmanned LPs. The army LZs in jungle forts were also sometimes under fire when supplies had to be taken in. Weapons training was carried out on a practice range in proper primary jungle near Kuching. The RAF Regiment armourer, Corporal Pierce, had set it up himself, with dummy soldiers – enemy and friendly (important to distinguish) – appearing from the vegetation for snapshot practice.

The practice firing range was also useful for showing new pilots the scale of jungle vegetation – grass could be fifteen feet high and bamboo forty feet. The former could look like green grass but could swallow up soldiers at the end of an abseil rope and the latter would tend to close over the rotors, drawn in by the downdraught. Rather than a normal hovering take-off – the trick was to sit on the pad and pop out like a cork from a bottle at full power, before the bamboo swept in overhead.

Jungle flying was second-nature to 225 pilots, on their own, in all weathers and often in the dark, on trooping, supply and casevac tasks – and there were a lot of the last one. We were amused when a visiting General was allegedly given an award just for 'flying over the jungle in single-engined aircraft regardless of personal risk'. It was of interest that when the Navy flew in from their carriers in their Wessex over the jungle they flew in pairs, as the RAF did when they flew over the sea to visit ships – to each his own element.

Corporal Pierce's Nord SS11 anti-tank missiles were wire-guided, with a range of 2,000 yards, designed for precision attacks on small, high value targets. They provided a small selection of modified Whirlwinds with the capability for aggressive patrolling. It was necessary to keep a cadre of pilots trained-up to fire them. Mick Charles was one:

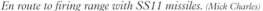

En route to firing range with SS11 missiles. (Mick Charles)

There was a simulator at Kuching, housed in a little hut. The kit comprised a screen, projector, chair and a control joystick. A spot of light was projected onto the screen and we had to learn to steer the spot around a track to reach the target. The controller didn't operate exactly intuitively and until you got used to it the spot would sometimes zip off at ninety degrees to where you had intended. The missile fit on the aircraft was not very reliable but we did achieve some successful test firings.

The test firings were initiated by Pete Bulford, using as a target a limestone cliff near the town of Bau. Corporal Pierce and his team would peg a white parachute onto the cliff and the pilots, operating the controller from the left-hand seat with the cyclic stick removed, would let fly – with practice rounds that on impact exploded with white powder.

Mike McKinley was another of the pilots selected for training:

I fired off four or five of them and became a fully qualified missile man. In time, I trained the next generation of missilers. It was all in truth great fun – but the SS11 was a lethal little weapon and we were never cleared to use it in anger in Borneo.

Martin Mayer, a Borneo Boy who arrived on 225 in July, confirms the power of the SS11 shells:

When we were reasonably competent, we were allowed to fire the real missiles. The warhead on these rounds consisted of what was basically a big round grenade designed to fragment into many pieces of steel for anti-personnel. Understandably these played havoc with the parachute targets and after about three rounds left it completely shredded. There was a disused goldmine at the bottom of the cliff and one session, when there was no 'chute left, we decided to try firing our remaining rounds into the entrance of the shaft. The idea was that the explosion might bring down some of the roof and, who knows, perhaps some gold as well! After the firing, I dropped off my crewman at the entrance – he dashed inside the mine and came out with a big grin holding shiny bits of rock. He was most disappointed later to discover that it was pyrites and worthless – fool's gold!

Martin was twenty-four when he joined the squadron. As a lad the RAF was in his blood. Just ten months after his birth in Lancashire in 1941, his father was lost in a Stirling bomber over Frankfurt. From 1945 he lived with his mother and stepfather (also RAF aircrew, on Sunderlands in Coastal

Pilot Officer Martin Mayer, kitted out in latest fashion army combats and desert boots, complete with side arm. (Martin Mayer)

Command) and one of his earliest memories was being allowed to sit in the tail turret with four Browning guns while his dad inspected the rest of the line. Life at various RAF stations, close to Mosquitoes, Lancasters and other iconic aircraft, ensured that, after boarding school and the CCF in Fleetwood, he applied for Cranwell.

He wasn't, however, selected for the College and, instead, after University he joined up on a Direct Entry Commission under the B scheme which gave him leaving options after eight, twelve and sixteen years of service. He was awarded Wings on the Jet Provost, coming second in the order of merit on his course, before becoming the first of three to experience the sixty-five-hour straight-through rotary conversion on the Whirlwind. He comments:

Hovering was for me something of a black art – all that whirling and thrashing around – and to go solo, you had to show competence in engine-off landings. For a fixed-wing man, that was something else again. You had to set the rotor-speed lever to Ground Idle – deliberately, in flight! Then you'd auto-rotate inexorably downwards, with the collective pushed right down, ready to pull it back up again in the flare,

142

to cushion your hoped-for safe landing. You'd try for a steeper flare on rough ground – you could afford a longer landing-run on a runway.

Anyway, I coped with all that and passed out in June '65. In fact, this time I managed to come out top of the course – so they offered me a Permanent Commission, subject to an interview with the AOC Training Command. That turned out to be a formality and I accepted. Then I was able to fly out to Singapore and join my course colleagues – all Pilot Officers and all posted to Borneo!

Shortly before Martin, another Borneo Boy first-tourist had arrived, fresh from Tern Hill. Dick Holmes was born in India in 1945 on the Ganges plain between Delhi and Mount Everest into an Indian Civil Service family. Among thousands of others they left in a hurry when Partition came about in 1947 and emigrated to South Africa. Inspired by the 'Biggles' stories of Captain W. E. Johns after Matriculation at Hilton College, Natal in 1962, he applied to join the RAF.

At my father's suggestion, I seriously considered joining the Fleet Air Arm – that never transpired. Probably just as well as I am pretty sure I would have been killed by the law of averages prevailing at that time in carrier-borne ops. Instead, I arrived at RAF South Cerney in the Spring of 1963, and got my Wings before I passed my UK driving test.

Opting for rotaries was an easy decision. At Leeming, we'd had a Valiant crew on a recruiting visit – they described their routine to us, and that convinced me I'd be completely unsuited for the V-Force role. Contrast that with a Sergeant Signaller – he seemed old to me, probably all of twenty-six – telling me yarns about his helicopter-winching experiences and describing what was going on in Borneo. As a young, coming up twenty colonial, I was sold.

When I arrived at Labuan, the average age on 230 Squadron was about thirty-six. We Tern Hill tyros were bringing it down fast, and at the same time giving the Squadron Commander some supervisory headaches. We were all up for the task and the training at Tern Hill was top-notch, but we were so inexperienced. I had the good fortune to be taken in hand by Flight Lieutenant Bill McEachern, a very experienced Whirlwind pilot and the Squadron QHI. An Australian, he'd started as a Sergeant Pilot at the very end of the Second World War, on bombers, so he'd flown all types – piston and turbine, fixed and rotary wing. But even after the month of in-theatre conversion it took me another couple to be comfortable with the role.

Operational techniques in the jungle had to be cottoned onto quickly as they were mission and life-critical. For every lift-off we had to work out what the Whirlwind's performance would be – whether we'd clear the trees, and all that. Using the fuel-flow meter, we'd find out what our fuel flow was in the hover and see what the margin was between that and the red-line maximum for the altitude we were at. If the margin was great enough, we'd know we could clear the tops in a vertical lift-off – if not, we'd need an exit path where we could pick up forward speed and lift. We had to get it right – there was rarely a turn back option if we miscalculated. Some of those trees were two hundred feet!

Landing was much the same – working out by means of a level flight power-check at fifty knots on the approach, whether we had the margin to cope with the lack of ground-effect cushioning on top of the log pile landing-pad in front of us, for example. Landing at zero speed was a technique we just had to master as again, there was no overshoot option.

And all the time in between you'd be on the lookout for a possible landing spot in case of trouble. Paddy-field, jungle clearing, village *padang*, river-bank or shoal – anywhere reasonably flat would be better than into those hundred-foot trees. In a single-engine helicopter you just had to be proficient in the techniques of auto-rotating landing – both on land and when ditching into the sea, by day and at night. We had a lot to learn!

So did the ground crew, come to that. I noticed early on that some new arrivals seemed to reckon that they'd come down in the RAF maintenance hierarchy, being posted to helis, especially those who'd worked on the glamorous types, like Hunters and Javelins. They soon learned differently. When I flew out to Sepulot for the first time, two-up with Bill McE, there were airmen in the cabin going out on their first detachment. It was at least an hour's flight to Sepulot over continuous jungle. When we got there Bill asked them a question: 'Where do you think we'd land in an emergency?' Already shaken up by the trip, it made them think a bit. Bill's answer was 'Well, we usually aim to select a tree which looks like it might support the aircraft's weight.' That made them think a bit more. This was a posting and job they could be proud of, all right. I worked the same trick myself a few times, including on the two-and-a-half hour trip to Tawau. The change in the lads' attitude was almost visible – it never failed to work.

Dick Holmes had arrived on 230 Squadron just as the first repatriations had resulted in a lack of experience among the ground crew. That changeover, a bulge in aircraft undergoing routine servicing and a continuing lack of spares (in particular replacement Gnome engines), led to a reduction in hours flown in July. However, no tasks were cancelled at the Sepulot and Tawau detachments and at Labuan an aircraft was found to take part in a Red Cross

Fête on the Padang in Victoria town. But that Whirlwind, while hovering over the harbour with six on board, suffered a complete engine failure, and plunged into the sea in full sight of airmen relaxing at the Services Yacht Club. The sailors rushed to the rescue and all on the aircraft were saved but the ditching gave added urgency to Dick's engine-off landing practice.

Over in Tawau a British hovercraft, on trial for Borneo operations, also lost all power, and ran aground in the full heat of a tropical day. The 230 Squadron Whirlwind not only winched down cooling drinks to the unfortunate crew but also managed to rig a line to the hovercraft and tow it to its base at Tawau Sawmills for repair.

At Bario a pair of 110 Squadron Whirlwinds flew in to relieve the Mk 1 Wessex of 845 NAS which, despite losing 1,000lb in payload between the UK and the tropics, had managed everything expected of them. They clattered off to the waiting HMS *Bulwark* for repatriation where their squadron, after some fun in Aden en route, was to re-equip with the Wessex Mk 5, a much more powerful helicopter, with twin Gnome turbines[33].

In Kuching, following their tumultuous previous month of over sixty hours per aircraft, for 225 Squadron July turned out to be much quieter by comparison. This was mainly due to the over-tasking of the trial having disrupted the aircraft-servicing 'stagger line', the carefully-balanced interlocking of month-by-month scheduled maintenance on a forecast hours-flown basis. This had led to a shortage of engines, as Gnomes were pirated from aircraft under maintenance to aircraft on ground awaiting repair.

In the wake of the Plaman Mapu incursions, work continued for 225 and 103, in an action reminiscent of the Malaya Emergency, to move Chinese residents from the area to a series of secure compounds. All the helis and other aircraft in Sarawak were hampered by the start of the 'slash and burn' season, when the clearing of jungle by *parang* and fire created a dense smoke-filled inversion, trapping the haze and reducing visibility to a couple of miles.

225 Squadron gave more work to the Belvederes of 66 Squadron when two Whirlwinds crashed within a few days, each time flown by the same pilot. The first incident occured when a pair was tracking along the route home to base. Mike McKinley was there and wrote home about it:

Last Saturday, while returning to Kuching with Brian Skillicorn formating on my left, I was alarmed to hear him call 'Mayday – Mayday – Mayday' in a fairly unconcerned sort of way. I turned around to see him disappear into a hole in the trees and went down to see how he was. He had done a superb job and there was hardly any damage to the aircaft and none at all, physically, to the four occupants.

But, strange to tell, there was no tail rotor. It had fallen off, just like that! An inherently alarming situation in a helicopter... However, it says

145

Brian Skillicorn in his hole in the trees, and...   *(Mike McKinley)*

... on the beach, before...

... wreckage is hauled back to Kuching by Belvedere.

(Fraser Skea)

(Mike McKinley)

a lot for the basic safety of the things, as well as the skill of the pilot, that he could get it down so well.

I had only the squadron Technical Officer on board and he was sitting up front with me. However, he got himself onto the floor and managed to squeeze down under the seat and into the back – a tricky operation – and instantly found himself converted into a winch operator. He winched them all up and we just came back. So easy! The aircraft was stripped down the next day and pulled out by a Belvedere. It should be flying again in a few days.

That adventure occured well inland, near a village called Tebakang. The next was on a coastal beach. Mike wrote this incident up in the Operations Record Book:

No sooner had the congratulations on the skill with which he had handled the [tail-rotor] situation died down, than he found himself with another forced landing on his hands.

This time, he was en-route HMS *Albion*, anchored about ten miles north-west of Santubong, when, crossing the coast, his aircraft developed acute engine problems and he had to force-land on the beach. Unfortunately this time, after a successful initial touch-down, he ran into soft sand and the nose dug in, causing considerable damage to the aircraft. However, no one inside was hurt.[34]

The Whirlwind's flailing rotors chopped off the tail boom before the blades went flying into the sea but Brian Skillicorn, crew and passengers survived to be picked up by an 848 NAS Wessex and flown to their original destination. Ironically, those on board comprised, in the words of Mike McKinley, 'a miscellaneous load of Belvedere, Whirlwind, Scout and Sioux pilots, sent to *Albion* to help the naval Wessex which were to carry out a battalion changeover in the Bau area'. The Wessex Mk 5 aircraft of 845 had arrived in Borneo in May, tasked with operating from *Albion* into Sibu, Tawau, Bario and Labuan. The Whirlwind crew and passengers having been rescued and declared by the ship's doctor as being fit to fly, the day proceeded as planned, and the changeover of Gurkhas for Australians was successfully completed. Mike remarked in his report: 'Helicopter enthusiasts might have thrilled that day to find five basic types of British military helicopter all operating in the Kuching area.'

At about this time a further 'soft-surface' landing, this time by a far heavier aircraft, was witnessed by John Davy:

They told 34 Squadron to try for a Beverley landing at Simanggang to see how it went – seemed somewhat extraordinary at the time as the dirt and grass runway used to sag under the weight of just a Twin Pioneer. Anyway, the Bev proved a bridge too far – literally ploughed its way down the strip. So the bulk stuff continued to get sent by boat up the Lupar River and they got on with improving the dirt road from Serian.

Colin Ford, on a roulement of three-week stints on the 103 Squadron Kuching detachment once every other month, very nearly added one more to the little spate of operating mishaps. As he recounts:

I was tasked to shuttle thirty or so Gurkhas from point A to point B. The pick-up was from a sloping LP and I was in two-wheel contact with the ground and about to pick up troops when their NCO suddenly disappeared around the front of the aircraft. Next thing I know, he appears in the left hand window, climbs in, bashes me with his Sterling SMG – and promptly sits on the collective lever. It was tricky enough controlling the Whirlwind on the slope without his fat backside on the controls! There was little I could do to move him, so I used the collective to hoist up his left buttock, managed to get airborne and continued with the troop lift.

There was another Whirlwind close call when, on a continuation training sortie at Kuching with Dave Reid, Hugh Lake set out to demonstrate a procedure for coping with engine failure after lift-off. It gave Dave a bit of a scare and the incident is still clear in his mind:

The idea was that at two-hundred feet and seventy knots climbing away from the airfield, you pulled the Rotor Speed Control Lever on the fuel-flow computer to Flight Idle, flared the rotor to trade speed for height, and turned one-eighty degrees for an auto-rotating downwind landing back on the runway. 'Done it many a time at Tern Hill,' Hugh said.

All went well at first – flare, speed for height, full left rudder and steep turn right the way around. But this time Hugh had done it too close to the runway and hadn't pulled hard enough. One-eighty turned into two-twenty. At the top of the descent, with no speed and no revs, a heavy landing was inevitable. With the collective fully up to try to cushion the landing he had to plonk it down across the tarmac, nose down, leaving the front oleos bent double, the back of the aircraft broken and us hanging in our straps.

Fortunately, the cambers at the edge of the runway meant that the rotors were undamaged but all hell broke loose. Apart from everything else, a civvie Fokker Friendship was on the approach and had to go round again as the airport blokes got us towed out of the way – embarrassment all round.

I suffered a damaged coccyx and Hugh had to endure a 'hats on' interview with the Station Commander. I reckon it was a daft manouevre anyway. I'd never have done it in an emergency – I would have landed straight ahead, in the nearest soft, friendly paddy-field or whatever. .

Dave had a further near miss, this time self-inflicted, while on re-supply out of Lundu:

I'd been detached to Lundu for three stints of a month each, where we'd an ongoing task – lifting water up to the thirsty Gurkhas in their hilltop base. If it was cloudy, as it usually was, the flying was a bit tricky – I found it useful to watch a chap by the name of Brian Danger do it. He'd creep up the side of the hill, tree to tree, knowing that they'd all meet, as it were, at the top. Then, when he wanted to come down, he'd launch his Whirlwind into the cloud, pointing away from the hill and, therefore, he reckoned, into a clear area. Then he'd lower the collective to the floor and drop down through the cloud.

I tried it and it worked. But once I didn't monitor either the compass or the turn-and-slip ball nearly closely enough. I got the Whirlwind right out of balance, and found myself coming out of cloud pointing straight back at the hill – not a good idea! I really scared myself that time but I stayed with the method. And later in my career I was able to refer to my stupid mistake when teaching instrument flying to students.

It was in Kuching that Colin Ford gave the RAF public relations machine some further assistance by participating in a short piece of filming for BBC TV News featuring helicopter supply to the Tanjong Po lighthouse on the north coast. He even did the voice-over. The programme went out in London following the six o'clock news – another small lift for the low media profile of Confrontation.

Chapter 15

Views from the Ground

Although independent entities, the RAF rotary squadrons operating out of Kuching could not function without support from the whole, now sizeable, base. A key element in that support was the Helicopter Handling Team, seconded from the Army Air Transport Training and Development Centre (AATDC) at Old Sarum. At the AATDC the Helicopter Section was tasked with developing USL equipment and procedures, together with handling and trooping drills and the training of joint-service personnel in all facets of helicopter operations. The job in Borneo was the same but the remit extended to airdrop if required. The Team Leader at Kuching from July 1964 was Sergeant Richard Nicholson.

Born in 1934 Richard signed on for the Royal Army Service Corps (RASC) at the age of eighteen and, as a private, served on operations in Malaya, driving a truck. His first action came in a terrorist ambush in March 1953 – within minutes he was twice wounded, once by hostile and once by friendly fire. Back in the UK in 1956 he became a corporal in Air Despatch (AD) and had a twelve-month tour in Aden. His next was to be in Kuching. Richard explains the job:

> In the team we had a second sergeant RASC AD, a Royal Marine sergeant, and a corporal Royal Engineers. All kinds of loads needed clearance – on the spot and in the field – mainly defence stores and equipment for the construction of the border forts. Coils of barbed wire, sand bags, timber and even some railway lines were lifted in vast quantities as USLs and all had to have the team's 'Authority to Carry'. We'd devise a lashing and lifting method, test it under a crane to make sure the load hung level then fly it under a helicopter to get the pilot's opinion. If that was all satisfactory the clearance would be authorized on the spot.
>
> We worked with the RAF Whirlwind and Belvedere, the Royal Navy Wessex, and the Army Scout. Very versatile, helicopters – they could carry most things, internal or under-slung, to most destinations. All

150

except the Belvedere were also cleared for airdrop of personnel and cargo by parachute, a very useful method of accurate delivery into very small drop zones. The Scout even had a special 'chute fitted in the door to ensure that the load being despatched cleared the landing skid.

When operations began, we'd work out each payload with the aircrew according to how much the aircraft could carry over the required distance. The team would then often fly with the helicopters to their destinations to supervise off-loading and de-rigging.

We'd also train soldiers in the forward area in the preparation of LPs and DZs, and in helicopter reception, communications, marshalling and trooping drills. The Royal Marines were very good at working with helicopters but some of the army units needed a fair bit of instruction. We also worked with Commonwealth Special Forces and MI6 people – you had to be sure they were well-briefed.

On one occasion at an LP, we found Gurkhas, who always do exactly as they're told, cutting the grass short with their *kukris* because the book said 'clear to ground level'. They were mightily relieved when we stopped them – it was heartbreaking work. We explained that long grass was not a hazard to a helicopter but that cut grass blowing around could be. On another occasion, a Gurkha sergeant was so impressed with the training we'd given his platoon that he presented me with his kukri – a rare and special gift. When I asked if there was anything we could give him in return, the Gurkha said he couldn't carry any souvenirs but could he have a roll of twelve-hundred pound nylon cord for bivouacs. It was willingly given.

Retrieval of airdrop and slung-load equipment was always a headache and often parachutes and rope-nets were abandoned. They deteriorated if left exposed to the sun for too long, but could still be put to good use around the forts and longhouses, for anything from hammocks and roofs, to sun hats.

At one time there was a call for cats from a fort which had a rat problem. The AD lads caught as many cats as they could around Kuching, crated them up and airdropped them to the said fort. Unfortunately, as soon as they opened the crate, all the terrified cats rushed off into the jungle, never to be seen again. Better results came when an enterprising Air Despatch Officer decided to drop them a python – that immediately got to work on the rats. He said he had got the idea from Robinson Crusoe.

Air Despatchers had a trick or two themselves. There was an SAS officer who kept requesting replacement Omega timepieces on the basis that the airdrop had malfunctioned. The lads knew it was a cheat. They went down to Kuching market and bought a large, heavy old clock for ten dollars which they airdropped to his patrol. There were no more requests for timepieces. Some years later I met the said SAS officer, who was by then a brigadier. He said that he still had the clock – it had turned out to be a valuable antique and was one of his prized possessions.

That was a good tour, in Borneo. Of course, we knew it was all most uncomfortable for the British soldiers, under the dark jungle canopy, bitten by insects and snakes, in the pouring rain and steamy heat – liable to be ambushed at any time by Indo Commandos, or guerrillas wielding *parangs*. But we enjoyed it, being in the front-line of things. And we reckoned we did our bit for the fighting men.

In March 1965 the RASC morphed into the Royal Corps of Transport but the tasks remained the same. In September the same year, at the end of his Borneo stint, Richard Nicholson moved back to Old Sarum after a job well done. In 1975 he was commissioned and, following forty-four years spent in varied and successful colour service, he retired in the rank of major. He was awarded an MBE in 1989 for his outstanding contribution to Air Despatch training and logistic re-supply to the Army by helicopter.

'Not bad,' he says, 'for a man who only wanted to drive a truck!'

★ ★ ★ ★ ★

One of the soldiers lifted by Whirlwind to the Plaman Mapu action in April 1965 was twenty-three-year-old platoon Sergeant Danny Hunt of 2nd Battalion, the Green Jackets (KRRC),[35] the battalion that had taken part in the operations to quell the Brunei Rebellion. Danny arrived in Borneo just before the Paras came under attack:

This was my first operational tour. I'd joined the Army as a Boy Entrant in 1958 and had seen some time in the Green Jackets in Northern Ireland and Berlin. But twelve days' acclimatization in Nee Soon Transit Camp, Singapore, and a bit of jungle training at Kota Tinggi was all I'd seen of the Far East before joining my Battalion in Penang on the sixth of February '65. Prior to moving to Borneo the Battalion completed the jungle course and in addition I was lucky enough to attend a ten-day survival course living with a tribe of aborigines in North Malaya close to the Thai border.

We moved to Kuching at the start of May, an uncomfortable five-day journey on a flat-bottomed converted steamer, the *Auby*. On arrival Battalion Headquarters was set up close to the airport at Kuching while our Company was trucked down the road to Tebedu and lifted by heli to the FOB at Tepoi.

We were close enough to hoof it to the border on patrol, where we were re-supplied by helicopter – Whirlwind, Wessex and the occasional Belvedere. But we could be shunted about by Whirlwind, like that morning when the Paras were bounced at Plaman Mapu.

In August we were to experience our own action. We had been in an ambush position for a week and were on the point of pulling out when it became obvious that our quarry were close. The Platoon commander initiated the ambush mid-morning and for a short while all hell broke loose. The Indonesians fired back with great accuracy and it became clear that on our withdrawal one of the riflemen had been hit. We managed to sort his leg wounds out, administered morphine and then set off back carrying the lad on our makeshift stretcher. We didn't arrive back at our RV until nearly midnight.

It seemed that we had ambushed some thirty Indonesians, killing fourteen of them. The story for them did not get any better when they arrived back at their base – they were greeted with some 105-millimetre shells from our artillery. The Platoon Commander, Lieutenant Mike Robinson, was awarded the MC and the wounded rifleman was eventually medically discharged.

After refuelling at Gunang Gajak, an RAF Whirlwind...

... departs, before...

... Navy Wessex arrives.

(pictures Dick Hayes: by kind permission of the Royal Green Jackets Museum, Winchester)

We were mightily pleased that the 105-calibre pack howitzers were there – gave us really effective cover in some tricky situations. Some moved around but the one at Tepoi didn't – it was always there when we needed it and the gunners knew every nook and cranny of that part of the border, and where to aim.

You hear all these stories about the beautiful native girls of Borneo – well some of them could be true. We were strictly forbidden to interfere with them – although for my Company at Tepoi there was precious little opportunity. There was a *kampong* across the river, but little contact – and in the forts and on the border there were no girls, nor anyone else come to that. But all the same I know that one or two of the soldiers would smuggle some of their beer ration into their patrol kit, hoping for a chance of getting their leg over in exchange for a couple of cans.

Danny Hunt remained in Sarawak until the end of September 1965 when he again enjoyed 'the dubious delights of the *Auby*' before returning to barracks in Penang for rest and recuperation. In due course he returned to Borneo for more action, leaving the Far East in 1967. In July 1980 he was commissioned and retired to Wiltshire in 1996 in the rank of major.

★ ★ ★ ★ ★

July 1965 saw the arrival in Kuching of Dick Hayes, a platoon sergeant in 3rd Battalion the Green Jackets (The Rifle Brigade). Born in 1937 in Hammersmith, Dick reported for National Service in January 1959, after a six-year apprenticeship as a carpenter/joiner. He remembers the day clearly:

Medical examination was a mass-production affair, with a hallful of rows of naked lads being processed like cattle. I was found fit and they accepted me for service. I loved it all – the drill and the boot camp. I found myself so much at home that within two months I'd signed up for twenty-two years as a regular soldier – with a nine-year option to leave that right from the start I never even thought about taking up.

In early January '65, the battalion – all personnel unaccompanied – was sent for four months of acclimatization and pre-detachment training in Fan Gardens at Fan Ling in the New Territories, Hong Kong. Then in May it was on to Malaya for a further two months' training at the Jungle Warfare School in Kota Tinggi. While we were there we took the opportunity to buy up all of the lightweight kit from the markets in Singapore that we might need for the upcoming stint in the ulu before arriving in Borneo on the third of July, for a six-month tour of duty.

It took us three days at sea to get to Kuching, in the MV *Auby*. That ship was a sight to behold – red with rust. And the captain had a flaming red beard to match! Still, she did us better than the Beverley that took the advance party – that lost three of its four engines halfway there and had to go back to Changi to try again!

The whole battalion then climbed into 3-tonners for ferrying to Balai Ringin HQ – it was clear we were on active service as we had to sit in the trucks with our rifles loaded, pointing outwards with one up the spout. We were there to replace 2 Para on the left-forward position in 99 Gurkha Brigade in the 1st Division of Sarawak. It took us days to clear up after those guys – it seems they'd had it rough up at Plaman Mapu so perhaps housekeeping wasn't their priority. The huts were pretty basic, bamboo with *attap* and banana-leaf walls, and corrugated-iron roofs. The Sergeants' Mess had a 'boot boy', a local *Dayak* who cleaned the rooms, made the beds and was the general 'gofer', all for about five bob a week in old money. And he walked ten miles into work each day, and ten back.

I was the Signals Platoon Sergeant but I wasn't at HQ for long. We had two forward bases, at Nibong and Gunan Gajak, and because of poor radio communications with the forward patrols, the Signals Officer decided that we needed a mobile relay station and that I was just the bloke to run it. So for all but six weeks of our tour, I and my 'jungle buddy' Rifleman Danny Finn were on patrol, humping packs that weighed a hundred pounds each, what with radios, rebroadcast kit, spare batteries and aerial kits, not to mention night clothing, ammo and food. We lost pounds, keeping up with those fast-moving patrols and climbing hills to get reception.

Most of those patrols were special CLARET missions, and forward airlift was by helicopter. There were two RAF Whirlwinds based at Balai Ringin, parked on a playing-field about a hundred-yards square. Both pilots were WO1 Masters in their mid-forties. Doug Ponsonby was an avid collector of butterflies and moths and Jack Trigg was a former jet-jockey. He was famous for a dusk landing made by torch signals when he had a bit of trouble – his glasses fell off and got lost on the cockpit floor. He survived that, and countless other skin-of-the-teeth troop-lifts at border DZs – many a time having to go out backwards.[36]

A lot of people say that there were no air-strikes in Borneo. I contest that. There was this Indo AA-gun, horizontally mounted on top of a tree-covered hill that was about five hundred yards inside Kalimantan, that was giving our patrols a hard time when returning from operations. So an FAA Buccaneer was called in. Time elapsed between the calls of 'Target recognized' and 'Target destroyed' was seven seconds precisely

Belvedere brings Santa Claus and Christmas mail to a welcoming RSM Nick Carter (RB) at 'Beak's Field', the school playground cum helicopter pad at Balai Ringin. All helicopter pads are named and registered worldwide – this one after a KRRC officer.

Green Jackets using alternative form of Borneo transport.

(pictures Dick Hayes: by kind permission of the Royal Green Jackets Museum, Winchester)

157

'Clearing a ridge of jungle was a major task.' (Colin Ford)

– I measured it. In a puff of smoke the gun emplacement was eliminated and the Indos gave no more trouble. The Riflemen on the patrol were treated to some naval humour on this occasion when the RN Ops Officer was asked 'Where's your Buccaneers?' He replied, 'On my buckin' head.'

At the end of his six months in Borneo Dick Hayes was posted as a signals instructor to the School of Infantry in Hythe and then Warminster where it later became the College of Land Warfare. Having risen to the rank of WO2 (RQMS) he left the Army in 1981 for seventeen years in Her Majesty's Prison Service. He retired to Wiltshire to edit a book[37] about the 3rd Green Jackets' Borneo adventures, its last campaign as the Rifle Brigade.

★ ★ ★ ★ ★

In that book is a story from one of Dick's colleagues in the 3rd Battalion, Corporal 'Geordie' Anderson of 12 Platoon, giving the soldier's angle on building helicopter landing pads on the border:

It was a task we occasionally got stuck with and although it was looked upon as something like a week's holiday compared to slogging up and down mountains every day, clearing a ridge of jungle was a major task. Jungle trees are gigantic hardwoods of teak, mahogany and ironwood over a hundred-and-fifty feet tall, with massive buttressed supports that slope down from about fifteen to twenty feet up, like a rocket ship's fins. Large chainsaws coped with lesser trees but we had to use plastic explosives in a series of ever-larger charges to blow down the big ones. This was highly dangerous in itself, but when they were falling the risks weren't over.

The sight of one of those jungle giants coming down was both awesome and terrifying – added to that, the weight distribution of the branches could sometimes take them the wrong way. Then, dodging a very tall tree weighing a couple of hundred tons required speed and judgement. In the working party I was in, one chap didn't manage it.

It was all a tragic stroke of bad luck – the tree went the right way but then it glanced off a dead one and fell towards us. Corporal Dickie Poole couldn't move fast enough over all the cut branches and logs and it caught him, crushing his head and neck – but he was still alive.

We called up a helicopter, while two of our medic-trained lads gave him an emergency tracheotomy – with a clasp knife. The Whirlwind came down through the clearing we'd made, and hovered low as we got Dickie into the cabin and off to hospital. But it turned out he was severely brain-damaged and sadly died a year later, in the British Military Hospital in Colchester.

Chapter 16

The Sparring Continues

August 1965 opened with the momentous announcement, first a rumour, then confirmed through official channels, that Singapore had decided to secede from the Malaysian Federation. The Prime Minister of the island state, Lee Kwan Yu, asserted that political tensions between his Chinese establishment and the Malay majority in Kuala Lumpur had given him no option. Despite banner headlines in the *Straits Times* and in Djakarta, where Sukarno insisted the move showed the fatal weakness of Malaysia, this development had little effect in the Borneo Campaign. Singapore soon confirmed that the British Sovereign Bases on the island would continue to operate as normal and that the Singapore Regiment would remain available for Commonwealth service in Borneo. The fact that the Federation had lost one member was soon put to the back of everyone's mind.

The squadrons in northern Borneo had concerns other than the political machinations of eastern potentates. Early in the month a CLARET patrol ran into trouble and two dead and three wounded Gurkhas were extracted from the border. There was heavier tasking in the Bario area than of late and the 110 Squadron detachment of three pilots in two machines found themselves flying on average, sixty sorties a day. At the same time the strain on squadron assets was eased a little when the instruction came to hand over the SAR commitment at Butterworth to 103.

In Tawau news came from the border of an overdue army patrol. 230 Squadron's Pete Chadwick flew to the rescue from Tawau, picked up a SARBE signal and plucked the lads out of a border LP. On the same detachment Dick Holmes brought back a downed AAC Sioux as a USL from Kalabakan before himself carrying out an emergency landing later in the month. In the last week, Squadron Leader Keith Cawdron took over as Officer Commanding, and before month-end he was moved to report: 'Aircrews' and technicians' staggered changeovers are leaving us short in both departments. At this rate, the squadron is in peril of being out of action within five months.'

For Flying Officers Davy and Morgan on 225 Squadron, August was special in that each, in turn, did a stint as Officer Commanding the busy Lundu detachment. The Borneo Boys had come of age and just as John and Ian moved up in the pecking-order three brand-new tyros from Tern Hill, including Martin Mayer, became operational.

The two Lundu Whirlwinds were fully employed with moving out the 1st Battalion Argyll and Sutherland Highlanders and moving in the much larger King Edward VII's Own Gurkhas, at the same time as shifting large amounts of defence stores into the new base position at Biawak. In the latter, they were again assisted by 848 NAS and four of their Wessex. The month was a record for the unit, with over 167 hours flown, 1,800 troops and 408,000lb of freight moved. Fortunately for all concerned, August was a quieter month for incursons – less than a score of casevac missions was flown.

Mike McKinley also took his turn as OC in Lundu:

The 225 Squadron Detached Flight Office was in a small *attap* hut on the Battalion HQ at Lundu base. I was in charge of two aircraft, nine airmen and one other pilot and I enjoyed the opportunity, as a twenty-four-year-old Flying Officer with just six months in theatre, to exercise independent authority for the first time. I was able to prioritize operations for myself – there was an HF radio that had patchy communication with Squadron HQ in Kuching, and the occasional 'Message not understood' could be convenient.

The flying up there was superb. There is a five-thousand-foot range to the west which rises almost sheer from sea level and is most impressive. The border runs along the top. A few panics while I was there necessitated our flying a lot on and around that range, with large clouds scudding all over the place and, it being the beginning of the wet season, bad visibility. One can do a lot with a helicopter but those sorts of conditions teach one the best ways of doing things. I feel a wiser pilot for the loss of a little bit of surplus confidence!

There was in general a noticeable stand-off between the Army and the RAF in Borneo – the Army felt they should be flying the rotaries themselves and the RAF's increasingly top-heavy operational command structure made the general lack of fast response from us a continuous issue. It didn't help that the Navy's helis weren't so bound up in clearance procedures. But although we may have been wearing different uniforms, we certainly managed to work closely with the soldiers at Lundu, especially the Gurkhas. Perhaps I 'went a bit khaki' myself out there.

Mick Charles found the same sense of cooperation when detached to Simanggang:

I spent several months up there, working primarily with the 2/2nd Gurkhas and 1/10th Gurkhas who operated mainly to the east of Simanggang towards the Jambu area. I even managed to go on a couple of patrols with them – one up the mountains to the border area and another downriver towards the sea. That was a wonderful experience. On one occasion Colonel Nick Neil MC – CO of the 1/10th and a veteran of Burma and Malaya, quite a guy – wanted to get a good look at enemy territory and asked me to fly along the border with him in the left-hand seat so that he could see clearly. The weather was fine and I flew at five thousand feet to give him a better view. It was not until we had landed that troops on the ground reported that the Indonesians had been firing at us with a heavy machine gun. Fortunately, they missed. But the Colonel was not impressed and muttered something about 'sorting them out'!

We were used to carrying all sorts of freight which sometimes brought undesirables into the aircraft with it. On one occasion I was in the back, wearing just shorts and chukka boots, acting as crewman while we retrieved an airdrop at Jambu. After the flight as I was about to get out of the aircraft I noticed something close to my bare left knee – a scorpion! We caught it with care, put some elastoplast over its sting, tied a bow around its middle, tethered it with a short piece of string to the middle of the Company Commander's table and covered it with a mess tin. The note on the top said, 'Happy Birthday Chris'. Chris Campbell-Thompson took it all in good part.

John Davy was also at Simanggang:

Simanggang was not a bad place at all for a detachment. The Gurkhas had made the camp habitable and built us a crew bungalow. And the girls in the local hospital were very attractive – more and more so as the weeks went by.

Many of the Whirlwind men speak fondly of jungle bases – Pete Chadwick for one:

At the beginning of September '65 my name came up on the 230 Squadron duty roster for a spell at Bario. We relieved the 845 NAS Wessex detachment and when I first got there I flew with a Jungly in the left-hand seat for area familiarization.

It was idyllic up there on the Plain of Bah – rice paddy, distant mountains, native lovelies... They all made up for the slightly primitive lodgings and messing of a remote army base. I was there for three weeks

1/10th Gurkhas with 81mm mortar at Lubok Antu...

... and Head Man at Jambu.

(pictures Mick Charles)

– we left when 848 NAS arrived with their new Mark Five Wessex. I was sorry to go.

In Kuching the Ops Officers found an hour or two of air time to allocate to hosting a journalist looking for stories of Confrontation. A Whirlwind was detailed for the task and up front was Mike McKinley. The experience gave him something else out of the usual to write home about:

I did a job the other other day flying a journalist around to have a look at the 'war'. He had a photographer with him, and a chap from Command Public Relations who was keen to play up the 'hearts and minds' angle. We landed at one of the most primitive *kampongs* in this area and I had a much better look around than I have ever had time for before. When the headman, no less, told me that his wife was having pregnancy problems and asked if I could take her to Kuching the PR man was thrilled. We'd even laid on an impromptu casevac for him! It was all great fun, and fascinating.

Mike McKinley makes it to Malta Times. (Crown Copyright)

The PR man got the coverage he wanted, and Mike's picture made it to the *Malta Times*.[38]

★　★　★　★　★

The crew of a 66 Squadron Belvedere had a busy day on 8 September 1965, flying most of the daylight hours while lifting just on 59,000lb of freight and thirty passengers to a building project in the Lundu-Biawak area. Later, another clattered up to Labuan to lift a UPS1 radar installation to Bario but, generally, a shortage of Gazelle engines and vital spares continued to limit the squadron's effort.

For 103 Squadron it was a relatively quiet month in both Seletar and Kuching, although significantly for the personnel there was a change of command underway. The OC designate, Squadron Leader Fred Hoskins, arrived early in the month to be given an introduction to Kuching by Pete Davis and his men. Fred had already had a varied RAF career. He enlisted in the Royal Air Force in 1945 as an Aircraft Apprentice at Number 1 Radio School, RAF Cranwell, and, after three-and-a-half years, qualified as a Radio Fitter before being awarded a cadetship and moving to the other end of the Cranwell establishment, joining 54 Entry at the RAF College.

Commissioned as a Pilot Officer in the General Duties Branch, with Wings gained on the Percival Prentice and the Harvard, his first tour in the Far East was from 1952 to 1955. He flew fighter and ground attack sorties in the Malayan Emergency, operating the Hornets of 33 Squadron Butterworth. He was a QFI on Vampires at Cranwell before converting to photo-recce Canberras in 1958 followed by Staff College as a Squadron Leader. After three years in Air Intelligence at the Air Ministry (morphing into the Ministry of Defence) he converted in 1965 to rotaries – the Sycamore and the Whirlwind 10.

As Fred arrived on 103 Pete Davis[39] left for his first spell in Whitehall – following slap-up parties at the Airport Lounge in Kuching and the rather more posh Mandarin Room in downtown Singapore.

★　★　★　★　★

Two years after the birth of the Malaysian Federation, Confrontation had by late 1965 in essence changed from a series of sporadic anti-terrorist encounters with determined but lightly-armed IBTs to a continuous action against battle-hardened professional Indonesian soldiers, equipped with the latest in Russian weaponry and dug into well-fortified permanent bases. The commanders on the security forces' side had responded with a move to pre-determined, well-planned forays from company-strength forts.

165

At this watershed in the campaign there was a change of command in the joint HQ in Brunei. At the beginning of September, after close on three years as Director of Operations, Walter Walker handed over to Major General George Lea. The new man came directly from the command of 22 SAS, and continued the successful strategy and tactics developed by General Walker, carrying the fight to the Indonesians. CLARET cross-border operations were by now occupying the majority of the security forces' foot patrols, and the enemy were increasingly on the back foot.

There were changes, too, for the Whirlwind squadrons in northern Borneo. The detachments of 110 moved from Labuan to Sibu, and from Bario to Nanga Gaat, while 230 transferred its aircraft at Tawau temporarily to Bario, pending the arrival of 848 NAS Wessex on the Plain of Bah. These moves were aimed at equalizing the disposition of support helicopters in Mid-West Brigade. A side benefit for 110 was that they found the rations, water and accommodation at the Gaat much better than they were used to up in Bario.

At Bario there was a fright for a *Kelabit* community when, on the fourth of the month, two Indonesian Invader ground-attack aircraft strafed a longhouse at Pa Umor, no more than four miles to the east of the base. The Whirlwinds inserted a reassuring squad of Gurkhas and, once more, President Sukarno's air force had failed to make any Malaysian friends.

For both 103 and 110 Squadrons the imminent introduction of centralized servicing back at their Seletar base was proving ominously bad for morale. In contrast, the well-motivated engineers of 230 at Labuan achieved an availability of one engine per airframe for the first time in four months and everyone cheered when one of their Whirlwinds flew to the rescue of stranded members of the Sub-Aqua Club. The swimmers were lifted from a remote sandbank before the helicopter succeeded in towing their boat back to the safety of Victoria Harbour.

At his headquarters at Seletar Fred Hoskins was taking stock of the wide area of operations of his new command. Having acquired the SAR duties at Butterworth, he likened 103 Squadron's task to one of 'running operations over distances the equivalent of Edinburgh to London, and on to Hamburg'.[40] At Seletar serious salt-corrosion was discovered in the SAR Whirlwinds and the crews were ordered not to carry out 'wet-winchings' except in cases of extreme emergency.

For the Kuching Belvederes and Whirlwinds September was a busy month – the Gurkha Battalions were at full stretch on CLARET operations and the daily round of insertions and extractions noticeably increased in intensity. The helicopter pilots were never briefed on the detail of what was planned on the far side of the frontier. For one thing, the patrols' missions were a closely guarded secret. For another, the less the aircrews knew the fewer the beans they could spill if captured. But they were becoming aware that clandestine ops were in progress – it was impossible not to be. Mick Charles expands:

> I was on the Lundu det, working with the King Edward's Own Gurkhas. We carried a good number of them to and from the border, and we assumed they were there to cross it.
>
> Some of our tasks took us to landing sites on top of the Pueh range which formed the border west of Lundu. At a height of five thousand feet we had to be a bit more careful with the more limited performance of the aircraft.
>
> But we found that by shuttling troops over the relatively short distances to the frontier and maintaining a lowish fuel state, we could deploy more men in a given period than a Belvedere which could carry about twice as many but took longer to load.

Whirlwind and Belvedere formed a good team, as they did at the end of August when an SAS patrol identified heavy Indonesian military river traffic in the area of Siluas. A major CLARET operation was launched, codenamed HELL FIRE. The Whirlwinds of 225 Squadron inserted an advance party of signallers on top of a 1,000-foot hill at Kandai before a Belvedere moved in a howitzer. Then Whirlwinds landed a recce party at a landing site to the north-east of the hill, near the border swamps, before shuttling in the rest of the company.

On 28 August the Gurkhas crossed the border, tasked with laying an ambush and taking out a sizeable convoy if they could find one. After two days of uncomfortable advance across swampy ground, fording streams eight-feet deep, they had achieved their objective, raking a small flotilla of boats with withering fire.

Indonesian counter-attack was immediate and fierce and Company Sergeant Major Hariprasad took five machine-gun bullets in his leg and thigh. With heroic support from his comrades he evaded capture. But he was still hugely at risk from loss of blood and the imminent onset of gangrene. It would take a stretcher party at least a day to haul him back over the swamps to the border, so on 4 September, the Battalion Commander, Colonel Nick Neil MC, a veteran of Burma and Malaya, took it upon himself to authorize a cross-border helicopter lift. A Lundu Whirlwind was scrambled, flown by Mick Charles:

> Still pursued by the enemy, the Gurkhas were trying to cut a clearing for us and it was not until very late in the day that we were given the clearance to go. John Davy was in the left-hand seat and Brian Skillicorn down the back on the winch. Colonel Nick was in the cabin too – as usual, leading in the forefront of the action.

167

We flew first to Kandai. It was already getting dark and there were thunderstorms threatening all around as we set off across the border. Given the conditions it was difficult to know how far into Kalimantan we flew but it was probably about three miles before, using the SARBE signal, we homed in on the landing site.

Although the troops had worked hard with their saws and kukris, the clearing was nowhere near large enough for us. So in the failing light we decided to lower a two-hundred-foot abseil tape, with a Neil-Robertson stretcher attached, through the trees. There then followed quite an interval of hovering while the troops struggled with the stretcher but eventually they managed to secure the Sergeant Major and we were ready to go.

Being unable to pull the stretcher up into the aircraft on the tape, we lifted straight up and, when clear of the trees, set off at a moderate speed with the poor Sergeant Major dangling way below. The thunderstorms were making things rather dramatic but in fact the lightning flashes were essential to enable us to see enough in the darkness to find our way back to Kandai.

We flew around the hill and from a high hover Brian talked me down into the clearing where we gently lowered the casualty down to the ground. We then landed alongside, brought the stretcher into the cabin and flew back to Lundu. Overall it was a great team effort.

I don't know where the Indons were hiding through it all – perhaps they thought we were bringing in reinforcements and were keeping their heads down. Just as well. Colonel Nick got a rocket from the Brigadier for sending a helicopter over the border.

John and Brian flew the Sergeant Major on through the dark to hospital in Kuching. John reports:

They told us he made a good recovery. There were casevacs all the time but, to tell the truth, what was probably a greater hazard than the enemy was leptospirosis – Weil's disease. It's carried in water by rats' piss.

It was always tragic to fly back to Kuching base with a dead soldier in the back. We used to land out of sight of the airport buildings so the bodybag could be transferred to an ambulance. Then the long-suffering ground crew would clean up the aircraft where necessary – bodybags had a tendency to leak.

Mick Charles remembers another Sarawak casevac:

It was a mission that highlighted the limitations of the aircraft radio fit. Somewhere south-east of Kuching, probably near Tebedu, a patrol high up on the border needed to evacuate an injured soldier. Cloud obscured much of the hill but I knew there was an RAF forward controller sitting next to the army signaller at the base landing-site and I could speak to him on my VHF set. So I flew up the hill until I reached the cloud base where, fortunately, the patrol could hear the clatter of my rotor blades. They were able to tell their signaller on their UHF radio that I needed to be higher up the hill and further to the east. The RAF controller relayed this vital information to me as I slowly climbed the slope. I went from tree to tree in cloud following the relayed directions through this cumbersome but effective link. We eventually found the patrol and picked up the injured soldier.

Another search in September was for an SAS trooper who was reportedly lost – he was on his first patrol and he also had no SARBE. A recce was made of all LPs and areas for which he might have made but, in the dry words of the reporting officer, Martin Mayer: 'He eluded all potential rescuers. He finally turned up a few days later at Sematan, somewhat undernourished but otherwise fit.'

Two further searches in 1st Division that month, which drew in aircraft of both 103 and 225 Squadrons, were to have tragic consequences, for both the Army and the RAF. Late in the day, on 20 September, an AAC Scout in transit from Lundu to Kuching was reported well overdue. The 225 Squadron stand-by Whirlwind was scrambled but the crew returned to base at nightfall with nothing found. The search continued next day, interpreters being landed and winched into villages in a vain quest for information.

On the afternoon of the 25th, Flying Officer Sam Smith of 225 Squadron took off in XP327 to continue the air search, in what turned out to be fateful circumstances. That same morning, Sam's colleague, Dave Reid had carried out an air test on that machine following a major overhaul and he had declared that all was as it should be with the airframe. Another colleague, Hugh Lake, was rostered to carry out the air search in the Serian area but Sam, on the final day of his two-year tour, and having completed 498 hours, had persuaded Hugh to let him make the sortie to bring his hours up to the round 500 before he left the island.

Sam lifted off for his sector recce, carrying the Navigation Officer, Flight Lieutenant Jack Canham, in the left-hand seat, and three volunteer airmen, ground crew and a clerk, in the cabin as observers. They found no trace of the missing machine and Sam turned for base. They never arrived.

At twenty minutes past four, a local man contacted the authorities at Serian saying that he'd seen a helicopter plummet into the jungle on a hillside three miles south-east of the town. A two-ship formation of Whirlwinds was immediately sent off from Kuching, led by Chunky Lord. Arriving after dark,

Chunky hovered his machine over the crash site, illuminating the jungle with his landing-light, while the second aircraft, piloted by Hugh Lake, with Mick Charles down in the cabin, succeeded in abseiling a three-man SAS team through the forest canopy to the crippled machine.

That in itself was a considerable achievement. It was quite a trick to maintain an unstabilized Whirlwind in the hover in the dark, without external references, and Chunky managed it while at the same time directing his landing-light so as to assist the Whirlwind below, being careful not to destroy that crew's night vision. The circumstances were also a challenge for Hugh Lake, having to keep his machine steady while no fewer than three strapping lads went down the tape into the trees.

But, for all that, there was nothing to be done for Sam Smith and the others. The SAS team found a completely wrecked Whirlwind pancaked on the forest floor. A foot party arrived from Serian and carried away the bodies. No one on board had survived.

It was discovered that the crash had been caused by a nut loosening and disconnecting a fore-and-aft control rod – the rotor had immediately flipped backwards and severed the tailboom. The men on board had died immediately on impact. Two of them had been on their last scheduled mission before posting home – Jack Canham, one of the 'old and bold' with an Observer's brevet from the Second World War, and Sam Smith, one of the original Tern Hill tyros.[41]

To deal with their personal effects, Fred Hoskins tasked, the junior officer on the squadron, Martin Mayer:

> This was an extremely sad task. I had to go through every tiny item that they possessed and read all their personal letters so that nothing which would offend the family should be sent back to the UK. That job quickly brought home to me the fact that flying could be a dangerous business.

Mick Charles, now tour-expired and on his way back for the QHI course at Tern Hill, attended Sam's funeral at the British Military Cemetery in Singapore at Ulu Pandan. Colin Ford visited the grave a week later. Not much more than two years before, Colin had set off with Sam from Platform 1, Paddington Station, for Lyneham and the Comet to the Far East.

The crash at Serian was the first for 225 Squadron on its Borneo tour. There were to be no more, for orders had come in that at the end of the following month the unit was to be disbanded. The air and ground crews, together with the Whirlwinds, would be transferred to 103 and 110 Squadrons. The 225 Squadron experience was to end.[42]

Chapter 17

Stalemate

On the first day of October 1965, *Radio Djakarta* came on the air with the riveting news that in the small hours that morning, the so-called Revolutionary Council of pro-Communist officials, including the Chiefs-of-Staff of the Navy and Air Force, had staged a coup, spearheaded by a Palace Guard battalion. President Sukarno was under 'protective guard' at an air base, and six army generals were under arrest.

The Indonesian Army had long been a bulwark against the country's three million-strong pro-Peking Communist Party, and the coup was instigated on the grounds that the generals allegedly were planning their own power takeover the following month. A few hours of mayhem ensued in Djakarta, with Communist youth and women's armed factions taking to the streets and exchanging fire with regular troops, and the six generals being summarily executed.

But, the same day, General Nasution, the Commander of the Armed Forces, who had himself escaped capture, made a radio announcement to the effect that the coup had been crushed and the President was safe.

There followed ten days of confusion. Their coup having failed, the Communists incited riots throughout Indonesia and resorted to terrorism. Kidnapping, arson and armed robbery were rampant and, in Central and East Java alone, an estimated 170 right-wingers lost their lives. Retaliation by the Army was swift and heavy-handed. Upwards of 200,000 militant Communists were reportedly massacred but Sukarno himself was careful not to alienate either the Communist leaders or their Chinese patrons and began once more to divide and rule his cabinet.

In Malaysia these momentous events were closely followed and analysed endlessly, both politicians and military men second-guessing the Indonesians' will to pursue Sukarno's *Konfrontasi*. In the last months of 1965, at least, there were no apparent effects in Borneo, Indonesian troops on the border still appearing to be fully committed to the struggle.

The Whirlwinds flew on.

* * * * *

From its Labuan base, in October 230 Squadron was maintaining detachments at Tawau and Sepulot, and temporarily at Sibu where an aircraft was positioned on casevac standby as enemy action was expected on the border. By mid-month it was obvious that the unit, despite a shortage of pilots due to repatriations, was on course for the first time to total forty flying hours per Whirlwind within a month. Life on the squadron continued to be a continuous round of challenging missions interspersed with relaxation in a pilot-friendly Far Eastern environment. Out of Sepulot Dick Holmes certainly had his full quota of the former:

> Alongside the strip there was this four-hundred-yard-long stack of forty-two gallon empty fuel drums, three deep. Despite the camp's best efforts, the dregs of fuel and the drums themselves were continually recycled by locals for cooking stoves – often they'd float them down the river at night to the nearest village.
>
> Then there was the saga of 'Kabul', the honey bear. It was given to the Mess as a baby and somehow managed to grow into an incredibly strong animal about the size of a large bull terrier with claws to match. He desperately needed a one-to-one relationship with someone and found our itinerant movements difficult to live with. At times he could be quite irascible. Then General Walker's wife heard about him and said she would take him on, so I was the one detailed to accompany him on the next Twin Pioneer flight to Brunei.
>
> He was in a stout wooden cage which by the end of the flight was looking anything but stout – another fifteen minutes and a very frightened and angry Kabul would have had the freedom of the Twin Pioneer. I think he finished his days in Nepal.
>
> Another time I was tasked to lift a huge amount of food, beer, and kit for some Australian engineers building the new road to Sepulot town – they were moving about five miles to a new camp.
>
> The pick-up point turned out to be a small flat-top hill about fifty metres long and a hundred feet high, surrounded by two-hundred-foot trees. There was an incentive to take maximum load – it looked like there were going to be some twenty runs needed in any event. So I worked out a technique – load up to a point where I could just manage to hover taxi and then use the fifty-metre flat-top to get sufficient translational lift to fly off over the edge and climb away over the treetops.
>
> All went well until about the fifteenth go, when I set off to find myself at the edge of the hill with no airspeed but lots of ground speed – a strong tail wind must have sprung up out of nowhere.
>
> I was hurtling towards the surrounding trees, and in deep trouble. But just in time I spotted a gap just wide enough to squeeze through

Sepulot airstrip with adjacent river. (Colin Ford)

with the rotor banked steeply over. I was lucky – there was just enough rotor power to make the manoeuvre and I was through and clear.

Needless to say, for the rest of the job the incentive was not maximum payload, it was to stay alive! I made sure from then on that I always gave myself a comfortable power margin.

It was at Sepulot again that Dick experienced what was possibly his most challenging mission:

The final container in an airdrop, the one with the beer ration, had floated off the DZ into the Talankai river, which was in spate at the time. Four brave RAF Regiment 'Rock Apes' immediately and heroically jumped into the water to rescue the precious pallet. They got on top of it but were promptly swept down-stream before, luckily, the airdrop 'chute snagged on a rock.

It so happened that Trevor Wood was overhead at the time, returning from a task in his Whirlwind, and spotted them in difficulties in the river. He landed immediately and with the rotors still turning beckoned over

Pa Tik, south of Pensiangan: river is the border and Murut longhouse sits right in front line.
(Colin Ford)

to me and a burly Flight Sergeant crewman, Jock Hood, to form a crew
to go and winch them out. After a hasty brief, we decided that I'd operate
the winch and Jock would go down on the wire with the strop.

One of the Rock Apes had abandoned the container and struggled
to the safety of the river bank. From a height of eight feet we winched
up our first survivor in the strop in copybook fashion. The next lift,
however, was a near disaster.

The guy grabbed Jock by the leg and let go of the pallet – both were
immediately swept out of sight under the belly of the aircraft. I was
unable to see and control what was going on because I was wearing a
passenger headset with a short connection lead. I conned Trevor to try
and keep up with them in the fifteen-knot current, but he was
complaining about taking tip-strikes from overhanging branches. I
realized that the situation was getting out of hand and gave Trevor 'Up!
– Up!'

Jock came up upside-down with the winch wire between his legs and
the survivor grimly hanging on to the strop with both hands. I was so

relieved to see them that I grinned – Jock never really forgave me, as he thought I found it funny for nearly drowning him.

Fortunately it all ended well. A naval Wessex picked up the fourth man downstream and following a rotor-blade change the Whirlwind was as good as new. And the squadron instituted some winch training for the pilots.[43]

*   *   *   *   *

For 110 Squadron, tasking in October was dominated by the takeover from the 3rd Royal Malay Regiment in the 1st Division, Sarawak by the 1st Battalion King's Own Scottish Borderers, during which the squadron passed a total of 7,000 operational hours in Borneo. But, for both 110 and 103, there were difficulties with the adverse effect on morale and serviceability caused by the introduction of centralized servicing at Seletar and Kuching. At the same time, an influx of new pilots and a brace of air engineer crewmen demanded attention. But, the main issue was the imminent disbandment of 225 Squadron and the transfer of its personnel and equipment to the sister units.

*   *   *   *   *

The transfer date was to be 1 November but the effects were felt from the start of October, when two 225 Squadron aircraft were despatched from Kuching back to Seletar to be absorbed into the centralized servicing arrangements. The deal was that personnel were to be headquartered at RAF Seletar, with crews despatched to Borneo detachments for a month at a time. But those still on one-year unaccompanied tours were to remain in Borneo continuously and, at the end of their year, there would be the possibility of an eighteen-month accompanied extension.

The Borneo Boys were given notice of their new units. Mike McKinley, Martin Mayer, Bob Turner and Dave Collinson were among those destined for 103 and Dave Reid, Fraser Skea and John Davy were detailed for 110. Some were for posting back to the UK – the iconic leaders, Pete Bulford and Chunky Lord[44] were off to CFS(H) and the QHI course where they would be joined by Ian Morgan, the second of the Tern Hill Tyros to be tour-expired.

Ian has good memories of his time on 225:

Arriving back at Kuching in October '64, I bumped into the Sarawak government's Director of Civil Aviation, John Seale, whom I'd first met a year earlier. He told me that a flying club was being formed in Kuching with a Cessna 152, and would I like to be the instructor? A wartime RAF pilot, he was also a botanical specialist, and he'd married a local *Dayak* girl who owned a family rice farm – together they enabled the village to grow record crops. Anyway, John lent me his Second World War QFI notes and duly signed me up with the necessary licences. After a nominal check-ride with Bob Sattelle, a departing Ops Officer who happened to be an RAF flying instructor, I became the club's first chief instructor.

I was also from time to time asked to fly as co-pilot on the 52 Squadron Valettas detached from Butterworth to Kuching for border supply drops. My value as an emergency pilot was reckoned to outweigh any rustiness in twin-engine fixed-wing flying and, of course, by now I had a photographic knowledge of the terrain of large areas of Sarawak.

We ate well in Kuching. Malaysian Airways had initiated the Comet 4, 'Silver Kris' First Class service from Singapore. But it was often cancelled for bad weather – the landing aids at the airfield were minimal – leaving surplus in-flight meals in the Air Terminal office of Malaysian, whereupon Lettie would call in friends, including me, to gorge on lobster and caviar.

At the same time we 225 Squadron pilots discovered that our trooping flights in theory qualified for the provision of in-flight snack meals for the passengers – just a coffee and a chocolate bar if the trip was less than two hours – and the Catering Officer cooperated by letting us have the equivalent in other rations, subject to the submission of a mountain of paperwork. This proved sufficient for a slap-up curry party on the squadron every two to three weeks.

At least three nights a week the boys would eat out downtown with Chunky Lord and it was not unknown for him to hand out the following day's tasking over supper before he dropped off to sleep with his moustache in his rice.

In the end I was pleased to be leaving for Tern Hill and with Borneo colleagues. It wouldn't have been the same at Seletar.

Ian's adventures with Pete Bulford continued on the QHI course at Tern Hill where together they wrote off a Sycamore. Ian tells the story:

It was a combination of that single collective lever amidships, the instructor in the left-hand seat having to operate the cyclic counter-intuitively with the left hand and the fact that Pete Bulford's rather large bodyweight had thrown the lateral centre of gravity out of the safe range, that made the aircraft virtually uncontrollable. The Sycamore rolled rapidly to port and the rotors thrashed themselves against the ground, reducing in length with each revolution. By the time we got the engine stopped they were down to a few feet in length.

No one was hurt, save that Pete, with his head against the ground, was slightly concussed. Notwithstanding, the OC Flying appeared in the Land Rover and took us off to the Mess for a restorative. That's where the doctor found us – too late for a blood-test!

Within weeks, following more crashes, the Sycamore was withdrawn from service and Ian finished the course on the Sioux, which he found a pleasure to fly by comparison. He was to serve in the RAF until age fifty-five, and retired as a wing commander, a relatively high rank for a 1960s rotary man[45].

Mick Charles, the first Tern Hill Tyro to return to the UK, has compiled some telling statistics from his logbook:

I'd always felt that most of our time in Borneo was spent flying solo – it turns out that that was indeed the case. In my final month, September '65, I flew seventy-two hours, sixty-one of them without another crew member. However, the average for the previous time in Borneo, on 103 and 225 Squadrons, was nearer just forty per cent solo – of course the remaining sixty included training and categorization checks, all dual.

I've also found that, as a generalization, flights from Labuan or Kuching were usually two-pilot whereas from a detachment, Lundu, Simanggang, Long Semado and so on, they were much more likely to be solo. And those sixty-one hours in September were on detachment at Lundu operating into sites right on the border – Kandai, Biawak and those patrol bases on the top of the Pueh range.

Whether we followed that Order Book requirement for two pilots or two pilots plus Bren gunner slips my memory – I think that we just got on with the job.

Hugh Lake has a final story of the Chunky Lord days:

The squadron decided to throw a Mess party. As well as importing huge fronds of vegetation to transform the building into a jungle setting, it was decided to serve a Chef's Special melon dish. As good melons were about fifty cents each in the market Chunky set off up-country to get a cheaper bulk supply.

He flew around until he spotted a melon farm deep in the countryside. On landing he waved a five-dollar note at the advancing Chinese farmer, pointing at his melons and then the aircraft. As he had served in Hong Kong he knew the correct protocol and set off with the man's wife to have a bowl or two of tea before inspecting the farm's carp pool.

On returning to the Whirlwind he found the whole family waiting to bid him farewell. He climbed aboard, started up, took off, performed the obligatory flypast and returned to base. Back in the crew room, he hailed the first pilot he spotted with 'Get 'em them unloaded and over to the Mess. By the way, the aircraft seems to be handling a bit oddly.'

Equipped with a Land Rover the young pilot and a driver advanced on the machine. On opening the door they were pretty well buried in an avalanche of melons. The cabin had been filled almost to the top – there were about three hundred melons in there. The whole base was eating nothing but melon for a week.

In 225 Squadron's final month, October 1965, the Simanggang detachment carried out the changeover of New Zealanders for the Askar Renjer Malaysia (1st Malaysian Rangers), while, at Lundu, Dashera Festival parties with the 2/2nd Gurkhas were on offer, complete with goat sacrifices and blessing of weapons. For the month the squadron logged 419 operational hours, hauling 250,000lb of freight (10 per cent underslung) together with 1,000 chickens, four goats, two tracker dogs (which went down in harness on the winch) and one snake (a stowaway). For the tour, 225 had lifted 99,968 troops, 5,618 passengers, 9.4 million pounds of freight, and 1,514 casevacs, all in 56,153 sorties and 10,743 hours – a proud record for the men to take to their new squadrons.

★ ★ ★ ★ ★

Throughout November Chunky Lord's crews had no choice but to knuckle down to a different way of life. Seletar was huge. It housed six flying squadrons, missile and RAF Regiment squadrons, Royal Corps of Transport, Maintenance and Marine Craft units, as well as the Far East School of Joint Warfare. For the Borneo boys there were now secondary duties (a first for some of them), AOC's inspections and even, from time to time, a Station Parade. For relaxation there were yacht, golf and other clubs and a range of sports and activities. And the place was teeming with people – service families, school pupils and a veritable force of locally-employed civilians.

For Dave Reid, who in his year on 225 Squadron had completed 700 operational hours, flying all day, practically every day, it was a wrench. It was no longer the *attap* single room with the beetles and bunk-bed, it was a double shared with Brian Skillicorn in the mahogany Mess. Dave found things different on the squadron, too:

It was a more regulated outfit, 110. We did continuation training – it was back to the clearing at Lombong – and flew security patrols against potential insurgents in up-country Malaya. There was also search and rescue duty, but mercifully I managed to keep off that roster. For the first time we had a proper schedule of categorizations – fortunately with our own Training

Officer. We steered clear of the standards guys, the 'Trappers'. A plus point was that the crewmen could now be properly trained – but they were mostly ex-signallers and not always that keen on the job.

But it wasn't long before we were back in Borneo. The Seletar squadrons maintained a rota of monthly detachments and for me that meant time at Kuching, Sibu and Nanga Gaat. We got to the Gaat via a direct Argosy flight to Sibu and took over up there from the Navy. There was no handover period and we had problems keeping hold of bits of kit that the naval guys had pledged to the locals.

Of course, on 225 we'd got into relationships with a series of local lovelies – easy to do and manage when we were all the time in Borneo. We kept those going but it was more difficult when you flew off back to Seletar after four weeks. And then there were the girls at Seletar to manage too. We now met European ladies, and that made a change, but we'd got used to the Asian girls and continued to court them in Singapore. We met them in the general social circle and racial problems just didn't occur to us – but they did to the Service Establishment.

I took a lovely Chinese girl to the Mess, and also a Muslim beauty who worked in a hotel downtown. I couldn't see any problem but the Station Commander could – carpeted me and said that it was frowned on for officers to fraternize with local girls. Brian Skillicorn didn't take any notice. He and his local sweetheart became happily married![46]

At the end of his first month on 103 Squadron Mike McKinley ran into trouble:

Perhaps I was still smarting from the disbandment of the best squadron in the RAF and also I'd had a couple of boring days doing lots of short air tests with Jack Feeley, our Engineering Officer. Anyway, I was flying yet another test when I guess I just decided to let off a bit of twenty-four-year-old steam, with some low flying along the Kuching River.

Unfortunately, I didn't notice the thin telephone wires strung across it. The best I could offer my new boss, Fred Hoskins, by way of mitigation was that I felt I'd handled the subsequent emergency rather well. The Whirlwind was not easy to fly with telephone wire wound around the rotor head and I did get it back in one piece.

Bluey Atherton was not amused by my exploit – I had cut off half the telephones in Kuching. Nor was he persuaded by my emergency-handling argument. Or perhaps he was – I probably deserved a lot more than just the full-blooded Aussie bollocking I got in his office!

★ ★ ★ ★ ★

November saw an increase in the number of 66 Squadron Belvederes on the dispersal in Kuching – there were now five operational. But as a back-up for the positioning of 105mm howitzers, the Whirlwinds were practising a new loading sequence. This, involving a split of the load between two aircraft, was devised by a Major Beeton of the Royal Artillery.

110 Squadron, from its main Kuching base, opened a detachment at Balai Ringin. The Squadron Commander was hoping to receive a new batch of pilots as repatriations had again made a dent in the establishment. He was pleased with the new boys he got. In his monthly report he declared: 'The quality of graduates from Tern Hill is excellent' – fine testimony to the continuing high standards of training at the rotary school.

The Tern Hill production line was still in full flow. Reporting for rotary training this November was a young man destined to join 110 Squadron in due course. Rick Atkinson had joined up at RAF Locking as an apprentice but, after three years of rigorous training was selected to go before the Officer Selection Board. He still recalls that interview:

'So Atkinson,' they said, 'what makes you think that you are a leader of men?' Somewhat non-plussed, I said the first thing that came into my head. 'Well sir, my name begins with "A" so I'm always at the front!'

Despite that gaffe, Rick was selected for aircrew and gained his commission at South Cerney. He flew Jet Provosts at No. 7 FTS RAF Church Fenton and was awarded his Wings in October 1965.

He and his twelve newly-qualified colleagues were anxiously awaiting their postings when the Officer Commanding came into the Crew Room and said, 'Right, five of you chaps are going to fly helicopters.' Jaws dropped, Rick's amongst them. He had never been near a helicopter and had his heart set on flying Canberras. In order to help him come to terms with this move, still regarded as far from career-friendly, Rick's instructor organized a flight in a helicopter at RAF Leconfield.

Awaiting his turn, Rick was offered a ride in a two-seater English-Electric Lightning T.5, the training version of the twin-jet interceptor. As he recalls:

The rocket-ride take-off in the 'Stovepipe' was a noisy, exciting affair but at five-hundred feet we were already into cloud. The mission was a practice intercept. I watched the altimeter windmilling around – in minutes we were levelling out at forty thousand! The pilot homed in using his radar and reported, 'Missiles Gone', before rolling over and plunging back down through the clag. We broke out of cloud at five-hundred feet and there was just enough fuel for one circuit and overshoot – no roller landings permitted. Just forty-three minutes from take-off, we were back on the ground. As we taxied back to dispersal I was thinking, 'This isn't for me – take me to the helicopter!'

It was a yellow Search and Rescue Whirlwind 10. Suddenly, tarmac and hangar roofs were magically falling away below, and we were off for a sortie out at sea, winching off the back of an RAF launch. Then it was a low level transit skimming over seashore and open fields and into a woodland clearing. I was very favourably impressed and volunteered! In November '65 I joined ten other pilots at Tern Hill for rotary training.

★ ★ ★ ★ ★

There was now no shortage of crews on 103 Squadron. Fred Hoskins had received six Whirlwinds and five pilots from 225 and with those reinforcements the Kuching contingent could be boosted to a dozen aircraft and crews, giving them the strength to take over the forward detachments at Simanggang and Lundu. In Kuching, the squadron moved into the former accommodation of 225, and found the buildings required a good deal of redecoration, as well as new toilets. Building materials were in short supply and the air and ground crews had to go on the scrounge. One of the pilots, Flight Lieutenant Tim Nicoll, one of three engineers on a flying tour, proved to be particularly acquisitive. He liberated WC pedestal bowls from the Marines and in order to cut timber for the Crew Room floor, borrowed a chain saw from 1/7th Gurkhas.

Bob Turner, one of the 225 Squadron pilots transferred to 103, reckoned that the new operating arrangements had not much changed his schedule – he found himself in Borneo almost continuously:

The squadron ops staff at Seletar tended to send out to Borneo the blokes who were on one-year unaccompanied tours – the fellows with families in Singapore were not that keen to go off to the bundu and bullets. I, however, was happy to go, especially when I was appointed Detachment Commander at Simanggang.

This was a fantastic job for a Flying Officer at such an early stage in his career. The det consisted of three aircraft, four pilots including me, one crewman and eight airmen. The role was to operate in support of the infantry battalion covering Sarawak's Second Division. With one hundred nautical miles between Simanggang and Kuching we had to be self-reliant.

There was a landing strip where the aircraft were kept and the crews lived in a requisitioned civilian bungalow in the town nearby and close to Battalion HQ.

The soldiers were deployed along some hundred-and-fifty miles of Indonesian border, in four major company bases. The only way to move between those sub-units was by river boat or helicopter – our Whirlwinds were much in demand.

There was very close liaison with the Army at all levels and I agreed our daily tasks in detail with the Battalion Ops Room. When I got there, the resident infantry were the Royal New Zealanders – they were later relieved by the 1st Malaysian Renjers.[47]

We'd be tasked with troop and freight moves throughout the Division and with supporting the covert ops of the SAS. We'd fly frequent casevac missions, mostly for military personnel but also quite often for local people – the arrival of a helicopter on a remote village *padang* was a major event and usually drew a large crowd.

Mike McKinley was in Kuching on 17 November 1965, a day that turned out to be a black one for the squadron. He tells the story:

Flight Lieutenant Bert Fraser had set off with an artillery man on board, Gunner Martin, down to the border in the Bau district to deliver him to a company of Gurkha riflemen on a clandestine op. He went overdue. We waited and we waited – it looked bad. Then, fairly late in the day, a report came in from the Gurkha Company Commander.

His men were dug in on the hillocks overlooking the frontier area, recceing for an ambush on one of the river routes the Indons used. They had set up a radio-relay station on a nearby peak and the men up there reported having seen a helicopter fly from the Sarawak side, straight over the border into Kalimantan. They identified it as a Whirlwind – they could see the RAF roundels. Next thing, there was the sound of heavy machine-gun fire and the helicopter flew off and disappeared, trailing smoke.

I was on standby and was scrambled to search. The Gurkha officer had given a pretty accurate position to the east of a big Indonesian base at Kindau and over the border from an area we all knew well. There was a high ridge with little sugarloaf rock formations on the crest. You could hardly miss it, but Bert obviously had. We all knew there was a 12.7-millimetre calibre gun there and you made sure you kept low behind the hills and trees. Bert must have become disorientated or distracted, or maybe he mistook one hill for another – who knows?

We flew until the light had gone, but found nothing. I went back next morning and switched on the Violet Picture more in hope than expectation and, sure enough, there was no SARBE signal. Neither Bert, nor Gunner Martin, was ever seen again.

After a memorial service at Seletar in early December, Bert Fraser's widow and her two young children were repatriated to the UK.

★ ★ ★ ★ ★

Fred Hoskins himself was by now earning his rotary spurs in Borneo, leading from the front. In the first week of November he flew a Full Precautions sortie to withdraw Marines from contact with the enemy at Pang Amo as well as a casevac mission to lift out a pair of 1/7th Gurkhas from Tebedu. Later in the month he led the search for Bert Fraser before taking on a challenging night-time extraction of 2/10th Gurkha wounded from Serikin, close to the border and at night. Those casualties had been in the CLARET action in which Lance Corporal Rambahadur Limbu won what turned out to be the sole Victoria Cross of the Borneo Campaign.[48]

December proved a quieter month for 103. For a highlight there was Colin Ford's evacuation of two young ladies from an island off the east coast of Singapore:

> I took a call from the RCC saying that there was a medevac request from Pulau Ubin, a favourite beach-ringed island in the Johore Straits between Seletar and Changi. Apparently, a young woman over there was lying unconscious. We scrambled and flew to the Ubin but couldn't find the casualty at the reported grid reference. As it was popular for its beaches, I decided to do a quick sweep around the island just in case.
>
> As we rounded a headland we saw a group of Europeans gathered around a girl, prostrate on the beach. We landed alongside and saw that she was in trouble. So, without further ado, we picked her up and put her on board the helicopter. I told RCC that we had the casualty and were taking her to the RAF Hospital at Changi, which we did.
>
> After leaving the hospital, I left Changi ATC local frequency and checked in again with RCC. They told me that they had just had another phone call which said that the condition of the young lady on Pulau Ubin was worsening. Question: who had we picked up?
>
> We went back to Ubin, and started a search at the original grid reference where we saw someone waving at us. We landed nearby and another young woman was carried from under the trees to the aircraft. We flew her to Changi hospital as well.
>
> Later we unearthed what had happened. The original casualty had trodden on a poisonous stone fish in shallow water and was very groggy with the pain. Her friends had taken her inland to find a phone. Meanwhile, a bunch of Royal Navy guys were on the other side of the island having a banyan – a beach party. When it was time for their boat

Beach on Pulau Tioman: one of many Malayan offshore islands. (Dave Lanigan)

pick-up, they discovered one of the girls had fallen asleep in the open and was suffering from sun stroke. They were discussing what to do when, out of the blue, we appeared in our yellow SAR helicopter, grabbed her and whisked her away to hospital.

Both girls soon recovered and I think we got a tick in the box from the Navy.

In the unaccustomed lull in West Malaysia, the opportunity was taken to address the backlog in the 103 Squadron training programme, spearheaded by the new if, as it turned out, temporary Training Officer, Hugh Lake. Halfway through his year in Borneo, in July, he had been called back from 225 Squadron to Farnborough, Hampshire, for an interview at the Empire Test Pilots' School, ETPS. As he says:

The boss, understandably, was not happy, but I got a seat on the next Comet home and was temporarily reunited with my 'wife of ten days'.

At the final interview, in front of all sorts of Brass and Brains, I was asked what I thought of the Whirlwind 10. Well, I just let rip about the performance, the lack of yaw control, the need to clamber up the side to get to the cockpit, the lack of contact with the cabin and the positioning of the instruments – finishing with a long lecture on the difficulties of using fuel flow to measure performance in the field and how I would like to meet the bizarre mind who thought that up. After a long pause, the Group Captain chairing the panel said quietly 'I think that might be arranged.' But I did get accepted for the course!

I returned to Kuching and 225 Squadron but then got caught up in the transfer and spent my final ten weeks in the Far East as Training Officer at Seletar on Fred Hoskins' 103 Squadron.

John Dowling, in many ways the daddy of RAF rotary operations, was OC Flying at the Helicopter Wing at the time and I learnt a lot from him. In that post, I went up to Butterworth and flew jungle familiarization sorties for the Australian Huey pilots. I remember being very impressed with the performance and pilot-friendliness of the American aircraft as compared with the Whirlwind. It made me realize how well our group of aviators had done to get the work that they did out of the machines.

I left Seletar on December twenty-first – home in time for Christmas.

★ ★ ★ ★ ★

110 also had a quiet December at Seletar. Much attention was given to the presentation of a new Squadron Standard at a parade enhanced by the music of the 2/6th Gurkha Rifles' band. Some of the gloss was taken off by the torrential rain which forced the whole affair into a hangar but it was still, by all acounts, a grand occasion.

★ ★ ★ ★ ★

For the final two months of 1965, 230 Squadron had Labuan and the north of Borneo to itself. There was a wide area to cover, the farthest eastern outpost being the 180-mile-distant Tawau – difficult to reinforce in the event of aircraft unserviceability. The south-western limit was marked by Bario and, early in November, the squadron aircraft at that forward detachment was scrambled to search for a missing army helicopter.

The Sioux was duly found, perched on a rocky riverbed outcrop a few miles short of Bario base. The pilot had made three attempts to cross the ridge north of the Plain of Bah but had been foiled by low cloud and thunderstorms. Short of fuel, he had been forced to land wherever he could. Out of radio contact in the deep valley, the clatter of an approaching Whirlwind must have sounded sweet indeed.

Later in the month two squadron aircraft were tasked to escort a pair of Belvederes carrying USLs from Bario back to Labuan. 66 Squadron had been boosted at the beginning of the month by the arrival on HMS *Albion* of four additional aircraft from Aden and were on course to make a 50 per cent year-on-year increase in operational hours. On this occasion the Whirlwinds were able to carry the 66 Squadron servicing team, as well as their two portable fuel pumps and survival equipment, thus increasing the Belvedere crews' sense of security and maximizing their underslung payload.

The heavy workload carried on for 230 Squadron into December when, a few weeks after his twenty-first birthday, Pete Chadwick was involved in an SAR mission that turned into a wild-goose chase. As he remembers:

> It was one of those chaotic incidents that happen in a military campaign. Right after a rather good lunch, I was scrambled out of Labuan to go to the aid of a hundred-foot-long decommissioned landing craft that was overdue at its destination. They failed to give us a grid-reference, just a place-name – can't remember it exactly but I do know it wasn't on our map. But I was told it was on the river Belail, and that was marked. So I picked up two of my colleagues as observers and off we went.
>
> We found the river all right, and flew up it – no hundred-foot landingcraft to be seen. We called Ops, only to be told that the boat had, after all, reached its destination. Curses all round and back to Lab double quick.
>
> It turned out that we'd abandoned the search only five miles short of the boat's destination. What a lash-up! A grid-ref wouldn't have helped us much in any case. It turned out we were all of us, the RAF Ops Centre, the Brunei Harbourmaster's Office and me, using different editions of the map – every one of them probably hugely inaccurate. And the boat wasn't in any trouble anyway! Heigh-ho – such is war.

Later in December the 230 Squadron standby aircraft at Sepulot was scrambled to a civilian motor car accident up in the Sabah highlands. Bad weather led to the need for two attempts at getting over the southern ridge out of the base but, finally arriving at the scene of the crash, the three-man crew – pilot, crewman and army medical orderly – found four casualties, one sitting and three prostrate and all in a bad way. Crewman and orderly got them onto stretchers and into the Whirlwind and it was back through the cloud and down to Jesselton airfield for onwards to the hospital.

Finding on arrival that the ambulance was manned by just a lone driver, the whole helicopter crew had to take over. They successfully transferred the casualties, one with a suspected broken back, from military to civilian stretchers before manhandling them safely into the vehicle, whereupon the orderly escorted them to further medical care. By such means four more hearts and minds had been well and truly won.

This was just one of forty-five casevac missions flown by 230 Squadron in December. At the end of a busy month, and year, the Squadron Commander wrote in his monthly report:

> The squadron is now beginning to pass its peak experience level. This month has seen the departure of two very experienced pilots and this trend will continue during the next few months. However, the freshly-trained younger pilots show great promise, and providing a leavening of older more experienced personnel can be found, the squadron should continue to be operationally effective in 1966.

Squadron Leader Cawdron had thus given a further plaudit for Tern Hill tyros.

* * * * *

As 1965 approached its end, the signals coming out of a still riot-torn Indonesia were confusing but surely, with the weakening of Sukarno's position and the lack of success in Borneo, something in his economically-disastrous *Konfrontasi* had to give before long. On the Borneo-Kalimantan border, the CLARET raids were forcing Indonesian units to move back from their forward bases, yet the fervour with which their soldiers fought against the incursions of Gurkhas, Paras and other British and Anzac infantry showed strong continuing commitment, at least in his army, to Sukarno's cause.

At Christmas 1965 Malaysia and its Commonwealth allies faced the likely prospect of continuing months of jungle fighting. The RAF's helicopter squadrons could see that, even after more than three years now of all-out action, they were not about to leave the mountains and swamps of Borneo any time soon.

Chapter 18

The High Tide Turns

By New Year's Day 1966, Sergeant Paul Moran, RAF was in his second month in Labuan as an engine fitter on 230 Squadron and quickly learning the ropes. Paul was born in Devonport and educated in St Ives, Cornwall where he joined the ATC. In 1955, he signed up with the RAF as a Boy Entrant Engine Mechanic. He satisfied all the criteria for adult service and had a spell in Malta before returning to RAF St Mawgan in the West Country and the maritime patrol Shackletons of 206 Squadron. It was from there that, in his twenty-sixth year and just five years married, he was sent out to the Far East to spend twelve months some 8,500 miles away from his young wife, on a one-year unaccompanied tour.

He reckoned he could cope:

From the Sergeants' Mess bar-chat, I had soon found out that 'Dear John' letters from the UK were pretty common. But I took no notice of all that – the post from home came in good and regularly and the hard work and action made the time fly by.

I was often detached for a fortnight at a time to RAF Tawau in eastern Sabah – the smallest RAF base in Borneo but the closest to the enemy. Over there, unlike at Labuan, they issued the airmen and Junior NCOs with a Sten gun or a Lee Enfield .303 rifle, and we SNCOs were given a Sterling submachine gun which we carried at all times. Two of our squadron pilots, Messrs Lamb and Lawn, were two of the last sergeant helicopter pilots in the RAF and they knew every wrinkle of the landscape of Sabah and had all the helipads by heart.

The Whirlwinds were good aircraft to work on – pretty reliable. We lost none of them in my time at Labuan through mechanical fault but I heard about the one that went down in the sea during an air display before I arrived. It seems that was a fuel-computer run-down. But both pilots, Flight Lieutenant John Atkinson and Sergeant Lawn, stepped out onto a motor boat and didn't even get their feet wet. All the same, the salt water had contaminated the aircraft and it had to be scrapped. The airframe was mostly magnesium alloy and prone to corrosion – had to be regularly washed down with a mixture of water and WD-40.

The Gnome engine was superb.[49] In flight it was virtually trouble-free – failures were not unknown but were very rare. There was a set maintenance programme and removal and installation was quick and easy. Minimal tools and equipment were needed and they could be carried in the Whirlwind. Once the cowlings were removed and a supporting strut fixed, all you did was undo all the appropriate connections, slide the engine along the strut and lower it onto its stand. Actually, if there were enough sun-tanned RAF 'erks around, it could be lifted up by hand. An engine change could be carried out in, say, two-and-a-half hours – the pilots barely had time for lunch before they were off across the jungle again!

Gnome engine change at Sepulot. (Mick Charles)

The Whirlwinds were cheap to run but the snag was that in the hot and humid mountains of Borneo it couldn't carry a great payload – with full fuel and two GPMGs mounted in the cabin, not more than four fully-equipped Gurkhas. With a lighter fuel load and no Bren guns on board, the aircraft managed a much more useful payload – six to seven troops. The guns were carried less and less when it became evident that Confrontation was easing down.

Confrontation action from over the border was indeed much quieter in January 1966. Tasking for 230 Squadron in the first weeks of the year consisted mainly of routine troop movement and re-supply. Outside of that, two highlights were the stranding in Sabah thunderstorms of Ted Heath, the visiting Tory opposition leader, and a casevac mission flown by Dick Holmes to retrieve two seriously wounded soldiers from Sebatik, within 400 yards of the border. Dick also had a further run-in with the multi-hoist system – this time, he was on the end of the line:

> The fully developed system of Jack Canham's tapes had recently arrived on the squadron and I volunteered with two others to test it out. We all successfully got ourselves down from a hundred-foot hover, I being the last to go. The pilot landed while we gathered up the loose tapes. After about thirty seconds on the ground we heard the engine run down, a complete engine failure. And a minute or so before, I was at fifty feet on the tape, with the Whirlwind fifty feet above me! That will always come back to haunt me.

When not on the tasking list, aircrews found various ways to ease the stresses and strains of Borneo. On Labuan Dick found escape on the water:

> I was into the squadron's pet project, the construction of a thirty-two-foot long, three-foot beam dug-out canoe, which we'd named '*Mimpi Sampan*' – they told me it meant 'Dream Boat'. It was successfully launched and with six men at the paddles it made the grand speed of five knots.
>
> It was decided that something should be done about that speed, which hopelessly restricted its range. So Bob Smith, our squadron Engineering Officer, got hold of an engine from a time-expired hydraulic rig and mounted it horizontally in the stern. We liberated a propshaft from a written-off fire extinguisher pump, and picked up a propellor from a downtown outboard-motor shop.
>
> The whole thing looked rather like the ramshackle boats that run about on the Bangkok River. But trailing a large pall of blue smoke and starting from the Membedai beach, the *Mimpi* now allowed tours of the island – highly enjoyable, sharks, rays and stonefish notwithstanding.

At the end of December Pete Chadwick had returned to Sepulot for his final four-week detachment and, before the end of January, his one-year tour came to an end. He has fond memories of his time in Borneo:

> My Far East experience was memorable in so many ways. It was outstanding, as first tours go, for individual responsibility. It was really

'Hearts and minds' with Dayak girls, and...   (Fraser Skea)

... Murut boys.   (Colin Ford)

Dhobi at Nibong. (Dick Hayes: by kind permission of the Royal Green Jackets Museum, Winchester)

a case of making it up as you went along, with no heavy hand of authority on a young man's back. The usual routine from beginning to end was to climb into the cockpit after breakfast and strap ourselves to the Whirlwind for what could on occasion be up to eight hours, after which we'd go off back to the Mess or wherever for an evening curry from the Gurkhas – and then retire to the bar for some beers.

There were no complications from female relationships – you'd get a mid-tour two-week leave in Bangkok or some such. There were the all-female staff at the hairdressers in Victoria – bra-less in tight T-shirts – and the professional Chinese girls in Jesselton. Despite the plethora of *Dayak* beauties in the longhouses, all those stories of helicopter pilots' nights of passion were mostly just that – fables.[50]

However, the natives in those longhouses – where the helis were often forced to stay for bad weather or other emergencies – were always very hospitable. Two-up with a mate, I remember being forced down by storms just a couple of ridges short of Sepulot, and treated to a ' tapai' session. Tapai's made from the leaves of the tapioca bush – they stuff them into a huge gourd, douse them in water straight from the river, and leave them to ferment for several weeks. My mate and I drew straws to decide who should drink the stuff, and I lost. It was lethal. When the weather cleared I could scarcely manage it up to the cockpit.

We'd be detailed to make hearts and minds trips – sweets for the children, gifts for the headman and all that, and always a medic on board. Wherever you landed, even in the smallest village, there was always a football pitch. Once, we went to this school where miles from any road, the teachers were under orders from the authorities from KL to teach the kids the Highway Code! There they were, pushing their desks around the floor to simulate cars – the cars they'd never seen. Come to that, they'd never even seen a road.

Working with the Gurkhas was a revelation. While I was detached to Bario it turned out their HQ at Seria needed a water buffalo for their annual good luck ceremony. A buffalo cost several dollars at Seria but you could get one up at Bario for a few bob and, would you believe it, I find myself tasked by ATOC[51] to fly one down to the HQ. I take Flight Sergeant Eddie Beacon as crewman, and together we manhandle this huge protesting animal into the cabin. We've got it lashed down with airdrop tape, but Eddie sits for the whole flight with his .38 muzzle to the beast's head, just in case.

We land at Anduki, where the Gurkha officer says that they really need the poor creature along the road at Seria. I say 'Not sure where that is' and he jumps into his racing-green MG and says 'Follow me!' So there I am in the Whirlwind, formating on the motor, low to the road when, for the first and last time in my life I get waved on by a car – a native driver chugging along in a clapped-out Austin 7!

The grateful Gurkhas stack the cabin with *Tiger* and off we go back to Bario. But we're forced down by weather at Long Semado and Eddie sits up all night with his revolver, guarding the precious cargo.

Tour-expired, Pete was airlifted back to Singapore for two weeks at the Changi Creek transit hotel and an opportunity – the first for a year – for gift shopping. Then it was the mind- and body-numbing experience of a chilly February in Yorkshire and RAF squadron life in the United Kingdom – a world away from the freedoms and exotica of the Far East.

★ ★ ★ ★ ★

January 1966 was also a quiet month on the border south of Kuching. The aircrews of 66 Squadron were more worried about their aircraft than they were about Indonesians. The Belvederes received from Aden arrived in a very poor state of repair and needed a great deal of ground crew care and attention, and the fleet overall had developed unacceptable levels of vibration in the rotor heads and flying controls. The whole led to a spate of unserviceabilities towards the end of the month.

Westland sent out a technical representative from the UK, who had discovered that a number of components received as spares had been incorrectly marked and were therefore accompanied by the wrong datasheets. Although disconcerting, this development did indicate one probable cause of the continuing serviceability problems and the hope was that, having been diagnosed, they could be solved.

The Squadron Commander, Squadron Leader 'Bunny' Austin, was something of an extrovert individualist who liked to lead from the front – he was well acquainted with flying Belvederes back to base from forward areas with one engine out, all on his own to save weight. But he was currently wrestling with a different sort of challenge – the make-up of his aircrews.

Those who had come from Aden contained many Masters who had completed mostly three tours on helicopters and they had brought the average age of pilots on the squadron up to forty-five. At the same time, a number of Borneo-experienced men were coming to the end of their tours and needed replacements – four younger men were expected in the next four weeks. But the Belvedere's RAF service life was being truncated and the OCU at Odiham was in the process of closing down. Despite 66 Squadron having no Operational Conversion establishment it was decided to send graduates direct from Tern Hill to Seletar, to be trained on the squadron itself.

One of the first to arrive, in January, and just short of his twenty-fifth birthday, was ex-Valiant man Dave Lanigan:

At Tern Hill I'd found the change from fixed-wing a distinct re-learning process, but after the two-day QRA [Quick Reaction Alert] standby periods on Valiants – sitting on fifteen-minute readiness for possible Armaggeddon – the new hands-on skill-based activities were most refreshing.

I'd come out of Tern Hill in October 1965 and reported to the Belvedere OCU at Odiham. In two weeks of ground school we were told about the advantages of tandem rotors over the conventional main and tail rotor configuration. A tail rotor is exposed to damage and takes away some twenty per cent of installed power just to keep the machine straight in the hover whereas in the Belvedere all the power goes to lift the machine and its payload. Then there's the obvious advantage of having two engines driving two rotors through synchronising gearboxes – if you lose one Gazelle turbine, the drive-shaft carries the power of the remaining one to both rotors at once and you stay airborne.

We were told the history of Belvedere accidents. In at least two cases the second pilots had switched off the remaining live engine after an in-flight engine failure. Changes to the engine control switches and management drills fixed that. There had also been cable failures in the yaw-control system. Those led to cable changes and more frequent servicing, which sorted that one out.

After ground school there was a dull pause – the two training machines at Odiham were both seemingly permanently unserviceable due to vibration. All that my fellow student Max Sceats and I could manage, right through to year-end, were numerous ground engine-runs, and a few short air tests. So, with Christmas over, Max and I plucked up the courage to ask to be sent out to the operational squadron in Singapore.

We found we were pushing on an open door – but it meant we arrived on 66 Squadron at Seletar almost completely untrained on the Belvedere.

Dave and Max were swiftly inducted onto Bunny Austin's squadron and started theatre conversion, alongside conversion to the Belvedere itself, on 8 February 1966.

* * * * *

For 103 Squadron the turn of the year had seen the repatriation of the last of the trio of Tern Hill tyros. After flying close on 900 hours in his thirty months in FEAF, working with most of the Gurkha and British battalions and 22nd Regiment SAS, Colin Ford followed Mick Charles and Ian Morgan to CFS(H).

January 1966 saw just the one incursion scare, at Long Jawi, which led to a 110 Squadron Whirlwind spending ten consecutive days up in the mountains on Full Precautions standby. The two pilots and their crewman had reason to report that the living conditions at this forward army base were primitive in the extreme but the expected incursion did not materialize. Downriver at the Gaat, other crews worked hard lifting underslung bags of river shingle for the foundations of a new Whirlwind servicing shelter. It opened to great acclaim from the ground crew and doubled in slack periods as a cinema.

Other than that, and a single 103 Squadron aircraft being detached to Balai Ringin, all was routine, and there being no Indonesian landings in Singapore or Malaya, the way was clear for the pilots in Borneo to be rostered for clearing the backlog of jungle survival training back on Changi beach.

However, the Sarawak workload for the Whirlwinds soon racked up again, for there was another peak in unserviceability for Belvederes and the AAC Scouts and Sioux. The pilots of 110 and 103 were once more tasked with a full programme of routine trooping and re-supply missions, hampered by torrential monsoon rain and heavy mud. At Nanga Gaat, the river rose to forty feet above normal. Helicopter pads and the hangar were in danger for a while as a further rise of a few feet would have washed away their foundations. As it was, the 110 Squadron detachment were distressed to watch their showers and toilets disappearing in the flood. The entire camp of the King's Own Scottish Borderers had swiftly to be moved farther up the hill and the Whirlwinds were called upon to lift replacement generators to the new position.

Such a temporary disruption to a camp and its cookhouse would have been a setback for the airmen as well as the soldiers. As Fred Hoskins explains:

Having received tasking orders by signal during the previous evening, Whirlwind crews would usually set out soon after dawn and might be away until early evening, doing what had to be done and refuelling from drums of Avtur stored around the place. Often it was simply not possible to calculate how long crews might be away from base but we never took any food with us. I think we simply became accustomed to being looked after by the Army.

Almost everywhere we landed at the forward bases the soldiers would offer us at least a drink of the lemonade made up from crystals and usually termed 'jungle juice'. I was told that, early on, before they had got used to the novelty of RAF helicopters, the Gurkhas used to offer mugs of rum, but jungle juice or tea were the usual refreshments.

But at Battalion Headquarters in the little town of Bau there was a permanent staff of locally employed labourers who virtually ran the landing site. The senior man had been given an RAF beret and was always known as 'Number One at Bau'. Not only could he be relied on for tea, coffee or jungle juice but he also supplied us with 'egg banjos' – two slices of bread with a fried egg in between. Number One would hand them up to the pilot while the rotors were turning if there was no time to stop. Payment was never required and I assume that Number One had a good contact in the army cookhouse.

Relying on local food, although cheap and delicious, sometimes had unwanted effects on the system. One morning when flying I was subject to an urge which would not be denied so, landing at a company base at Tepoi about a mile from Indonesia, I closed down and jumped out. On making my requirements clear I was shepherded through the barbed wire into the company fort, which was built around the summit of a small hill, and shown the way to the top where the Company Commander had his quarters. I ran up what seemed a very long path with steps made of ammo boxes and sand bags. At the top of the hill I was ushered to the 'seat of ease' – it was amazing!

Directly beneath the seat was a shaft lined with empty fuel drums with the tops and bottoms cut out and falling to a pit about forty feet below. The spacious convenience was constructed of sandbags and corrugated iron with what I can only describe as a huge unglazed picture window. The view was to the west where range after range of the mountains of Indonesia receded to the horizon, the colours changing from shades of green to shades of blue gradually getting paler and greyer with the distance. I believe it must have been one of the most magnificent views possible from such a facility – all so tranquil and beautiful that it was hard to realize that men were ranging all over those hills intent on war.[52]

So-called 'routine' helicopter tasks in Borneo could never be considered easy. For the 103 Simanggang Detachment there was one in particular that required more than usually high levels of concentration and endurance, as well as considerable flying skills. Bob Turner explains:

One of the almost daily tasks for one of the 103 Squadron Simanggang detachment Whirlwinds required an early take-off and a transit of about forty nautical miles east to Jambu, close to the Indonesian border.

The transit was usually uneventful, except that on more than one occasion, when cruising along at the Whirlwind's max permitted speed of ninety-five knots and a few hundred feet above the jungle, you'd be shaken out of the early morning 'mind in neutral' state as R/T silence was suddenly broken by a gutteral 'G'day'. Right alongside would be an RNZAF Bristol Freighter, or 'Frightener', no more than a rotor span to starboard. It was also progressing steadily towards Jambu, and an airdrop – its overtaking speed only a few knots faster than I was managing!

At Jambu, the company base was now well-developed, with a heli LZ and an artillery battery with two 105-millimetre howitzers. It was built on a long, steep and wooded ridge. The snag was that almost all supplies for the fort had to be parachuted in and the DZ was in the valley some three-hundred feet below.

The harness packs and one-ton containers delivered in the daily drops contained food, defence supplies, ammo for the guns, fuel for the helicopters – all sorts. Everything had to be unpacked and then repacked into cargo nets because the only way to get them to the top of the ridge was to sling them under a helicopter and haul them up – we spent many hours doing just that.

To save weight, we didn't carry a crewman – it was all done under pilot control. The procedure was to descend to the DZ and come to the

Malaysian Rengers Company Base at Jambu, where... (Martin Mayer)

...Whirlwind awaits arrival of... (Rick Atkinson)

... Kiwi Bristol Freighter with load.

Packs float down and...

...Whirlwind hauls them to top.

(pictures Rick Atkinson)

hover, aiming the fixed underslung-load hook below the fuselage as accurately as possible over each successive load. A soldier – often the company colour sergeant to ensure no pilfering – would then attach the net, containing about eight-hundred pounds of stores, to the hook. Then, it was full power and collective fully-up, and at about twenty-five knots forward speed we'd clatter steeply up to the helipad way above.

We'd drop the load, using the thumb-switch on the cyclic to release the hook. The stuff was then humped by soldier muscle-power to the appropriate place, except that the fuel barrels remained on the pad, for our future use. We'd then climb steeply into forward flight, bank into a wingover and in autorotation swoop back down to the DZ, where another steep turn would position the aircraft for the next load. It was great flying – almost a bit of helicopter aerobatics. And it needed skill in arriving in the hover with the hook in just the right place over a load you couldn't see. Each uplift took no more than five minutes, but there were a lot of them. This 'craning' work was always an hours-long affair and frequently continued into the afternoon, by which time we might have done forty to fifty lifts.

Then, there were the packs which had landed some distance from the marked DZ. Not infrequently these were in awkward positions, inaccessible for recovery on foot and needing helicopter-lift. Often, this meant hovering very close to high trees and vegetation in extremely rough terrain. It has to be admitted that the odd rotor-tip strike did occur but they rarely resulted in serious damage. Where the position was particularly difficult, the sixty-foot winch cable would be run out, by the pilot again, from a high hover. The load was then hauled over to the DZ and unpacked for lifting up to the LZ.

And there was the added business of refuelling. To allow the maximum weight to be lifted, the aircraft was fuelled for just twenty minutes. Well inside that, about every fifteen minutes, it was refuelled on the helipad from forty-four gallon drums, with rotors turning and using a portable pump. That gave us a chance of snatching a drink, and not quite so often, a pee!

At the end of the day, the rather wearied pilot flew the thirty-minute transit back to Simanggang, most times through the late afternoon thunderstorms which occurred almost daily. It was demanding and exciting flying, without a doubt!

Bob reinforces the points made by his colleagues on the Whirlwind's load-carrying limitations:

In the hot daytime temperatures – Simanggang is only about eighty miles north of the equator – much equipment was stripped out to maximize the payload. Most times, the cabin doors were left off, and some safety equipment. As well as the pilot-seat armour-plate, sometimes even the HF radio was removed. Even so, in the best case, carrying fuel for only thirty minutes, we could carry no more than about eight-hundred to a thousand pounds of freight, or some half-a-dozen troops – depending upon how much kit they were carrying. Mind you, Gurkhas were usually a little lighter – we could lift a couple more of them.

Such limitations, together with crew rotations meant that the Navy's squadrons were from time to time called in off their commando carriers to help out at periods of heavy tasking. In February a detachment of 845 NAS flew into Labuan off HMS *Bulwark*, now operating the twin Gnome-powered Westland Wessex Mk 5. Paul Moran remembers their arrival:

We had five experienced pilots repatriated in three weeks, all with three years and an average of one thousand hours in theatre. And to replace them, we got five tyros straight from training. They were competent to fly the Whirlwind, of course, but it was going to take some weeks to get them operational. At the same time, Central Brigade was crying out for more tasking – mostly routine freight and trooping, but our radius of operating had been widened, down to Seria and Anduki. So the Navy Junglies were called in.

We ground crew lads found the matelots a breath of fresh air with their more relaxed attitude to rules and life.[53] And their twin-engine Wessex Fives were so much more powerful than the Whirlwinds. I reckon the Whirlwind might be seen as a sort of London taxi cab and the Wessex perhaps a white van. But both had strengths within their own tasking envelope.

Because of its smaller size the Whirlwind was ideal for dropping into those tiny little jungle clearings – it just had to do more frequent trips, that's all. I'm sure the pilots found it a delight to fly and many a serviceman out in Sabah and Sarawak was glad to hear the familiar 'thwak, thwak, thwak' of the Westland Whirlwind on its way!

So we got a bit miffed in the Sergeants' Mess when the Navy ground crew labelled our outfit the 'Static Display Squadron'. But we laughed it all off. We didn't pick fights – we'd learnt to avoid fisticuffs. After all we'd had SAS guys in the Mess for months.

They were a race apart – strong and silent, with a fearsome reputation. Once, on Orderly Sergeant duties, I was required to shut down the Airmen's Mess bar at twenty-two thirty hours, sharp – a daunting task for one man against fifteen troops, fresh back from two months in the jungle. To my surprise, on command the raucous din stopped immediately and the SAS party trooped off to their *bashas*. Those guys were trained to obey orders without question – so I escaped, without serious injury!

By the way the Sergeants' Mess anthem of the time, to be sung when you could hardly walk, was a derivation of the Royal Naval hymn, 'For those in peril on the sea'. In this case 'on the sea' was changed to 'in the air'. The rest of the re-written lyrics were good, but now perhaps best forgotten.

In mid-January at the 103 Squadron Simanggang detachment, Bob Turner had a scare:

I began to suffer from a nagging abdominal pain. It got worse and the medico diagnosed appendicitis, saying that I needed to be evacuated to Kuching Hospital. I was at the time the only flight-authorising officer at Simanggang – so I duly cleared a casevac flight to take me there. But before an aircraft became available the attack became acute – it was a case of getting me straight down to the local civilian hospital in Simanggang town.

An Indian doctor removed the offending organ and I spent ten days in the recovery ward alongside nineteen other patients, most with terminal TB! That was an interesting experience to say the least, but completely successful. After a spot of leave in Singapore, I was back at Simanggang and operational by mid-February.

Bob got back to Sarawak just in time to see the lull in incursions on the Kalimantan frontier come dramatically to an end.

* * * * *

In January 1966 there had been no Indonesian attacks on Singapore and the Malayan peninsula. That strategy had failed, none of the Malaysian people having risen up in support of Sukarno's liberators. The President had in any case other matters on his mind for, in Djakarta, the power struggles continued. Sukarno was back in his *Merdeka* (Freedom) Palace but with his wings clipped by the increasingly influential Generals Suharto and Nasution and, halfway through February, affairs began to come to the boil.

President Sukarno had gone out of his way to give succour to the Indonesian Communist Party by commending them publicly for 'their sacrifices in the struggle of the Indonesian people for independence'. General Nasution chose what he thought was his moment and came forward to make a broadcast on *Radio Djakarta*, in which he strongly condemned the Communist Party for terrorism and crimes against the state. This constituted a direct challenge to a supposedly weakened President and proved to be a grave error of judgement. Within two days Sukarno had Nasution sacked from his position as Commander of the Armed Forces.

The governments in London and Kuala Lumpur soon saw Sukarno making fresh overtures to Communist China, North Korea and North Vietnam, soliciting their cooperation in a so-called 'Conference of the New Emerging Forces', and renewing his calls for the destruction of the Malaysian Federation.

The security forces in Borneo were put on high alert, ready to react against more attacks from pro-Sukarno army commanders and their remotivated troops. CLARET missions intensified their harrassing of Indonesian bases and patrols and there was a continuing heavy workload for the helicopters in support.

Many of the commanders in Kalimantan were fervently pro-Sukarno, and had taken heart from seeing him survive the post-coup storm. In reaction to the injuries and indignities being meted out to their troops by CLARET patrols, they hit back. On 16 February a fifty-strong party of Indonesian paratroops, supported by the CCO, crossed the frontier to strike at Tebedu, the target of that earliest attack in Confrontation, back in April 1963.

In his January letter home, Mike McKinley had written that operations in Western Sarawak, despite the testing weather conditions, were becoming somewhat humdrum but in his missive of 17 February all that had changed:

Ah well, my talk of monotony was premature. From midday yesterday to midday today, it's been about as active as one could ask for – and there's more to come. There's been an incursion that seems to have been quite a major effort on the Indon part and we've been moving troops all over the place to cut off their retreat routes.

The situation is somewhat blurred but this much is certain – there are something between fifty and seventy enemy further into Sarawak than they have been for a long time, but it's impossible to say what percentage is Indon and what local dissidents. People can melt so easily into this sort of country that it's impossible to guarantee catching them even though they are pretty well surrounded.

The Gurkha battalion that is running the show has had rather more casualties than they are wont to accept out here and are feeling distinctly annoyed about it. So if there is a real meeting between Indons and Gurkhas it will certainly be a nasty affair. We just await developments.

My own contribution so far has mainly been in pulling out casualties. Yesterday afternoon I went down for one who was in a bad way and then in the evening I had to go back to carry out a troop lift onto a sandbank in the middle of a river with dirty great trees on either side. After that, just as I was setting out to get back to Kuching before dark, I was informed of five more casevacs just off my planned course, so I went to look for them. They had no homing aids, were in the middle of scrub and jungle, darkness was falling and storms were moving in from all directions.

I hung around searching until it was hopelessly dark, and I had just enough fuel and light to get out of the hills around me. Then I found that a gigantic storm was blotting out the airfield so I used my dwindling fuel to divert to the only place I could – the HQ of the Argyll and Sutherland Highlanders. I landed by the headlights of two Land Rovers.

I then spent the night getting unwound on caviar and Glenfiddich. Gracious living is so much more fun when practised under such inauspicious conditions. I do admire the ability of the best elements of our Army to be so ridiculously British!

In the morning I was up at six o'clock waiting for news of the casualties and finally, after much nerve-racking cruising, in early-morning jungle mist and the treetops, I pulled out one Gurkha body, two badly hurt men and five others in various states of disrepair. I felt it was the best morning's work I had done out here and only wished I could have found them the previous night. I have never seen Gurkhas looking so grim before – normally they will grin under any circumstances, particularly for a 'helicopter sahib', so I don't fancy the chances of any Indon who might fall into their hands. It could be kukris out and heads off I'm afraid, though they've been discouraged from that practice out here.

Evidently, in the course of my searching, I flew within a few hundred yards of the Indons – who have Bren guns – a couple of times. It appears that, presumably for fear of pinpointing their own positions, they didn't shoot. I'm glad I didn't know all that at the time!

Martin Mayer adds a rider to Mike's account that shows the effect of the hearts and minds campaign:

When the Indonesians first came into the *kampong* at Tebedu they were welcomed by the local people. They were given food and accommodation and sent on their way in the morning with directions of how to get to Serian. However as soon as they were out of sight, one of the villagers cycled to the nearest telephone and reported all that they had seen to the security forces. The result was that an ambush line was put in ahead of them on their route.

They broke through this line with some losses but by using our helicopters we were able to reposition further ambush lines ahead of

Belvederes move troops, and …

(Dick Hayes: by kind permission of the Royal Green Jackets Museum, Winchester)

(Colin Ford)

… guns around, while…

…Whirlwinds carry in vital supplies.

(Colin Ford)

205

them. After some three days of this constant attrition they were very much reduced in number and decided to withdraw to the border. Their problems were exacerbated by a Shackleton aircraft being deployed from Singapore to remain over the combat area throughout the night, illuminating the ground with its brilliant parachute flares. Normally fighting operations would have to cease at dusk but the Shackleton effectively provided twenty-four-hour daylight. This wore them down to the extent that they seemed to be concerned only with making their way back to the border with the clothes they stood up in.

The first two weeks of February had seen 110 Squadron flying a volume of missions for West Brigade ten per cent above planned maximum, in logistical support of the Durhams but, from the middle of the month all RAF Whirlwinds and Belvederes in Western Sarawak were concentrated in the 1st Division, on dawn-to-dusk standby. There were six serviceable Belvederes in Kuching which, rejuvenated by the efforts of the ground crew and the visitor from Westland, managed 148 operational hours by month end, an out-and-out record for 66 Squadron. The 103 Squadron Whirlwind in Lundu was withdrawn to base to assist the Kuching and Simanggang aircraft in flying resupply, cut-off, and casevac missions. In one notable fifteen-minute long hover in a night rescue of two wounded soldiers of the Durham Light Infantry, the newly-trialled undernose searchlight more than proved its worth.

The Indonesians had headed for the Kuching-Serian road before splitting into small groups and proceeding in various directions and the helis succeeded in moving as many as 400 troops around the forward areas in the first two days of cut-off action. Again, the local population failed to rise up in support and the invaders were sent packing, many being captured or killed and many others perishing in the flooded rivers and swamps.

The dawn-to-dusk stand-by was lifted after a week but the withdrawal of all Western Brigade helicopters to the 1st Division action resulted in a backlog quickly building up elsewhere, guaranteeing work for the Kuching-based rotaries for weeks to come. It was on 21 February that Martin Mayer was tasked with carrying out a casevac at first light:

I was briefed that it was an injured Gurkha and that a landing site would be prepared for me. I only had a grid reference for the pick-up point and the ground and forest all around was covered by thick fog. I flew down the main road to Serian which was in the clear, and then by dead reckoning to the grid reference that I had been given. However, when I got there no ground was visible even though the fog was probably only a couple of hundred feet thick.

About a mile away to the southeast I could see a small hill sticking out of the fog and I flew to it and landed on the top. I then worked out a cunning plan. With my crewman, Sergeant Jack, leaning out of the door and directing me, I flew very slowly down the hillside and into the fog until I reached the base of the hill. I had calculated that the pick-up point was almost exactly one mile from the base of the hill in a north-westerly direction. I couldn't see very much through the windscreen so I decided to fly looking through the window, with the aircraft pointing forty-five degrees to port.

I then started the stopwatch and flew at thirty knots for exactly two minutes to the north-west whilst maintaining a heading on the compass of due west, Sergeant Jack giving me constant updates of the height of the trees beneath us. Would you believe it, as two minutes came up on the clock, we saw a small clearing in the primary forest beneath us with three or four Gurkhas waving furiously. We landed, and a single Gurkha jumped in and gave us the thumbs up to depart. We took him back to the hospital in Kuching but it turned out all he had was boils!

After the hubbub around Tebedu had died down there was another request for Martin's services. While delivering supplies near Lubok Antu he was asked to take a critically sick woman to hospital:

I said that was fine with me and, shortly after, a woman was lifted into the back of the aircraft and joined by her husband. I didn't have a crewman so had no way of knowing if they were okay but the door was closed and I trusted that they would be safe. I radioed ahead to the hospital in Kuching to have a stretcher waiting and she was soon in their care.

A couple of days later I was briefed by my Flight Commander to return to the hospital and pick up the woman and take her and her husband home. I duly went back to the hospital to pick them up and was delighted to see that now they were accompanied by a new baby. I hadn't realized when I took her in that she'd actually been in labour for over twenty-four hours.

I took them back to their *kampong* where they were met by a large crowd all smiling and clapping. I didn't shut down but was delighted to receive a few coconuts and bananas thrown into the back of the aircraft – hearts and minds again. I thought then that one could only compare Borneo with the situation in Vietnam where the Americans were in such terrible, escalating trouble.

★ ★ ★ ★ ★

Meanwhile, Dave Lanigan's Belvedere conversion on 66 Squadron at Seletar had been somewhat slow going, but progress was better than at Odiham:

207

'Hearts and minds' campaign rolls on: 2nd from right: Sqn Ldr Fred Hoskins, OC 103 Squadron, 3rd: Flt Lt Tim Nicoll, engineer turned Whirlwind pilot, far right: Flt Lt Bert Fraser, shot down and killed with his passneger shortly after this picture was taken. (Crown Copyright)

One of many medevac missions. (Colin Ford)

Jungle welcome for Whirlwind crew. (Paul Logan)

Murut ladies on parade for VIP visit. (Colin Ford)

By this time, I was a Flight Lieutenant, and married – I'd met Ann while she was a student at Nottingham University – but still under twenty-five, the age in the early 'sixties when the RAF started to support the married state fully. It cost forty-five quid for Ann to join me on an indulgence flight from the UK.

Max and I met our Flight Commander, Flight Lieutenant 'Dinger' Bell, who explained that for our first few months we new boys were to be closely supervised. We then at last started the process of learning to fly the Belvedere. There was a ladder up to the cockpit, where the two pilots were cut off from the crewman by the front engine. With the racket from that, the gearbox and the intermeshing rotors, it was noisy up there, with a lot of vibration. Flying in the hot, moist climate was normally done with the right-hand cockpit door open – cooler but draughty, so you needed to hang on to the maps and flight-plan. Performance at sea level was good – one hundred and twenty knots at maximum all-up-weight with an internal load. With a big external load like a Land Rover the maximum achievable speed was eighty.

209

There was a manual throttle to control rotor-rpm and no automatic stabilization or autopilot. As with all rotaries, ground-resonance was endemic with the Belvedere and the trick was to make all lift-offs and landings positive. And at thirty knots or below, the downwash was prone to recirculate through the rotors, causing a heavy vibration – you just had to get used to it and fly through it.

We did all right, because before long Dinger was talking about sending us out to the 66 Squadron operational detachment in Kuching to continue our training in Borneo.

By month end, Dave had accumulated nine precious hours of actual flying, and was slated to go out to Kuching in early March.

★ ★ ★ ★ ★

Up in the north and east of Malaysian Borneo, March 1966 was a busy month for 230 Squadron out of Labuan. The Whirlwinds flew 480 hours in the four weeks and this was well ahead of target, as was performance for the year as a whole. The frontier and Tawau were quiet, however, and tasking was mostly routine re-supply, given some variety by the lift of 4,600lb of radio and telephone equipment from the 3,000-foot 25th Milestone on the Ranau road to the 7,000-foot radio station of Sabah Post and Telegraph, halfway up Mount Kinabalu. Dick Holmes flew the mission with the squadron commander and they took off early, completing the task just before the clouds descended at the usual hour of ten o'clock. Later in the month, Flying Officers Holmes and Cheetham carried out a border casevac at night, the rescue pad being lit by flares dropped from an AAC Beaver.

In the Technical Section at Labuan Paul Moran had now been checked out on the standard drill for balancing the aerodynamics of Whirlwind rotors:

Tracking of the three blades was regularly checked in a simple way. The aircraft was first tethered to the ground. Then the tips of the rotor were each daubed in turn with a different coloured crayon – red, blue and yellow. The pilot started the engine, spun the rotor and applied full power, whereupon a technician bravely walked towards the spinning disc with a twelve-foot pole. On the far end of the pole was attached a long piece of heavy, white canvas. As the canvas strip was offered to the spinning disc, the blade tips briefly hit the canvas. If all the marks were together, tracking was deemed perfect. I'm not making this up!

★ ★ ★ ★ ★

On 8 March, Dave Lanigan duly arrived at the 66 Squadron Detachment in Kuching to start the process of Operational Conversion:

I was briefed by the Boss that there were to be no heroics as only two machines out of four were likely to be serviceable on any one day, and it was important to bring the machine back intact at the end of each day's flying ready for the next day's tasking. Oh dear!

I was issued with the infamous white maps of Borneo made up from aerial photos. These showed the coastline, rivers and latitude and longitude grids, but no contours, settlements or roads. So I started straight away making up my own set from other pilots' marking of details – riverside villages, mountains, airstrips, border forts and clearings for helicopter sites. On flying days we were issued with a Sterling and a full magazine in case we came down somewhere, though there was nowhere to stow it except shoved down behind the seat. Also issued was a flak jacket which was too cumbersome to wear so that, too, cluttered up the cockpit.

As a first tour pilot with thirty hours solo helicopter flying to my name I was happy to be looked after by the 'old and bold' Masters. The daily weather forecasts were vague, usually 'winds light and variable, and afternoon heavy showers dying out at dusk'. First thing in the morning a mist would rise from the jungle, reducing forward speed and obscuring the horizon, making navigation more difficult. We were ordered not to fly over the ill-defined border as the Indons had anti-aircraft guns and used them. It was also important not to fly in a direct line to a border fort but to change direction every five minutes or so while flying a hundred feet above the treetops. That way we'd avoid giving away our destination and hopefully not be welcomed by mortar rounds as we arrived! The destinations were referred to on the radio by a colour code – Red 3, Green 7, Blue 5 and so on.

The standard operational procedure was to fly two captains up, so there were no co-pilots. The chap in the right-hand seat at any time was the aircraft commander. The Belvedere at 120 knots cruising speed took a lot of stopping so a straight-in approach to a helipad started a mile away followed by a ninety-degree turn closer in. But this was not advisable with an underslung load. For that, a slow plodding approach was necessary to prevent a swing developing at the end of the eighty-foot strop.

Although the Belvedere was fully equipped for night flying, ninety-five per cent of our ops were carried out by day. But bad weather and clouds were avoided because turbulence led to problems trying to control rotor-rpm with the manual throttle and there was no stability system incorporated in the flying controls.

To build up my experience I volunteered for every flight and soon acquired the nickname of 'Dauntless Dave'. A typical working day at

Kuching would start the evening before when the army tasking officers would come up to the airfield and present their requirements for the morning. The pilots then worked out the most efficient way of transporting the troops, netted loads and sometimes 105-millimetre howitzers to their destinations. Our fuel load could be up to four thousand pounds, which left a margin of fifteen hundred pounds for payload at the start of the flight, increasing as fuel decreased.

For trooping flights Gurkhas and kit were listed at two hundred pounds and a normal soldier at two-fifty. But the SAS guys weighed in at three hundred – they carried machine guns and bands of ammunition, as well as the most enormous, bulging rucksacks. They wore a variety of military-style kit but they were clearly professional killers and looked the part. I was just glad that they were on our side!

Dave now began to rack up the hours. March turned out to be the month when the combined efforts of the Westland Aircraft Company, Rolls-Royce and the 66 Squadron ground engineers saw a dramatic and hugely welcome upturn in Belvedere serviceability. Despite a peak in spares shortage at Kuching, 250

'Dauntless Dave' ready for action. (Dave Lanigan)

operational hours were flown in Borneo, and an aircraft was found in Seletar to despatch to up-country Malaya for work on pre-Vietnam exercises with Australian and New Zealand forces in Trengganu and Butterworth.

★ ★ ★ ★ ★

In contrast, their servicing schedules thrown out by spares shortages and over-tasking, serviceable Whirlwinds in Sarawak were in short supply. Despite that 103 Squadron fulfilled its tasking for the King's Own Scottish Borderers ('Kosbies') and found the hours for Mike McKinley, Martin Mayer and Flight Sergeant Thatcher to blast two SS11 missiles each into the goldmine at Bau. On the same mission the flight sergeant successfully fired the GPMG newly mounted in the Whirlwind cabin. This was also the month when the ex-Signaller crewmen were for the first time categorized.

And when in the first week of March there was a further Indonesian incursion at the 24th mile on the border road in the 2nd Division, four 110 Squadron aircraft managed to fly close on twenty-four hours in one day out of Nanga Gaat, supporting the Gurkhas who successfully chased the invaders down.

★ ★ ★ ★ ★

The signals coming out of Djakarta remained confusing to the Malaysian side. General Suharto had said that *Konfrontasi* would continue but the Indonesian Foreign Minister, Dr Adam Malik, began to drop hints that it might end. It must have been obvious to the new Minister for Economics, the Sultan of Jogjakarta and one of the ruling triumvirate, that the costs of the conflict were becoming ruinous.

For the rotary pilots in Borneo, all that was not much more than background noise. Well into the fourth year of Confrontation, there were more troops to move in and out of border clearings, and re-supply at patrol bases, than ever before and the operating conditions required the usual vigilance and nerve.

Chapter 19

Jungly Mission to the Gaat

In March 1966 the JHC at Brunei had again called in the Royal Navy to reinforce the hard-pressed RAF rotaries and the new Officer Commanding 848 NAS, Lieutenant Commander Peter Craig, was given the chance to see the latest front-line action for himself.

He had taken over command of the 250 personnel of 848 with their Wessex 5s in early March, flying out to the Far East in an RAF Comet 4, in an epic journey of nearly six days from Lyneham to Singapore. This, as he worked it out, equated to an average speed of 'thirty-three and a half miles per hour'.

The squadron had disembarked from HMS *Albion* and installed itself at RNAS Sembawang with detachments operating from Labuan and Bario. As he took command, Peter Craig knew what he was in for – he had already spent nine months in Borneo in 1963. As he wrote in his diary:

Mere words are hardly adequate. Imagine yourself in conditions of 90% humidity and a temperature at midday approaching 100 degrees Fahrenheit, a seemingly endless carpet of dense primary rainforest with trees over 200ft high, mountains up to 8000ft along the border, gorges, no roads, remote longhouses and, overall, a pervading damp fed by morning mists wreathing about the trees, and rain – torrential slow-moving storms that you could hear approaching as they lashed down through the leaves. These were the conditions in which troops had to operate – and helicopters were essential to move them into a position to repel any incursion.

After settling in and being briefed on the current situation it was time to visit the Borneo detachments and I was flown over to Labuan on 23 March. That evening, over a plate of tiger prawns and a beer or two, the Senior Pilot and I discussed the operational details. We had just about covered everything when a signal message arrived, instructing the detachment to provide two Wessex 5s for a troop lift the following morning at Sibu, some 300 miles to the south.

Sibu was one of the two towns of any size in Sarawak – the other being the capital Kuching – and was situated in the flat mangrove swamp delta where the mighty Rajang river flowed into the sea. It was a major base for troops and had an airfield suitable for regional airlines.

As I read the signal, I wondered why the Wessex were required at all – Sibu was RAF helicopter territory. However, it all looked simple enough and an ideal chance for me to get back into business again so I told the Senior Pilot that I would grasp the opportunity.

At 0800 on 24 March we started the two twin-engined Wessex, taxied out and took off in bright sunshine along the main runway of Labuan airfield: vertical take-offs and landings were avoided where possible to reduce mechanical wear and tear. On board, we had a small snag team with some 'come in handy' spares, because we were going to be a long way away from our base maintenance.

The first part of the route was flown overland at 1,000ft but very soon we ran into heavy tropical rain which reduced the visibility to about a mile. The maps available (at the time) were not only lacking in detail but notoriously inaccurate as well, so rather than flying in conditions where we were unsure of our position I decided we should turn north and head for the coast.

Soon after, we were flying along the beach at 200ft in even heavier rain. In such conditions the windscreen wipers were useless but by opening the side window and flying slightly sideways at about 80kts we managed to see ahead for about half a mile.

I had hoped that the bad weather would clear but it was pouring down when we reached the airstrip at Bintulu where we planned to refuel from 40gal drums. Having landed, we topped up using hand-operated pumps – a slow process but the only one available; engines and rotors were kept turning just in case there were any restarting problems.

Airborne again we turned on to a more southerly heading for Sibu. About 25 miles away we broke out into clear weather and landed after what had been a very unpleasant flight of nearly 4 hours.

The Operations Staff briefed us on our main task which was to ferry 15 SAS troops and their equipment to Long Jawi, a remote longhouse deep in the interior about 25 miles from the Indonesian border. Because this was unknown territory for us it had been arranged that we would land at Nanga Gaat en route and pick up a guide from the detachment of RAF Whirlwinds based there.

As I listened to the briefing it was all too clear that what I thought would be a simple troop lift in the Sibu area was, in fact, going to be something far more interesting.

215

Leaving the snag team at Sibu with the majority of the stores and splitting the 15 SAS between the two Wessex, we got airborne again and headed east along the Rajang river passing the riverside settlements of Song and Kapit en-route and landed at Nanga Gaat 1¼ hours later.

Nanga Gaat was a forward helicopter base deep in the interior and had been established by 845 NAS in late 1963. It was situated on a promontory at an important river junction, strategically placed as far forward as possible to cover the border and still keep the vital river supply line; it was also the home of the Temenggang Jugan Paramount Chief of the *Ibans* and, therefore, politically important. The personnel of 845 Squadron, with the help of local labour, had developed Nanga Gaat into a first class base: living quarters, showers, electric light, galleys – even an 'Anchor Inn' – plus maintenance facilities and six landing pads for the helicopters.

On landing, there was a setback when my wing man flying 'Mike' reported that he was having tail-rotor problems and had to shut down. With the RAF pilot on board in the left-hand seat, plus three more SAS, I set off for Long Jawi as briefed but soon ran into the cloud that usually built up in the late afternoon. Our route was leading us towards the Hose Mountains and I was none too happy in view of the lack of any navigational aids.

As my RAF guide was beginning to look distinctly nervous I decided that discretion would be a wise move and turned back – there was no overriding reason to press on.

That evening, I asked the RAF detachment's Operations Officer for more details of what was afoot but got nowhere: 'I know what it's about but I'm not allowed to tell you,' was the only reply I could get. It was all very frustrating.

'Mike' was worked on that evening and the tail rotor trouble rectified, or so I thought.

We both got airborne early next morning with all the SAS on board and arrived at Long Jawi 30 minutes later after a flight in clear weather.

Long Jawi was a remote longhouse at the headwaters of the Balui river and had been the scene of one of the earliest raids by Indonesian troops during which five defenders were killed and seven murdered in cold blood after surrendering.

Retribution, by 1/2nd Gurkhas supported by helicopters of 845 Squadron, was swift and few of the attackers survived to get back to Indonesian territory. Since then, Long Jawi had been reinforced and was now a base of company strength.

Our task was finally revealed at the briefing: we were to lift 88 troops to a landing site cut out from the forest on a ridge about 25 miles away

Before long, remarkably quickly actually, there was the distinctive beat of a Belvedere's rotors coming towards us, flying very low – its size made it a favourite target for Indo machine guns. It joined us on the landing site and the technical crew at base had done the trick, for in the cabin was not only a new main rotor blade but also a ground crew team ready to swap it for Fred's broken one.

While they worked on that, the landing site filled up with children from the local *kampong*. The boys entertained us by whirling around their heads the stones that they'd tied to pieces of string, to catch birds and, in return, the boss's fellow-pilot, Peter Bogué, had them in fits of laughter by the simple trick of fastening and unfastening the Velcro tabs on the sleeves of his flying-suit.

In no time at all, the technicians changed the blade and successfully tracked it to make sure it was running in the same plane as the other blades. The panel-fasteners were snapped back into place and all was well. The children watched as everyone climbed back on board and the small flotilla clattered off to continue the business of the day.

It all seemed to me to sum up in many ways our efforts in Confrontation –professionalism, team work and a dollop of good luck, against a background of native goodwill.

The immediate availability of a spare Whirlwind rotor blade at Kuching could not be taken for granted. The RAF's logistic chain had been maintaining four squadrons of rotaries with up to more than sixty aircraft in far-off Borneo for year upon year, and helicopter spares were a continuing problem, particularly rotor blades. A recent series of heavy rainstorms had pitted their neoprene leading edges as they whirled around at high speed.

As April went on the month became notable for 103 Squadron casevac call-outs in Sarawak. In one of these an entire fever-ridden patrol of four SAS men had to be lifted out and in another a further SAS trooper was rescued in the nick of time, in the throes of a raging bout of leptospirosis. In yet another, the call-out was for a mission to bring down a wounded Gurkha from the lofty summit of Gunong Gajak at night. In addition, two stork missions were flown, resulting in happy events for two *Dayak* women each of whom in the longhouses might otherwise have lost both baby and her own life.

The Tern Hill production line was in full flow with four more tyros arriving on 103 Squadron in the month. The Squadron Commander reported that freeing up sufficient hours to make them operational was going to be a taxing task.

★ ★ ★ ★ ★

In April the Belvederes of 66 Squadron had one of their better months for aircraft availability and could send an additional machine out to Kuching. The detachment flew 290 hours in total, sufficient to bring Dave Lanigan to operational readiness:

> After the very controlled environment of the V-Force, the opportunity to plan trips and make decisions out in Borneo was refreshing. We flew leg-and-leg-about as First Pilot and, being new, for me each trip in Borneo was in the nature of an adventure. During daily tasking I enjoyed meeting the CO of the ground troops – more often than not an army captain, of equivalent rank to me – and agreeing how each task would be carried out.
>
> Then next day, it would be a different guy. The routes we'd fly would be different, too. We'd zig-zag outbound to the border forts and come back another way, to confuse any enemy surveillance. And we'd always fly at low level. The border was not to be overflown and we had to have an escape route ready just in case a fort came under mortar attack as we arrived.
>
> I was not aware that I was ever shot at – there were certainly no bullet holes found in my aircraft – but others were, for sure.

* * * * *

Up at Labuan 230 Squadron was rife with rumours concerning events in Djakarta, but expectations that Confrontation might come to an end were belied by a full tasking-sheet of freight and passenger lifts to and from forward areas. For these the squadron had sufficient Whirlwinds available, but the shortage of operationally-qualified pilots was acute. Two were borrowed from the FEAF squadrons to fill the gap and they were promptly despatched over to Tawau.

Time was found to organize some distractions for the men at Labuan, now in the dog-days of their unaccompanied tours. A CSE Concert Party put on a show, the Squadron Commander remarking that the 'aroma of perfume made a change from the stench of sweat'. And there was a hog-roast, made possible when, on a mission in deepest Sabah, one of the pilots succeeded in bartering one hundred 6-inch nails for a fat young pig.

But throughout these disorientating days when *Konfrontasi* was seemingly losing its momentum, it was as always vital not to let concentration slip in the Whirlwind cockpit. There was an incident on the Labuan dispersal that grabbed everyone's attention. Dick Holmes has the story:

> One hot and sweaty afternoon a pilot came into the 230 Squadron crew room looking thoughtful. He announced to the half-dozen of us sitting

222

there that during a ground run the engine had just failed, completely out of the blue. On investigation, the ground crew found that it was due to a lack of fuel. When asked what the collector-tank reading was at the time, they said it was showing one hundred pounds remaining. The total silence that followed spoke for itself.

The minimum fuel state for the Whirlwind's collector tank permitted at the time was eighty pounds remaining. Anything below that and there was a risk that even under normal manoeuvring the Avtur flow to the burners might develop air-locks and the engine would stop – with disastrous consequences.

We all knew that when you had say, fifty blokes to move and only one aircraft to do it, there was always the temptation to take five soldiers instead of four. Squeezing that extra man on board, or doing just one more shuttle we'd test our fuel endurance to the limit. This engine failure, fortunately on the ground, gave us all pause.

On investigation, it was found that condensation in the fuel-gauge tube was making the dial register as much as one hundred pounds remaining when the tank was actually empty. The minimum was hastily raised to a hundred and ten – ten percent of total usable. But from then on I always made sure there was a standard-sized RAF screwdriver in the aircraft tool kit – I'd use that as a dip stick to confirm that the reading on the collector-tank gauge was in fact correct!

Dick recalls a further unusual incident:

In the Labuan unit of the Army Intelligence Branch was a Staff Sergeant Steinitz, of Polish extraction, aged about forty-five and a brilliant linguist. The *lingua franca* of Borneo was Malay and we all picked up a few words of that, some more than others. But there were many dialects among the native tribes, often a different one for separate river-catchment areas, and that needed some dealing with. Fortunately, Sergeant Steinitz had learnt to converse in several of those dialects within a matter of months.

Anyway, one day I was tasked to take to him to an LS near the infamous Indon anti-aircraft gun on the border at Bantul, on the Pensiangan river. It was where some months earlier an AAC Scout had been shot up and the passenger, a padre, was shot in the knee.

I had no idea of the height of the LS in what was a very deep gorge, but naturally I went in at very low level to keep out of sight of the AA battery. It turned out that the LS was well above me, hidden by trees. I was beginning to feel very uncomfortable and thinking about what to do next, when a head came shooting up from the cabin, right between my knees, with a 'Get the f*** out!'

Needless to say, with a prompt like that, I executed a quick one-eighty. Despite all the stuff going on in Djakarta, the Indons were still trigger-happy.

In Sabah in May 1966 there were two signs of things to come. The first was the East Brigade Air Support Officer's reduction of the target number of hours to be flown by the 230 Squadron Whirlwinds. This was partly because all was quiet on the border but mostly it was aimed at getting the resident army units used to working with the Alouette helicopters of 5 Squadron RMAF, who had become operational in Eastern Sabah. The other was the completion of a section of new road from Keningau up to a point just twenty miles short of Sepulot. The work had required a monthly Whirlwind lift of up to 15,000lb of building supplies. That task had been completed and, in not many more months, the mountain ridges barring the way to this unspoiled longhouse-haven would be well and truly breached.

★ ★ ★ ★ ★

May 1966 saw the arrival in Labuan of a new Station Supply Officer, Colin Cummings. Born in February 1944, the RAF was in his blood – his father, a Halton apprentice, had enjoyed a twenty-five-year worldwide career as an airframe fitter. At school in Bristol Colin gained the qualifications to take up an engineering apprenticeship in Glasgow and, in 1963, aged nineteen, he approached the RAF:

> I was accepted for officer training but was found to be colour-blind. My hopes of being a navigator dashed, I remustered to the Supply Branch. I had sixteen weeks at Kirton in Lindsey in the summer of 1964 – sixteen weeks of boredom, the voucher stuff in particular being a living death. But then in September I was posted to Tern Hill, where the lines of helicopters really caught my imagination.
>
> It was just at the time when the RAF was introducing younger men to rotaries – Mike McKinley was there in training – and I lived among them in the Mess and started to fly as a passenger in their helis. An early flight was with Mike on his first night dual sortie. While I was hooking a USL onto a Whirlwind I was spotted by the Chief Flying Instructor who offered me a place on the five-day crewman's course. Naturally, I grabbed it.
>
> I was now pretty well qualified for supernumary aircrew duties and got my chance one Friday night when I was approached in a sparsely-

224

populated Mess to go as an observer on a dawn mission the next morning. It was a Search and Rescue flight in Wales for the crew of a Vulcan that had crashed the evening before. That mission turned out to be the very last time a Sycamore was used on SAR.

In June 1965 I had my first taste of the Far East, on reinforcement for five months at Kuantan on the east coast of Malaya, supporting six Canberras and their crews on detachment from Cyprus. It wasn't long after my return to Tern Hill before I was on the Eagle Brit again – this time to Singapore. Having 'stocked up' with new KD and other kit, there was the usual RAF Hastings out to Labuan.

I found what was, after close on three years of campaigning, a pretty substantial base. There were two Messes for officers – the Airport Hotel, where I first stayed, and the Shell Membedai Club, to which I moved as soon as a room became available. The HQ and admin buildings were semi-permanent as was the Sergeants' Mess. The airmen had *bashas*. Alongside the Membedai were bungalows for the Station Commander and other senior officers, including the Air Commander Borneo.

As Station Supply Officer, I pretty soon got myself issued with flying kit. With a set of 'jungle greens' – I still have the shirt! – flak jacket and .38 pistol, I was ready for anything.

★ ★ ★ ★ ★

In May 1966 the RMAF took over the 103 Squadron detachment at Butterworth, allowing the two Whirlwinds up there to return to the base at Seletar. This assisted Fred Hoskins in fulfilling the tasking commitment in Sarawak. In a busy month of 480 operational hours flown, 5,206 troops were moved around 1st and 2nd Divisions and fifty-two casualties were extracted, half of them as stretcher cases and half as walking wounded.

After a short few days off at Seletar, Mike McKinley was called back to Kuching for an unexpected extra task. In another letter home, he wrote:

I have been lumbered with the job of instructing on the SS11 missile and I've had to return to train up a couple of new pilots. I shall then, I suspect, be the sole missile instructor in the Far East, a pretty nebulous sort of qualification since the course specified by the manufacturers, Nord Aviation, is of six weeks – in Paris! My knowledge extends to what I have been able to pick up around the squadron from various people and booklets, as well as my experience of five shots and a lot of simulating. Five shots equal £2,500. On the Paris course you reckon to shoot at least ten. It is a strange way of training for what could be a very useful little weapon if things were to hot up again out here.

The month saw the announcement of awards for another 103 Squadron crew. The previous December Flight Lieutenant Jim Millar and his crewman, Sergeant Jones, had been sent on two missions to winch out Gurkha and Green Jacket casualties from an extended jungle firefight. In contact with the enemy, the soldiers had been unable to hack out landing pads, meaning that Jim had to control the winch from the cockpit while his crewman went down the cable. Even at its full extension, Sergeant Jones had had to work most of the time with his feet barely touching the ground and, unable to rig a stretcher, had no choice but to carry the casualties up on the wire in his arms. Despite the difficulties, they got them all out and, for their skill and courage, the sergeant earned a Mention in Despatches and the pilot was awarded the DFC.

The squadron's manning schedules in May were somewhat upset by another four tyro pilots arriving from Tern Hill, all requiring theatre familiarization, as well as by FEAF's insistence that a backlog in jungle survival training be addressed. This resulted in several already Borneo-experienced pilots being sent to the school at Changi. Both FEAF Whirlwind squadrons were detailed and on the 110 contingent was John Davy:

> I thought it strange that I should be detailed for jungle survival as I was very near the end of my tour, but it made a change. The first half involved an exercise immersed in the swamps of central Singapore after which, because of our disreputable condition, the collecting bus refused to take us on board. That didn't stop us. We somehow got ourselves back to Seletar and the Officers' Mess, where we sat defiantly down to lunch in our ragged and stinking jungle kit!

★ ★ ★ ★ ★

There was no shortage of pilots on 110 Squadron. In May 1966, a month that the reporting officer dubbed 'unexciting', the Operations Officer was able, after three years of 'one month in, one month out', to allow aircrews five weeks at Seletar for every four in Borneo.

One of the newcomers boosting the pilot numbers was the twenty-four-year-old Rick Atkinson, arrived for his first tour. He had been posted, along with two other tyros, to 66 Squadron and the Belvedere. His reaction to that was: 'Yet another beast to master before I'll be operational. When will I ever get to Borneo?'

But serviceability problems with the Belvedere had created such a backlog of pilot training that there were no hours to spare for first-tourists and so, after one familiarization sortie, all three were transferred. One went to 103 Squadron and two, including Rick, to 110. Delighted to be reunited with his pilot-friendly Whirlwind, he started in on a scheduled twenty-five-hour theatre conversion, including jungle landings at the long-suffering Lombong clearing.

The prospect of action for him in Borneo was not far away but the options were narrowing. On 22 May, as part of a general re-shuffling of helicopter resources, 110 Squadron packed its bags in Kuching and moved its Sarawak HQ to Simanggang.

Dave Reid found himself detailed to get the squadron car over there, along the road through Serian. Despite improvements to the surface, this was still a gravel road and had to be driven with immense care. In places it was positively dangerous, especially in wet weather as the camber had been laid deliberately the wrong-way round by Allied PoWs in the Second World War. There were stories of Japanese trucks flying off the road at the corners, leading to the execution of the offending drivers.

Dave describes the experience of travelling that road:

The car was a light blue Ford, a Zephyr Zodiac. It had been the 225 Squadron runabout and it was now definitely showing its age. Heaven only knows how it got to Borneo! It had a good engine but was rusting somewhat in the rear, and the brakes were definitely dodgy.

It was a hundred-mile journey, and twenty of them ran within touching distance of the frontier. I drove, taking along a mate from Air Traffic as co-driver. Halfway along, the brakes failed – but being young and foolish, we carried on, just using the handbrake and the gears. But I got overconfident and coming out of this tight left-hand bend, going too fast on the dodgy camber, we met an army convoy coming the other way, spread out in echelon right across the road. It was skin-of-the-teeth stuff but we squeezed through – wheels spinning on the dusty verge, army klaxons going like crazy.

We were really lucky there, and not much less so in a further close call down a steep hill with a sharp bend on a border riverbank – but we made it through to Simanggang in the end. There I found that my old mates from the off-the-runway incident were still running the technical shop. They owed me one so they fixed the brakes.

It was not long before Rick Atkinson, now operationally qualified, was on the roster to join Dave at the Simanggang detachment. As Rick remembers it:

The married men were not always keen to go to Borneo but I couldn't wait to get out there. As soon as I arrived they told me to get over to the armoury for my weapon. The armoury was an *attap* hut surrounded by barbed wire on a remote part of the airfield. A surly corporal reluctantly supplied me with a .38 revolver plus a handful, literally, of ammunition

– no holster or webbing to put them in. I managed to scrounge some webbing before taking the 'white-knuckle' ride in a Twin Pin up the Lupar River to the strip at Simanggang.

At my first appearance at morning briefing, Colonel Pounds, the boss of 42 Commando, took one look at my antique weapon and promptly had me issued with a 9-millimetre self loading pistol and a Sterling sub-machine gun. I practised in a quarry firing at beer cans and such but my guns never saw any action.

We got intelligence reports on Indon activities but I never saw any of their soldiers alive – just dead ones that we had to pick up. On one occasion we were waiting to load the bodies, rotors turning, when we noticed the Malay Renjers were pouncing on them with knives drawn – they were hacking out the gold teeth!

Much of the intelligence was obtained by the locally-recruited Border Scouts – their CO, a British Army major, seemed to have 'gone native'

Iban Border Scout in full fighting fig.
(Bob Turner)

but I suppose that went with the job! The Scouts' mission was to gather information on terrorist activity – ours was usually to pick them up and take them to a grid ref in the jungle. We didn't know where they went after we'd dropped them off, but we'd usually pick them up from another position several days later.

We were usually tasked by our RAF Air Liaison Officer who had to get authorisation from HQ in Kuching through several levels of authority. For routine sorties that was fine but for operations briefed directly by the mission commander it was a nightmare.[55]

At Simanggang orders and reports had to be transmitted verbally though the civil manual telephone exchange, housed in the police station downtown. You'd pick up the phone, and a high-pitched female Chinese voice would answer, 'Nummar pleeze?' It was a joke – the lines were terrible and we often had to shout the words out one at a time. A lot of times we just flew the mission, anyway.

But I remember an early trip with an ex-fixed-wing guy, married with kids. We were given a drop-off position by signal, but when we arrived at the point it was obvious that the patrol faced a long slog up a ridge. Embarrassingly, my skipper ignored the patrol commander's request to be dropped a couple of hundred metres higher up on the ridge, just out of sight of the border – 'Not authorized' was his excuse. I was dismayed at his lack of initiative – that sort of inflexibility didn't help the RAF's reputation in Borneo.

Another time, we'd gone through all the procedures and got clearance for two aircraft to go into a reportedly dodgy village near the border. We were instructed to go in the Full Precautions role: two pilots up, Sterlings at the ready and the crewman manning a Bren gun in the cabin doorway – the lot! We sneaked in as a pair, down the river, using all available cover, only to find all the locals had turned out to greet us, waving and grinning from ear to ear. It could, of course, have been a 'come-on', so one load of troops landed and moved in cautiously whilst we circled at a distance. They found no sign of terrorists – it turned out to be the friendliest village ever.

★ ★ ★ ★ ★

A Chunky Lord anecdote illustrating the onslaught of service bureaucracy is related by Ian Morgan:

Chunky was OC an early 110 Squadron detachment in Labuan when an inspection from HQ 224 Group was threatened. On going through the checklist of squadron reference publications, Chunky found that a copy of the Flying Order Book, the bosses' Bible as it were, which was held at Seletar, was also needed at the Labuan detachment. There wasn't such a copy, so he set about creating one. All by himself, he manufactured pages and back-dated the necessary signatures before 'distressing' his creation to give an appearance of authenticity. It worked, and Chunky and Co flew on.

* * * * *

By now there were five 66 Squadron Belvederes at Seletar, mopping up the work necessary to maintain aircrew categories and instrument ratings, and seven in Kuching, fully employed moving 105mm howitzers and soldiers around the frontier in the 1st Division of Sarawak. The Durham Light Infantry were replaced by New Zealanders and 42 Commando Royal Marines by Malay Renjers – fresh troops to guard the border, just in case the latest developments in Djakarta were yet another bluff.

Since the power-shift of February the position of Suharto and his supporters had been far from secure. The Communists remained a potential threat – the economic toll of *Konfrontasi* was pushing Indonesia towards potential bankruptcy, a situation ripe for left-wing exploitation. The conflict with Malaysia and the British had been a useful rallying-cry behind which to rally the people but it was isolating the rulers from the international community and the largesse needed to bail their country out.

The Foreign Minister, Malik, was the one in the triumvirate most firmly convinced that Confrontation should be brought to an end. He finally won his colleagues over and diplomatic feelers were put out to Kuala Lumpur. Things moved fast.

On 25 May there was an emotional encounter at KL Airport between eight Indonesian Army officers and the Parliamentary Secretary of the Malaysian Ministry of External Affairs. Meetings with the Tunku and between Ministers followed and talks began in Bangkok to find a formula for peace negotiations. Even before the end of the month, draft proposals had been exchanged regarding the recognition of each other's country. In Borneo the security forces crossed their fingers. Indonesia had feigned peace proposals three times in Confrontation already – was this to be another bluff?

Memories were still fresh of the contempt shown towards the January 1964 ceasefire by the more fanatical elements of the Indonesian Army. Although CLARET patrols were suspended to give the talks the best chance, whatever the outcome of the high-level negotiations, General Lea and his staff could not afford to let their guard drop.

It wasn't long before their fears were realized.

Chapter 21

The Bumpy Road to Peace

Early in June 1966 a group of Indonesian regular soldiers crossed the frontier through the Pang Gap south-west of Kuching and advanced into the Bau area, taking the shortest possible route to the Sarawak capital. Immediately, 103 Squadron Whirlwinds were scrambled to the support of the 4th Battalion Royal Australian Regiment (4RAR). Emergency tasking saw the helicopters lifting soldiers in the usual cut-off and flanking movements before the incursion went the way of all before it.

The CCO, in a move reminiscent of the Malayan Emergency, had long before been corralled into secure villages, and were powerless to assist the Indonesians. The Malay and *Iban* populations were quite sure by now where their loyalties lay. There was no popular uprising and the incursion fizzled out in the Sarawak oil-palm plantations.

For the aircrews of 103 the emergency tasking entailed long periods away from base. Their commitment was appreciated, however, as shown by the message received from the Aussies:

> In period 12th to 19th June, approx 2500 soldiers were moved in our area. Majority were moved by air at short notice. On 21st June, 231 soldiers and 3000 lbs stores moved in six hours. Magnificent, many thanks.

In that month 103 flew 550 operational hours in Sarawak, a record for the squadron. It now had the pilots to do it – aircrew numbers had climbed to thirty-one officers, nine Masters and eighteen Senior NCOs and the influx of tyros had outnumbered tour-end repatriations to the UK.

Bob Turner spent the last three weeks of his one-year unaccompanied tour at Lundu, operating the single Whirlwind detached in support of the Gurkhas:

> Although the intensity of enemy activity gradually reduced as the political changes in Indonesia occurred, the SH squadrons in the 1st and 2nd Divisions were still very busy with daily trooping and freight

AAC Sioux and RAF Whirlwind at Lundu base.

Fuel dump and Iban longhouse at Lundu base.

Lundu main street.

(pictures Mike McKinley)

lifts and frequent medevacs. I flew a hundred-and-seventy hours from February to June, continuously in Sarawak and mostly from Simanggang. For that final spell, as the detachment pilot at Lundu I supported army operations against the terrorists on the heights of Gunong Gading and at the border near Biawak.

Towards the end of my year, there was talk of my continuing with 103 Squadron at Seletar. That would have been difficult for me as I was still under twenty-five and would have been ineligible for a quarter or any married overseas allowances in Singapore. Perhaps it was the possible end of Confrontation that secured me a posting back to the UK instead. I was able to return to my wife and baby son, now eighteen-months old, and join the helicopter Instructors' Course at Tern Hill.

My year in Borneo had certainly been a fantastic experience, in so many respects.

Bob Turner was to have four years in Training Command before returning to Support Helicopter operations, culminating in command of 230 Squadron, which had by then returned to West Germany.

At the same time the youngest Borneo Boy was posted home from 110 Squadron – John Davy had completed a full two years in the campaign:

The work rota was generally ten-and-a-half days on, one half-day off, and even that was not usually taken. The effect was that by the end of my tour I'd accumulated four months' leave. I never got a suntan, just heat-rash – a touch of malaria too. The paludrin didn't always work and most of us went down with it. You were really ill for three days – never took less than a month to recover fully. No one got fat either – we ate well all right, but sweated it all off!

Relaxation in the jungle was on occasion fairly wild – there's a picture of Fraser Skea being hoisted up under a Whirlwind clinging onto a rope, an exploit of which he professes to have no memory. And the helicopter crews spent a lot of their time in Borneo surrounded by local teenage girls with little clothing. Happy days!

John was posted to CFS for training as an instructor, not on rotaries but on the fixed-wing Jet Provost. In a further twist in staffing policy, the need for squads of helicopter tyros had passed its peak, for the time being at least. By the time he was twenty-four, the lad who had made it to Labuan a few weeks after his twentieth birthday had qualified as an instructor, put in a stint in Flying Training and returned to join the staff at CFS. In 1974 he became one of the youngest Squadron Leaders in the RAF.

★ ★ ★ ★ ★

The first day of June 1966 was nominated officially in Sarawak as '*Dayak* Day' and the 110 Squadron Simanggang detachment had time to witness a sacrificial cow ceremony on the town waterfront. There was a significant decrease in tasking at all locations, Simanggang, Sibu and Nanga Gaat, as the Bangkok talks got under way.

But the squadron still had manning worries as a mysterious stomach complaint, originating at the Gaat, grounded every one of their pilots at one time or another in the month. This resulted in the OC Helicopter Wing, Wing Commander John Dowling, visiting from Seletar, being press-ganged into flying on an operational mission to Long Jawi, where bad weather forced him and the crew to overnight in a jungle base.

Later in the month Flying Officer Ramshaw hauled himself out of sick quarters to fly from the Gaat to Bario but on the return leg was forced by further storms to land in a riverbed alongside a longhouse. The local *Iban*, as usual more than willing to support any helicopter man, turned out to help cut a landing clearing up above the river bank. This saved the aircraft as, returning to the LP after an entertaining longhouse night, Ramshaw found that the waters had risen by eight feet.

Wherever a waterway was navigable boats were used to transport bulk goods. At Katilas no fewer than seventy barrels of Avtur had been delivered and needed hauling to the helicopter LP on the ridge above. A test lift of a single barrel by ten brawny Gurkhas took half-an-hour. A Whirlwind was called in and lifted the lot in two hours, a feat that, in the words of the reporting officer, 'pointed out the versatility of our helicopter force'.

It was time for a change of command on 110 – Squadron Leader John Price[56] was posted to Staff College in Bracknell, his squadron having reached the magnificent milestone of 10,000 operational hours since its first detachment to Borneo in July 1963.

★ ★ ★ ★ ★

July 1966 saw the event which signalled a certain end to Confrontation. On the fifth of the month, in Djakarta, Sukarno was stripped of his title of 'President for Life'. The way was now clear for Suharto and Malik to confirm that this time Indonesia really did intend to bring the undeclared war to an end. On the Borneo border all the signs were that the conflict was winding down – intelligence sources were reporting that the presence of the enemy near the frontier was barely noticeable. Tasking of the helicopters was all about troop movements prior to withdrawal, and preparation for pulling back from their own forward detachments.

★ ★ ★ ★ ★

The aircrews of 66 Squadron, under their new OC, Squadron Leader Paul Gray, had an out-of-the-ordinary task in Western Malaysia, the lift of a radio relay-station to the 4,187-foot summit of Mount Ophir, but the 154 operational hours in Kuching were all allocated to routine trooping missions. Nevertheless, the boss found ways to maintain morale. He certainly succeeded with Dave Lanigan, now past his twenty-fifth birthday:

> All at once a married quarter became a possibility and my overseas accompanied allowances rose by eighty per cent. Good news, as was becoming Squadron Flight Safety Officer. Flight Safety was high profile at the time due to the Vietnam War in which pilot error was resulting in nine times more losses than those caused by direct enemy action. The boss was keen on a new theme poster every month – 'Dehydration', 'Look-out', 'Assume nothing and check everything' and even 'Hard work burns fuel fast' – an encouragement to eat properly. Of course, I had to set an example and be safe, efficient and professional at all times – not a bad move in the scheme of things!
>
> As my experience increased I'd been allowed to go away from Kuching into the area to the east where there was almost continuous primary jungle, hills and wide rivers. The rivers were important for navigation, with the convention of keeping to the starboard bank when transiting along its course.
>
> After the serious work of the day it was down to Kuching Market Place for a squadron aircrew 'bash' with mountains of Chinese food cooked on the spot, and lots of *Tiger* beer, all among the noise of local families and the squawking of chickens waiting their turn in the wok.
>
> June sixth had provided an opportunity for everyone to let their hair down. The Squadron detachment of aircrew and ground crew had a big party at Kuching Airfield. Besides being the sixth of the sixth in nineteen-sixty-six for 66 Squadron, we were celebrating the continuing serviceability of the machines, the influx of new young pilots, and the leadership and positive attitude of the new Squadron Commander.
>
> He was different from Bunny Austin, more studied and thoughtful – but then he had responsibility for an operation spread over a range of a thousand miles or so. He carried on in the same spirit of supporting his men and was keen that everyone should relax when they came back from a detachment in Borneo or exercise up country – he himself was no mean driver of the squadron ski-boat, the *Rattler*.
>
> We felt the future looked good. Mind you, morale had been improving since the Army started using us more to move the troops around. We had been deployed on short detachments into the Second and Third Divisions of Sarawak in an area where the Navy were

operating with their Wessex. That had taken us right up near the front of the action – bringing back casualties and Indon PoWs from firefights deep in the jungle.

The troops we carried were listed at a standard two-fifty pounds each except for the SAS who merited three hundred. They carried huge Bergens and were festooned with weapons and ammunition belts. Each man seemed to wear highly individualistic kit, almost as if they'd been to an army-surplus store to get it.

But the firefights were a thing of the past, and the workload had diminished. By the last week of June the Kuching detachment had four Belvederes serviceable but tasks for only one. To break the tedium, volleyball tournaments were organized – at Seletar the ground crew were the victors but in Kuching the aircrew won. A good deal of attention had been given to the squadron's Fiftieth Anniversary Parade, due at month-end, and congratulations were sent to the previous 66 Squadron boss, Bunny Austin, awarded the Air Force Cross (AFC) for his work in Borneo.

★ ★ ★ ★ ★

On 103 Squadron the number of pilots rose again, to thirty-two officers and nine Masters, and there were now no fewer than twenty-one Senior NCO crewmen. The available trooping load in 1st Division provided just about enough work to keep them current.

The new boss on 110 Squadron, Squadron Leader Dick Hadlow, reported that all was quiet in 2nd and 3rd Divisions, adding that all operations were logistical.

★ ★ ★ ★ ★

In July 1966 Sergeant Paul Moran was detached to the 230 Squadron unit at RAF Tawau:

Tawau was about two hundred miles from Labuan. I clambered aboard a Twin Pioneer of 209 Squadron and off we went – what a ride! Sabah was virtually all trees, two-hundred feet high in places, and soon we were cruising along a green sea of treetops from horizon to horizon. The disconcerting thing was that there was no forced-landing site visible if the Alvis Leonides engines packed up – very unlikely, as it happens.

I arrived at Tawau to hear that there'd be a flying visit by the then Secretary for Defence, Denis Healey. So we hurriedly got our Whirlwind helicopters cleaned up, tidied up the PSP, hid away all the grotty ground equipment and bulled up the offices. As Senior NCO i/c I positioned an airman out with the aircraft in case the Secretary wanted to look them over, and doubled back to the now clean Line Office to man the phone myself.

A little later I heard the aircraft land with the VIPs. There was no one around and Tawau had suddenly become strangely quiet. Just then I heard footsteps approaching and in walked an RAF officer – a very high-ranking officer, and one whose right arm was missing from the shoulder. I had a one-armed Air Marshal perched on the corner of my desk!

He was part of the Denis Healey entourage – I waited for the rest of his party to appear, but they didn't show up. We talked about everything under the sun. He told me about his Second World War service and his rise up the ranks. He asked me my history, where I lived and what my plans were. Still no one appeared. I had the distinct feeling that this officer had come into the Line Office for a brief escape.

This was turning out to be the most genial conversation, and with a high ranker – normally sergeants didn't figure in their circle. It was very easy to forget who I was talking to. I am certain if there'd been beer in that office we'd have ended up slurping it! There was nothing at all pompous or superior about this officer.

I clearly remember one thing he said. We were talking about his wartime experiences and I suggested that his service was heroic. He replied, 'Not at all – I would have paid to be part of that war. When it was over I really missed it.'

I was itching to talk about his lost limb but it simply wasn't mentioned. The time went by but I refrained from offering him a cup of coffee – the 'tea swindle' in the office left much to be desired with its stained mugs and discoloured spoons.

Then, a phalanx of officers, warrant officers and RAF Police suddenly swarmed into the room to find out where their VIP charge had got to. He was whisked away and I was once again alone in the office wondering what had just happened. I never saw or heard of him again. Tawau returned to normal and the business of Confrontation took over.

It had been a very rare event. I mean, in the 'sixties ORs and NCOs just didn't talk for long periods with officers, not if they were above the rank of flight lieutenant. This impressively-ranked officer had spent time with me that was not on his itinerary. Our conversation was free of constraint, aggrandisement and status. I recall it as one of my more earthshaking moments in the Far East.[57]

Reinforcement at Bario. (Mick Charles)

Paul was not to be in Tawau much longer. In July, the officers and men of 230 Squadron were busy planning the forthcoming move out of Tawau and Sepulot and into Bario, scheduled from mid-month. The intention was that the whole of East Brigade should, as soon as possible, be supported by RMAF Alouettes. The Whirlwinds duly flew out of Sepulot on the 13th and into Bario, replacing two Wessex of 848 NAS, and another left Tawau on the 23rd. But, before their departure, a young first-tourist pilot had had an opportunity to demonstrate the quality of the Tern Hill graduates. The reporting officer wrote:

> Flying Officer C. P. Shaw had an uncomfortable incident while landing XP400 on the airstrip at Long Pa Sia. As he approached the hover, the aircraft began to rotate fairly rapidly, and refused to respond to rudder. By reducing height to only a few inches, thus allowing the ground-cushion effect to reduce the power needed and consequently the torque, the pilot managed to reduce the speed of rotation and land without further damage.
>
> The tricky situation was caused by a fractured balance-weight on the tail rotor. It was very well handled, especially as the pilot had less than 200 hours on helicopters.

As the stream of first-tourist pilots continued to arrive, tour-expired men left for home. Before the end of July Dick Holmes had come to the end of his year in Borneo and departed 230 Squadron in Labuan to continue his RAF career, eventually joining the Professional Aircrew stream. He took with him long-lasting memories, particularly of Sabah:

> Pensiangan was a favourite destination – lovely location, lovely girls, and plenty of tapai. Like Sepulot, Pensiangan base was relatively sophisticated. It was run by the Gurkhas, who would cook up eye-watering baht with merciless spices. Once, when they discovered they were paid less than the Border Scouts, there was a near-mutiny. Fortunately, the anomaly was swiftly righted and all was well.

In the same month, July 1966, a new pilot signed in on 656 Squadron AAC at Kluang. Slightly older than the Borneo Boy average at twenty-seven years, Sergeant John Richards had arrived to fly the Scout. Posted at short notice, and newly married, he had just one day of jungle survival training, and another of theatre role conversion, before being sent on the three-month roulement detachment to Borneo. The squadron had four Scout flights, two of which were at any one time in Borneo – one operating under West Brigade out of Kuching and the other under Central, out of Brunei. John picks up the story:

> I was posted to 10 Flight in Brunei, under the umbrella of 99 Gurkha Brigade. We had five Scouts on strength, manned by six pilots, two of whom were officers and four NCOs.
>
> The AAC didn't have a two-man crew set-up, so for the newcomer it was a case of 'in at the deep end'. The Scout AH1, powered by a Nimbus free gas-turbine, had entered service only in 1962 and had had engine serviceability problems. But by 1966, assisted by Rolls-Royce specialists, those were mostly ironed out. Away from base, if there was a problem starting the engine then the drill was to get the passenger, or a Gurkha, to depress the starter button while the pilot walloped the starter solenoid with a rubber mallet, ready to spring back into his seat as the engine began to wind up.
>
> The airframe was reassuringly robust. It had an uncomplicated landing skid, and simple linear drive shafts to the metal, four-bladed main and two-bladed tail rotors. There was an easy-access cabin and the usual rig for troop movements was a net, fastened to the cargo loops on the rear cabin floor, in which the Gurkhas would stow their giant rucksacks. Two guys would then sit each side on the sill with their feet on the skid if they could reach it, their rifles or Stens pointing out for protection, and chests leaning on harness straps attached across the

aperture. A third man could squeeze in between them and a fourth sat in the passenger seat.

Visibility from the cockpit was superb. The controls and flight instruments in the passenger position were removed to save weight, save for the foot pedals, which were locked. The pilot had a standard cyclic attached through the floor and a collective with twist-grip throttle. After take-off, the throttle was set at fully open and the fuel control system kept the rotor speed steady at some 400rpm. The radio fit was VHF, but in Borneo this had a very limited range and was practically useless in the valleys. An army B47 VHF/FM radio was also fitted to facilitate contact with forward bases.

Like the RAF we wore bone-dome helmets and throat mikes, as well as Australian model jungle-green lightweight flying suits, white chamois-leather gloves – soon stained green with sweat – and jungle boots, which lasted not much more than three weeks on ops.

My missions were primarily the insertion and extraction of Gurkha patrols. The Scout had the power to lift a troop of four from the base at Long Pa Sia – where, if I remember correctly, there was an RAF Single Pin spreadeagled in a tree at the end of the strip – to the highest, eight-thousand-foot ridges of the border range. The trick was to approach the LZ at a slant, so that your escape route if you couldn't make it to the summit would be downwards, away from the border. The all-round view from the pilot's seat was a great advantage as the LPs were usually not much more than a small platform constructed of bamboo.

The Standing Order of the day was 'Don't come back empty if you can help it', and a frequent return load was a bundle of retrieved airdrop 'chutes. Any of those bundles could carry a snake, or worse, which could be a nasty surprise for a lone pilot! We had our hands full, literally, at all times. The right could never let go of the cyclic, and the left was needed to do the rest, handling maps, instruments, radio and the collective – that at least had a friction hold. The map box was unhandily placed on the far side of the central instrument console – just in reach if you stretched right over.

The Scout had no particular handling vices, and dampers on the skid minimized any risk of ground-resonance. But the engine, the sole engine, was in the early days prone to turbine failures. Being fully-exposed on top of the fuselage didn't seem to trouble it – it liked the rain, which cleaned out the compressors – and it made for easier maintenance.

Like the Whirlwinds, we had all that business of manually pumping Avtur from 42-gallon drums. Our pump was mounted alongside the engine, to starboard.

Bukit Batu Lawi. (Rick Atkinson)

Navigating the Scout was by the time-honoured compass, stop-watch and 'mark one eyeball method', together with 'IFR – I follow rivers'! Fortunately, as the maps were so basic, there were some unique mountain features. One in particular, Bukit Batu Lawi, also known as 'Big Dick', was helpfully right on track from Brunei to Bario[58].

A sensible rule for us single operators was to inform the forward bases of our 'flight plan' on every move, many of them unscheduled as we'd often be diverted by a 'hearts and minds' opportunity.

We were encouraged to assist the locals where necessary and do-able. We had plenty of opportunities, often on chance overnight stops at their longhouses. Of course, some made free with this privilege, but many personal inconveniences were avoided – a five-day hike through the jungle to get to a neighbouring longhouse wedding, for example, became a five-minute hop in the Scout.

I was very pleased to be in Borneo. I revelled in the common determination to get the job done, and in the humour that provides a morale-booster to soldiers in action.

★ ★ ★ ★ ★

In July 1966, there was little action for John Richards, nor much for anyone else, for that matter. Mike McKinley very nearly had some excitement, setting out with the boss of 103 Squadron on a planned search for a possible airborne hostile near Tebedu. Fred Hoskins tells the story:

> The Royal Artillery had a 'Green Archer' radar installation near the border which was able to locate the positions of enemy mortars by tracking incoming rounds. On several successive nights this radar had detected a large echo of an object crossing the border and it was suspected that it might be an Indonesian helicopter, probably the heavy-lift Russian Mi-6, possibly bringing in men for an incursion. To verify this it was decided that a helicopter should be sent to Tebedu, ready to investigate should the trace appear on Green Archer again.
>
> Thus, in the evening of the eleventh of July, I flew a Full Precautions Whirlwind to Tebedu with second pilot and crewman and a third pilot, Mike McKinley, in the cabin with a lash-up radio ready to establish communication with the Army on the ground. He had one earpiece connected to the intercom and the other plugged in to an army A41 set.
>
> As well as a GPMG we had a de-planing rope which I felt might have had a better effect than bullets if we could get over the top of the enemy and drop it into its main rotor!
>
> When we landed at Tebedu we found an irate Company Commander, furious because he had not been told of this scheme. He made it obvious that he wanted nothing to do with it and did not want us on his patch. In the event, we were recalled to Kuching. The Green Archer reported seeing the echo again but it had broken up – it was deduced that the fuss had been caused by a flock of birds.

In retrospect Fred wondered whether birds flew together in flocks at night. Mike reckoned it was more likely to have been a swarm of the ubiquitous Borneo fruit-bats.

For most of July Dave Reid was detached to Sibu:

> The mood was unusually subdued – the only people giving trouble in the area were the rumbustious troopers of the Kosbies. I remember that

on the 30th of the month, I had the time to get hold of a radio and listen the the England soccer team winning the World Cup!

★ ★ ★ ★ ★

On the very next day, in the 4th Division of Sarawak, the silence on the Borneo border was broken. A company commander of the 'Rebel Faction' decided to take matters into his own hands. Lieutenant Sumbi had bought Sukarno's rhetoric lock, stock and barrel from the start, and he firmly believed that the people over the other side of the frontier were ripe for insurrection. On the last day of July he led a party of Indonesian Paras over the Bario Range and down the slopes to Ba Kelalan, bristling with aggressive intent.

Sumbi was known to be a man to be reckoned with. According to Colin Cummings, who was watching developments with interest from Labuan, 'Sumbi knew what he was doing. He'd earlier got a Second Class mark for his paper on Jungle Warfare at the British Army Jungle Warfare school!'

The Brunei Joint HQ had been expecting incursions such as this. Their intelligence network had heard that there were groups determined to infiltrate the CCO in Malaysian Borneo, aiming to set up cells in preparation for post-treaty subversion. Ba Kelalan, the group of native villages evacuated in late 1963, standing at 3,000 feet up in the mountains and just a couple of miles over the frontier, was an ideal point of access. The insurgents had chosen their moment well, as political necessity had just then taken a considerable upper hand over the military.

Early in August the Malaysian Deputy Prime Minister, Tun Abdul Razak, accompanied by no fewer than five cabinet ministers, flew to Djakarta. In talks with General Suharto, Foreign Minister Malik, and their fellow Ministers, they progressed swiftly towards a Peace Agreement.

The text stipulated that diplomatic relations were to be restored with immediate effect and the exchange of ambassadors was to take place as soon as possible. In addition, the Malaysian side agreed to give the people of Sabah and Sarawak an opportunity to re-affirm as soon as practicable their previous decision about their status in the Federation by holding general elections. Finally, all hostile acts were to cease. Ministers Malik and Razak signed the agreement on 11 August and, at noon that day, Confrontation effectively came to an end.

Although the Peace Agreement was not yet ratified, all offensive military operations on the Malaysian side were halted and command was handed over by General Lea to General Ibraham, who assumed the title of Director of Operations East Malaysia.

★ ★ ★ ★ ★

As the security forces continued to hold their fire, the Ba Kelalan insurgents marched on towards their intended objective, Brunei. But they were being watched.

Despite all the political shenanigans, right from the first reports of sightings Central Brigade had sent a tracking party to follow the rebels as they moved north-west. On 2 August their camp was found and the trackers estimated the Indonesians had a two-day start. To contain them, stop lines were put out across their most likely heading – down the Trusan Valley.

On the 4th the first positive encounter had been made when a party of twelve Indonesians attacked a Gurkha outpost – one insurgent was killed and one wounded and a Gurkha with a head-wound was whisked out by helicopter to Brunei. The Indonesians scattered to the west where later, two-day old tracks were found. On the 7th the tracking party had reported that they were one day behind the enemy who were indeed moving down the Trusan River.

On the 6th a second incursion had taken place south-east of Long Pa Sia. Again, stop lines were placed and contact was made on the 8th when one Indonesian was captured. Later, tracks of the remainder were found, heading back to Kalimantan.

News of the first incursion continued to be spasmodic until the 12th when three stragglers were captured at Long Lopeng. Under interrogation they disclosed that the party had split into two groups. One of these was led by a Corporal Rampingi and, on that same day, four of his men were captured and soon he and his remaining colleagues had surrendered. The other band was led by Lieutenant Sumbi.

The security forces still stayed their arm pending Treaty ratification but General Lea and his staff had had the foresight to initiate large-scale movement of troops into the area, based on Long Semado, where three 110 Squadron Whirlwinds had been detached from Simanggang for ten days in reinforcement of 230 and the FAA rotaries. Dave Reid was caught up in that, with unexpected consequences for one army officer. As Dave recounts:

At Simanggang in early August, we were detailed for a mapping exercise based out of Belaga strip – Belaga by this time being non-fortified, just a fuel dump. The drill was that one Whirlwind would hover up above to keep watch while the other abseiled an army guy down to river level with an altimeter to get the datum. Then off we'd go to survey the summits.

At the end of one day, we got back to Belaga to refuel, only to find no fuel there! It had all been pinched by the natives, who'd opened up the barrels with their *parangs*. I put out a call to Simanggang on the HF and, as darkness was falling, an AAC Beaver arrived with two small barrels on board – Lord knows how the pilot found the place in the gloom – before smartly lifting off to grope its way back to base.

By the time we'd pumped the Avtur into our tanks, it was too dark for us to fly, so we had to stay there. After a while, a line of twinkling lights comes up the hill towards us. It's the local *Ibans*, who've come to invite us to their longhouse for a party.

First, they pack us all into their outboard longboats to take us up the Rajang to Belaga village – for what turns out to be a memorable evening. After a few shots of their firewater there's not a lot I remember, except these cute schoolchildren singing nursery rhymes – in English. And then there was the trip back from the longhouse – the quiet waters of the Rajang at night, frogs, cicadas, bats, the lights on the banks and the stars all bright up above.

The next day, we leave the army guy at Belaga to work on his charts while we go down to Long Jawi to fill up the tanks. There we find the LZ crammed full of helis, eight of them, including two more 110 Whirlwinds We're told the Ba Kelalan insurgency's on and that we're impounded for immediate action. They send us up to Long Semado and we move scores of Gurkhas around the ulu, chasing the baddies.

We don't get back to Belaga until a week later, and find our army guy still there. He's somewhat bemused as he's had no comms to tell him what's been going on but he's nevertheless perfectly happy. While we've been roughing it at Long Semado, he's had seven mind-bending days on roast pig and firewater in the longhouse – being magnificently entertained by the headman's unmarried daughter!

On 17 August, the Peace Treaty was ratified and British forces were free to pursue the insurgents in full strength. A good number of Sumbi's group was captured in the Long Semado area but he and a hard-core of his followers scattered into the jungle and mangrove swamps. This brought a heavy tasking load for the 230 Squadron Whirlwinds, the Scouts of 656 Squadron AAC and the Junglies of 845 NAS and meant exhausting work in the swamps for the pursuing soldiers but, after a month of hand-to-hand fighting, the insurgents were finally rounded up.[59]

At that moment Confrontation was indeed at an end. For the British and Malaysian governments, as well as the Australians and New Zealanders, the Indonesians were now allies, to be welcomed into the anti-Communist bloc in South East Asia.

Chapter 22

Mopping Up

Despite the shifts of power in Djakarta and the patchy efforts of Indonesian troops in Kalimantan, both during and following the peace negotiations, the workload for the support helicopters remained demanding. As well as continuous freighting and trooping flights in the withdrawal from the border, there were numerous leaflet-dropping missions to be flown. The Malaysian government used these to set out for the Indonesian rebels on both sides of the frontier the terms of the Peace Agreement while calling on them to surrender their arms to the authorities.

The efforts of General Lea's security forces were now concentrated on withdrawal from Malaysian Borneo and handing over town barracks and jungle forts to Malaysian units. As troops were lifted from the forward areas, movements were completed wherever possible by river and the much-improved roads. As a result, by the end of August 1966 the RAF helicopter squadrons were rapidly finding their tasking schedules decidedly less crowded.

★ ★ ★ ★ ★

August saw the closure of the 103 detachments at Lundu and Balai Ringin but not before Brian Skillicorn had been forced to dump yet another ailing Whirlwind, this time on a hilltop LZ. He was unscathed despite his aircraft suffering serious Category 3 damage. Back at Seletar the lightened tension was signified by the opening of a new coffee bar in the squadron Crew Room, now teeming with under-employed aircrews. Families were invited and there was a short flying display.

It wasn't long before the OC was finding ways to maintain morale. Fred Hoskins organized Land Rovers and trailers, camping equipment and rations and sent some of the men off to mainland Malaya to explore – it didn't matter where they went as long as they got back on a specified date. He brought the two Butterworth SAR pilots down to Seletar before sending them on to Kuching for a change of duties and scene, allocating ex-Borneo men to the Search and Rescue role with the same purpose.

Overall, his 'endless belt' scheme, designed to ensure a trickle feed to Kuching of the right number of pilots and crewmen with the right mix of experience, continued. Regardless of marital status, it was fair shares for all 103 Squadron men of the remaining opportunities for Borneo detachment.

★　★　★　★　★

On 14 August the boss of 110 Squadron, Squadron Leader Hadlow, flew the mission from Nanga Gaat to extract from off the border to the south of Bankit the 2/2nd Gurkhas who had mounted the final patrol in the 3rd Division. Later in the month he accepted a presentation *kukri* in appreciation of 'the cooperation and help the Gurkhas had received from the squadron'. In exchange, the boss presented a squadron plaque as a 'memento of association'.

In a further signal that hostilities were at an end, a BBC 'Blue Peter' team arrived at the Gaat for three days filming, featuring the local longhouse and a starring role for Bunso – affectionately known as 'Bonzo' – the *Iban* who had for many months been batman to 110 Squadron's officer aircrew. It was the last visit to the Gaat – by the end of the month, the base that had become symbolic of both the RAF and Royal Navy helicopters' pioneering front-line role in the Borneo conflict closed down.

As with 103 Squadron, the 110 unit at Seletar was becoming somewhat overmanned with pilots, with insufficient hours available to keep all thirty-five current. But a boost to operational activity was in the pipeline – replacing the departing 230 Squadron, 110 was slated to take over Whirlwind duties at Labuan.

★　★　★　★　★

In September the activity for 230 Squadron was all about withdrawal. In a daily flurry of signals, orders were received to begin re-locating back to Odiham as early as the end of the month. The first four 110 aircraft flew up to Labuan from Kuching on the 20th of the month. Colin Cummings was involved:

> It was a high-profile operation and getting the fuel positioned at Anduki needed a great deal of ingenuity and determination, and not a little creative help from the Movements Section. It was another of the tasks that gave me a great deal of satisfaction. I felt that I was really able to make a difference – helping to bring the campaign to a successful conclusion. I had enjoyed working with 230 Squadron – I'd managed to put in quite a few hours airborne with them, including one memorable trip into deepest Sabah as a supernumerary crewman.

★　★　★　★　★

247

Withdrawal from Borneo was also on the near horizon for 103 Squadron. In his September report the Squadron Commander remarked on 'the swift and complete run-down of British forces, organization and equipment' from the forward bases. The squadron's detachments were to return to Seletar by no later than the end of October.

Before departure, in a further sign of the times, the squadron hosted a three-week visit by two of a group of Cranwell cadets sent to Borneo specifically to learn about helicopter operations – graduates of the RAF College were now being posted direct to rotaries. They travelled to Kuching and on to Balai Ringin, now manned by the 1st New Zealand Infantry Regiment. There they saw some casevac sorties (accidents to serving men and civilians were an unavoidable continuing occurrence) but two of their colleagues who were visiting 66 Squadron, won first prize. The young lads were lucky enough to get an educational night in a Sarawak longhouse.

★ ★ ★ ★ ★

The fort at Jambu, which had taken so much effort to build, closed in September. The Simanggang Detachment of 110 Squadron set up a shuttle service to fly troops and material out, and Rick Atkinson had the task of lifting the final load. He remembers 'staggering off on max power with several locals on board, plus a monkey, two cockerels and a python in a cage'.

Back at Seletar the 110 Squadron HQ was 'knee-deep in aircrew, all clamouring to fly'. For two crews, their wish was granted, with work in Western Malaysia on the joint-service Exercise SHARP KUKRI – one of the Whirlwinds was piloted by Fraser Skea, now a flight lieutenant, who flew on each of the eleven days. But, in a month that saw just 209 operational hours, the squadron was seriously under-tasked. There were now thirty-five Whirlwind pilots on strength and, to narrow the width of the command structure, there was a restructuring into three flights. At the same time an agreement was reached with 103 Squadron that Seletar tasking would be shared – 110 would take on those scheduled for Tuesdays and Thursdays, and 103 would take the rest.

By month-end the detachment at Sibu had closed, as had Simanggang, out of which the industrious Fraser Skea had the honour of flying the last Whirlwind, receiving 'many spontaneous demonstrations of gratitude' from the local inhabitants.

★ ★ ★ ★ ★

September tasking for 103 Squadron in West Malaysia was limited to operations in support of Malaysian and Commonwealth units, although one aircraft did fly all the way north to Vientiane to assist in flood relief efforts. In the last few days of the squadron's tenure of the Kuching base in October, there seemed in the local area to be a 'last chance' proliferation of knife wounds, appendicitis, hernias and pregnancies, all of which were serviced by Whirlwind missions.

At the end of the month Squadron Leader Hoskins presented a squadron crest to the Sarawak Museum before his final three Whirlwinds flew off to Kuching docks. The town and its grateful citizens said farewell with a flurry of balloons.

★ ★ ★ ★ ★

In Labuan the 110 Squadron detachment found itself taking the lion's share of the tasking – the 230 aircrews had their minds set on repatriation. For three weeks there were three aircraft detached forward to Bario, returning disbanding Border Scouts to their familes in 'obscure and primitive longhouses', and mounting the changeover from 2/7th Gurkhas to Malaysian troops. At Bario, Malaysian Caribou aircraft were now handling the shuttle down to the coast alongside the 209 Squadron Pioneers.

The 110 boys grabbed the work on offer with enthusiasm. When the captain of a Malaysian Airways Dakota spotted a dozen Australian signallers clinging to their capsized boat in the Bay of Brunei it was a 110 crew that got there first.

By this time Rick Atkinson had flown his Whirlwind up to Labuan from Kuching, via Bario:

Now that was quite a trip – mountain ridges, Plain of Bah, dusky maidens and all that.

From Labuan we worked on the mapping surveys. We'd fly over the sea to the main island and down into the interior to put Royal Engineer surveyors onto potential trig points. When the sea breeze was building up in the heat of the day, we'd watch the orographic lifting, seeding a line of thunderstorms along the coast.

To get through the range of the hills we'd follow the logging railway through the Tenom Gap. On the way back, once we were down to the coast again we could skirt around the storms. One time over Brunei Bay I had an electrical failure and my instruments went haywire – one of the few times I ever had a problem with the Whirlwind.

We were now working alongside RMAF Alouette helis, and Caribou light transports. One of the latter had a nasty crash in the jungle after a fuel system cock-up – the pilot feathered one engine, failed to cross-feed and lost the other. I got the story from an RAF pay officer who was on his rounds. He was sitting at the forward end of the cabin and watched

249

the terrifying cockpit drama as it developed – shouting, arms waving, and the pilot trying to haul the plane up with brute strength. The Caribou sliced through the jungle canopy and came to rest with its nose crumpled against a massive tree – the captain was injured but the co-pilot died. The fuselage had broken in two, so a sergeant policeman who was sitting by the wing could get everyone else out unscathed.

I flew over the crash site the next day but could see very little evidence of the wreck or a break in the jungle canopy which had swallowed up the aircraft. The survivors had had the presence of mind to spread out a red dinghy on a knoll, which was the only thing visible from the air, and only when right overhead. A sobering experience for us, clattering around above the jungle in a single engine helicopter!

On 13 October Flying Officer Geoff Leeming, another Tern Hill trained first-tourist on 110 Squadron, had a scare when that single engine for once let him down in flight. He was en route for Miri on the North Sarawak coast and in the left-hand seat was a newly-arrived colleague, along for familiarization. In the cabin, together with a youthful male relative as escort, was an elderly Chinese lady bound for hospital.

Just ten miles short of destination the pilots' ears and nerves were attacked by the squall of a warning klaxon, telling them that something was seriously wrong with the fuel-flow computer. Sure enough, the engine began to wind down and the Whirlwind embarked on its inevitable descent towards almost certain destruction in the treetops. But, in the nick of time, a glint of water appeared through the branches – a wide river was off to port. Geoff achieved just sufficient control to haul the aircraft round and make it to the river bank and a gravel shoal above water. With flaring rotors he dumped the Whirlwind down – more or less intact and with no harm coming to crew and passengers.

It was another skilled bit of flying to be marked up for a Tern Hill Tyro. Unfortunately, in the laconic words of the Reporting Officer: 'The river Flying Officer Leeming chose to park in rose soon after the incident.' But Geoff's SARBE beacon did its work and he and his colleague, as well as the two Chinese, were winched safely out before the flood. In due course, so was the sodden but eventually serviceable helicopter. But 'anti-leptospirosis injections had to be given to those people who worked on the aircraft in the water'.[60]

In the same report it was noted that the work generated at Labuan enabled every 110 Squadron pilot to achieve eighteen operational hours in the month, with each aircraft logging the targeted forty.

★ ★ ★ ★ ★

October 1966 saw the Junglies finally and reluctantly completing their pull-back from the Far East. Lieutenant Commander Craig and the Wessex of 848 had sailed for Gan and the UK in August, a month or so before the Wessex of 845 arrived back in the Far East on HMS *Bulwark* in time to assist in mopping up the Sumbi incursion. They mounted operations from Bario and Sepulot before, on 9 October, re-embarking at Labuan. They saw no further action in Borneo.

The Whirlwinds of 846 NAS, having returned to Tawau, ceased operational flying on the same day. There was a farewell party at the Tawau Sports Club and, on 12 October, four Whirlwinds in finger formation flew over the town and out to join 845 on *Bulwark* off the eastern Sabah coast. Their CO wrote: 'Car horns were blowing and the locals waving with great gusto. The squadron feels that it was noticed while at Tawau and we can look back to a tremendous send-off.'

Their 10,000 square-miles of territory were handed over to the Alouettes of the RMAF and 846 was itself disbanded a week later, having completed over 6,000 hours of operational flying since being commissioned in 1962.

The departure occasioned a signal from the Commander Far East Fleet:

Nearly four years of Fleet Air Arm helicopter operations have been brought to a close in Borneo – 845 and 848 in the Wessex days, 846 in the more hazardous missions with the Whirlwind 7. Step proudly all of you, for you helped to write a noble page in FAA history.

* * * * *

Work for the AAC Scouts continued, much of it welfare work for the native population. Their loyalty had been such that few requests were ignored. John Richards recalls one such:

Many disasters were deflected courtesy of the 'Army Airline'. I was called out to carry the son of a powerful longhouse chief to hospital in Brunei where it was discovered he had peritonitis. After an emergency operation and recovery, I was tasked to deliver the lad back to his village, where a great reception awaited us both.

I was able to politely refuse the rice brew on the grounds that I had to get the aircraft home in one piece, but found it difficult to do anything other than accept the prize pig offered as a gift of gratitude.

The beast was duly made fairly secure in the cargo net, but en-route base, a combination of its strenuous efforts and bumpy weather freed it enough for its snout to appear by my left elbow. The pig did what pigs do when terrified and I arrived at base with the cockpit covered in porcine shit and piss.

The ground crew presented me with a mop and bucket to clear up
– and the Gurkha cookhouse prepared a splendid barbecue.

★ ★ ★ ★ ★

The Belvederes of 66 Squadron were also managing to keep busy enough. As
with the Whirlwinds, the expected heavy workload in association with the
withdrawal of Commonwealth forces from the western Sarawak front-line had
not materialized, but good serviceability allowed a vigorous attack on the
training backlog. The last of the Odiham-trained pilots arrived at the beginning
of September and by the end of the month all but the new arrivals were
operational and the squadron was celebrating a record 294 hours flown.

But tasking in Kuching had fallen right away and it was decided to reduce
the detached strength to four aircraft, with eight at Seletar. At the same time
detachments for aircrew were reduced to a fortnight at a time. In Borneo
highlights were now such achievements as the darts team winning the inter-
section shield and in Seletar the talk was all about overcrowding in the HQ and
the creation of inter-section hockey and ten-pin bowling teams.

However, in October tasking in Western Malaysia picked up, mainly down
to the freighting and trooping missions flown with the 1st Battalion Scots
Guards and the 2/7th Gurkha Rifles on the counter-revolutionary exercise
WINGED HAGGIS in Terendak, 120 nautical miles north of Seletar. Six-ship
formation flying around Singapore was another fillip for morale. As Squadron
Leader Gray reported: 'The Belvedere performs best when it is worked hard.'

★ ★ ★ ★ ★

For 230 Squadron the tour in Labuan came to an end as planned in November
1966. The eleven Whirlwinds were stripped down, loaded into four 53
Squadron Belfast transports and flown to Odiham. In their two years in Borneo
the aircraft had achieved 8,558 flying hours, hauling 3.3Mlb of freight and
carrying just under 40,000 troops and 414 casualties.

Delivered back to the arms of their loved ones, the men of 230 prepared
themselves to trade the excitement and warmth of the Far East for the
privations of national economic crisis and the trials of an English winter.

★ ★ ★ ★ ★

For the over-manned 103 Squadron, now based at Seletar, there remained just
the one detachment, the SAR commitment at Butterworth but participation in
WINGED HAGGIS alongside the Belvederes provided relief. Nine pilots and
seven crewmen with four Whirlwinds had thirteen days of hard work and, in

his November report, the Squadron Commander wrote that a great deal of experience was gained, and valuable lessons learnt:

> The first and foremost is that a tactical squadron which is intended to be fully mobile ought to be completely self-contained, able to move itself by road, eat, live, work and sleep right on the job and, in conjunction with an associated unit of the RAF Regiment, defend itself.

In December 1966 notable events for the squadron were a visit from six officers of the South Vietnamese Air Force and the departure for the benighted United Kingdom of two of the redoubtable Borneo Boys – Martin Mayer and Mike McKinley.

Martin left for Tern Hill and the QHI course. He was to fly helicopters for twenty-five more years, both as instructor and test pilot.

Mike has a few final thoughts on his time in Sarawak:

> I was inspired by my experiences with the Army at Lundu – we went to all their briefings and always knew as well as anyone what was going on. Later on, I never ceased arguing the case for close cooperation with the soldiers.
>
> I was also impressed by my experiences with the SS11 missiles. Some years later I found myself arguing in RAF circles another case, the one for armed helicopters. Of course the fast-jet boys thought I was being silly – so the Army got the Apache. The rest is history still being played out!
>
> Where I was lucky in Borneo was that I never once caught any of the usual jungle diseases such as scrub typhus, leptospirosis and malaria. But I missed out on Gurkha festival celebrations, none of which coincided with my Lundu detachments.
>
> There wasn't much chance to fraternize with the locals either. I took the whole Flight up-river for a party in a rare quiet period but we found no lissom *Dayak* maidens bathing in the stream.
>
> Actually, there was a better chance to meet Malaysians in Kuching. The market square was always full of people, including girls, of course. Mind you, the midnight curfew was a bind. Chunky Lord used to climb back over the perimeter fence – he could have been shot!

Mike was also posted to CFS but, as with John Davy, not to Tern Hill but rather Little Rissington for fixed-wing Chipmunks. He was to return to rotaries, flying the Puma before leaving the RAF at the age of thirty-eight. Never far from the world of aviation, he was to become a Borneo Boy with half a century of flying to his name.

★ ★ ★ ★ ★

December saw Dave Reid leaving 110 Squadron after two-and-a-half years in Borneo. He was to remain on rotaries for the whole of his Air Force career but is still puzzled about how he came to be selected for 'choppers' in the first place:

> I've never been sure what the criteria were. I suppose I had good motor skills and was very aware – missed nothing that was going on around me. And I showed right away that I realized the main hazard to safety in the air was yourself – it was down to you and no one else to continually evaluate any risks you were running.
>
> I was never overawed by the Borneo environment – the distances we flew, the mountains and jungles, and the swamps. I was helped by the Whirlwind 10 being so reliable – it came from the Sikorsky S55 and that was overbuilt in the American way and very robust. The only time I remember being a bit fazed was the straight-line transit over mountains from Belaga to the Gaat – it was less hairy when you followed the river. And operating at night was also somewhat dodgy – all those SHNAP lights floating around in front of you... We were known to call them 'Seletar Helicopter International Torchlight Systems' – perhaps providing a more appropriate acronym.
>
> But the selection procedures obviously worked. We had lots of confidence – a bit like kids given new sports cars. It's amazing we didn't have more crashes.

Dave Reid was posted to CFS(H) and was to become a successful QHI and helicopter test pilot before retiring from the RAF aged fifty-five and joining his ex-110 Squadron colleagues Fraser Skea and Rick Atkinson as an instructor on the rotary simulators at RAF Benson – each of them was to complete close on fifty years in aviation.

★ ★ ★ ★ ★

For 66 Squadron December 1966 brought an upturn in workload and spirits in Borneo, now firmly renamed East Malaysia. Operations with Malaysian forces now ranged over the whole of the 1st, 2nd and 3rd Divisions of Sarawak. LPs close to the border, previously the domain of Whirlwinds, Wessex, Scouts and Sioux, were now being used by the Belvederes. In the 3rd Division sites abandoned by the RAF, such as Long Jawi, Nanga Gaat and Kapit, were being reopened. Dave Lanigan expands:

> The Belvedere was a sleek machine, and took some time to slow down, so from a hundred-and-twenty knots, it was necessary to start the flare

a mile out to bring the speed down to 40 knots for the approach. Then, with these new LPs, you had to watch out for hills on the way in and the way out and for the trees and sloping landing pads when you got in there. With the tandem-rotor layout and our size it was all pretty tight for us, to say the least. Our problem was that we sat right up the front end and couldn't see what was happening to the back end. We depended entirely on our crewmen talking us down from the cabin door.

MAOTs were sent in to recce LZs for suitability for Belvedere operations. It was as well not to build them too close to the villages and forts as our downdraught was so powerful. One day I got too close to a village schoolhouse and took the roof off – fortunately, the squaddies on the base were able put it back the next day.

Another time I was tasked to land on a longhouse *padang*. We got down successfully and, while our army passengers went about their task, my crew had a three-hour stopover which gave us an opportunity to meet the locals. We had a long conversation using sign language, showed them our maps and gave the children sweets. They showed us pictures on the walls of the British Royal Family taken from magazines from about the 1930s to the 1950s. They showed us the knives they used for hunting deer. They told us they'd been given them by our troops and in return they'd provided trackers to help our soldiers follow the raiding parties returning to the Border.

The army guys told us that over the years the locals had accepted helicopters but were still startled by motor vehicles on the rare occasions they appeared. They added that the natives in this part of Borneo had been headhunters until very recently. As I lifted off, I was doubly careful with the downwash – didn't want to be blowing their roofs off!

In December Wing Commander Dowling flew in a mission to place a spire on the top of the Hakka Methodist Church in Singapore, his final flight in a Belvedere. Three Whirlwind pilots transferred for conversion to the larger machine, and 300 hours was topped by the squadron for the month. At the same time, cooperation with the Alouettes of the RMAF was increasing, in a spirit of what the reporting officer called 'friendly rivalry'.

★ ★ ★ ★ ★

In November and December 1966 a spell of poor serviceability for the 110 Squadron Whirlwinds, coupled with the now endemic operational situation meant that tasking out of Labuan was light. But the survey work continued and it was on such a mission that, at the beginning of November, Fraser Skea found himself once more plunged into the perils of jungle flying – literally:

I was on a mission to insert two engineer surveyors at the top of the three-thousand-foot Tinkar Hill, over one hundred nautical miles east-north-east of Labuan, near Tongod in deepest Sabah. I had Flight Sergeant McDonald downstairs as crewman. We flew through the Tenom Gap, refuelled at Tenom itself and pressed on for the summit.

On top, I went into the hover and told McDonald to begin winching down the surveying kit, bundled up in a cargo-net. That went all right and he started on the heavy concrete trig-point. We're on the way down when there's a loud crack from the tail-boom and the Whirlwind begins spinning round on its axis. I don't have a choice – I have to dump the helicopter on the summit, quick as I can.

We go down like a stone – the dead weight of the trig-point as ballast – and hit the summit-ridge, where a snapped-off tree trunk pierces the battery bay, saving our bacon. The trunk holds the machine fast – just as well as there's steep cliffs both sides of us. If we'd gone down there, we'd've been gonners. As it is, we're perched at three thousand feet and balanced on a tree stump – still far from what you might call safe.

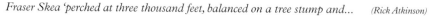

Fraser Skea 'perched at three thousand feet, balanced on a tree stump and...   *(Rick Atkinson)*

The tail rotor's stopped – the crack we heard was the gear-shaft snapping – but the rotors are still running. McDonald jumps out and ties a rope from a picketing point on the helicopter down to a tree, and I very carefully close the aircraft down, keeping the machine as stable as possible. I then get on the HF radio and send out my first ever 'Mayday' message: 'Impaled on a Mountain Top'.

We clamber out of the aircraft with great care and picking our way along the ridge get ourselves clear of our forlorn-looking machine. Funny how you don't feel vertigo in an aeroplane, but as soon as you're on a mountain crag, blimey!

It's not too long before there's a clatter of rotors and the welcome sight of the Brunei stand-by Whirlwind, edging up the forested mountain slopes to winch us off our perch. But I realize that's not going to be straightforward. Four of us and at least two in the standby crew – that's a lot of weight to lift at three thousand feet.

We get the engineers and crewman on board and there's only me left to go. The pilot's running out of power but he's just got enough of a margin to lift me a foot or two before dragging me through the scrub and clear of the ridge. Then he plunges down the crags to pick up speed and lift – with me dangling thirty feet below at the end of a wire. They start to wind me in but then the winch begins to stutter – that's all we need. But it picks up again and I'm finally dragged aboard. Thank God for Westland engineering! We land at Tongod where everything suddenly gets better – there's a bevy of pretty VSO [Voluntary Service Overseas] girls ready to look after us.

Rick Atkinson flew over to Tinkar Hill the next day to pick up the pieces:

I'm authorized for a one-off sortie to fly out to the crash site, taking some ground crew to recover all the valuable removable items from the wreck. It's a long way out in the ulu and we have to stage through Tenom and Sook for fuel. At Sook we find that most of the fuel drums have been punctured by locals with machetes, intent on getting hold of aviation fuel for their cooking stoves. But we reckon there are just enough intact drums for the next stage and the return trip – provided the thieves don't get at it whilst we're away!

We stagger off at max permissable weight and head for the village of Tongod which sits on a river bend down below Tinkar Hill. As we make our approach, the locals come running down on to the grassy knoll, led by two white girls. I'm amazed to see white women so far out in the interior of Borneo. One's an Australian, immaculate in her nurse's uniform, and the other a student from the UK, working for the VSO.

... come to rest at a precarious angle.'

(Fraser Skea)

After a brief introduction I fly the ground crew up to the wreck where they bravely 'hover jump' out of the cabin door and onto the narrow ridge. It's a miracle Fraser managed to get the Whirlwind down without it rolling over and crashing down the tree-covered hillside. It had come to rest at a precarious angle – the tree stump helped of course. Leaving the lads to see what they can salvage, I fly back to Tongod and shut down.

Down there, the Aussie nurse asks me if I could take a mother and her sick baby to hospital at Tenom. I reckon I might just manage to get airborne with mum, baby, ground crew and salvaged equipment but when they insist that I have to take dad and another child too I reluctantly have to refuse.

It turns out the lads can't work on the engine to get it out as there's not enough room on the peak I regret to this day that I didn't just ditch all that equipment and take the whole family to Tenom – I never did hear if the baby survived.

Fraser's aircraft was abandoned where it lay. He and I have talked about returning to Tongod and climbing Tinkar Hill to see if the old Whirlwind is still there – perhaps one day we will.

That ill-fated mission to Tinkar Hill was Fraser's final sortie with 110 in Borneo. His colleagues completed the survey work in December, including fixing the height of the summit of Trus Madi, the second highest in Borneo which involved winching at an altitude of 8,200 feet. But Fraser returned to Singapore to spend the final month of his tour operating from Seletar.

At the end of November Rick Atkinson also returned to Seletar, one of a quartet of pilots returning Whirlwinds to base via Kuching and HMS *Bulwark*:

We routed through Brunei and Miri. On board my aircraft were a couple of pet dogs that the ground crew would not leave behind. One was a lovable mongrel called Jinx, but he hated helicopters and had to be dragged aboard. There he lay flat on the floor with one paw over his head. But while we were refuelling at Miri, Jinx leaped out and made a run for it across the airfield. Try as they might, the boys couldn't get him back and reluctantly we had to leave him there, knowing that it was highly unlikely that we would ever return to Miri.

At Kuching we got a garbled signal all in 'Navy speak'. It was: 'RV with'(incomprehensible codename) 'at lat/long 110deg E, 1deg 55min N'. We plotted the lat and long – it was some way offshore, but were they working in GMT or not?

We take a chance and lift off at dawn – I'm at Number Four. After twenty minutes or so the leader starts calling the ship on VHF – no response. He keeps on calling and after a few more minutes I can hear them coming back to us, loud and clear. So I tell the leader and he comes back with: 'Number Four, you have radio contact – you have the comms'.

I'm talking to the ship when he says, 'Have you the ship in sight?' 'No,' says I. He comes back with: 'Making smoke – making smoke', and a thin wisp of black smoke appears on the horizon in my one o'clock. As we draw nearer there's no mistaking her as HMS *Bulwark*, the RN's helicopter carrier.

Now we have to get on board and none of us has done it before. But we've looked up the procedure in a very tattered book back at Kuching. We have to overfly the ship and then turn and approach into wind off the port side. Then we follow the marshaller's instructions and move sideways on to the deck, the Boss first then each in turn, upwind. But I have this terrible feeling after I touch down that I'm rolling backwards into Number Three. I stand on the brakes in desperation, only to realize, after a quick glance to my starboard, that I'm not moving – it's the enormous swell pitching the bow up in front of me. I've never been on a carrier-deck before.

When I've clambered down from the cockpit I get yelled at by a rating, 'Hats off and sleeves down on the flight-deck – Sir'. It's a different world on a carrier.

Over on the island there's a lieutenant commander waiting for us. He leads us down to the Ops Room and briefs us on our activities over the twenty-four hours it's going to take us to get to Singapore. Very officious, he is: 'Stand to attention when a senior officer comes into the room' – and all that. He says there'll be lectures and warfare seminars and PT in the morning before breakfast. We're aghast. Then he says 'We'll now start off with a training film.'

We all groan inwardly as the projector starts to whirr and the screen flickers into life. But blow me, if it isn't Mickey Mouse and Donald Duck! The lights go on and the projector dies. 'Right gentlemen,' says the grinning lieutenant commander, the bar's down this way.' We have a memorable voyage back to Singapore.

In December Rick's colleague Fraser Skea was posted, as were so many of their Borneo Boy mates, back to Tern Hill for the helicopter instructor's course and a long and distinguished career on rotaries. But, in a note of bathos, symbolizing the somewhat downbeat ending of the Borneo Campaign, Fraser overslept after his farewell party, missed his scheduled flight home and eventually made it just five days before Christmas.

Postlude

Despite the shooting war of Confrontation being a thing of the past, as operations in Malaysia, Singapore and Brunei got under way in January 1967 there could be no let up in the aircrews' concentration. The weather and terrain were no less challenging and every sortie still needed the highest standards of airmanship. A firm grasp of a helicopter's cyclic stick continued to be a non-negotiable requirement.

There was a good deal of airborne work to do. Transports still needed to parachute in rations for the withdrawing troops before flying shuttles between Borneo and barracks in West Malaysia, Singapore and Brunei. Fuel was still airdropped for helicopters on support missions. For the rotaries, the howitzers that had proved so crucial to military success needed to be lifted out along with large quantities of other equipment – although many military-surplus goods appeared in the local market, including corrugated-metal sheeting rescued from the jungle, beer barrels and, on one occasion 7,000 sheets of PSP at a couple of Malaysian dollars a piece. Medevacs were a continuing task – soldiers were still catching jungle diseases, falling in rivers or needing appendectomies. In addition Commonwealth military exercises and helicopter training for jungle warfare commanded a growing commitment as Malaysia, Britain, Australia and New Zealand were not about to drop their guard in the still-fragile Far Eastern scene.

★ ★ ★ ★ ★

January 1967 brought monsoon floods to North-East Malaya. Dave Lanigan reported:

> 66 Squadron despatched a Belvedere to assist. However, the press of men, women and children rushing up to the machine as it approached, regardless of rotor blades, wheels and hot exhausts, forced the crew to drop off the supplies in the hover. The aircraft came back to base with a long list of unserviceabilities having operated and been parked in heavy rain for days.

In the same month the squadron flew training sorties at Terendak with Australian and New Zealand forces bound for Vietnam. In the first week of

Full formation of 66 Squadron Belvederes flies out of Kuching for final time. (Crown Copyright)

February a Belvedere made a marathon Borneo tour from Kuching to Labuan, tasked with lifting the engines and undercarriage from the crashed RMAF Caribou before carrying them over to the airstrip at Meligan. On the return trip an enforced night-stop at Sibu happily coincided with celebrations for Chinese New Year. However, that sortie proved to be a last hurrah for the Belvederes in Borneo – before the end of the month the Sarawak detachment was to be withdrawn.

The ground crew toiled manfully to get every one of the aircraft serviceable and on 20 February, in pouring rain, a full formation of Belvederes flew proudly over local villages and Kuching docks before landing on the deck of the LST *Maxwell Brander* for ferrying to Seletar. The squadron was able to boast that in the Borneo Campaign its tandem-rotor machines had lifted all of 95,000 troops and 10Mlbs of freight while putting in no fewer than 4,500 operational hours.

★ ★ ★ ★ ★

The Scout pilots of 656 Squadron AAC also left Borneo in February, handing over to the Alouettes of the RMAF.[61] Sergeant John Richards returned with his colleagues to Kluang to complete his two-year tour before posting for a second stint abroad, in West Germany.

★ ★ ★ ★ ★

POSTLUDE

Four 103 Squadron Whirlwinds out of Seletar were detached in January to the flood-hit swamps of North Malaya and in the same month took part in a 28 (Commonwealth) Brigade exercise with the Sabres of 77 Squadron RAAF. It soon became apparent that, against a hostile high-performance interceptor, the unarmed helicopter stood little chance. In February four Whirlwinds and their crews were ferried up to Hong Kong on *Bulwark*. Up there they were reunited with their old friends the Royal Marines and mounted reconnaissance sorties along another sensitive frontier – this time with another would-be expansionist empire, China.

Cracks in the airframes of the SAR aircraft at Butterworth showed that the Whirlwinds were feeling the strain of Far East operations and on 8 March, the detachment was withdrawn. But in April six 103 Squadron Whirlwinds, accompanied by seven pilots, four crewmen and a ground crew team, found themselves back in Kuching. They'd been called in to supplement the Alouette helicopters of 5 Squadron RMAF – a unit known to the RAF guys as 'Tunku's Tigers' – in support of Malaysian troops and, in a monthly rotation with 110, they were to be tasked on average with one mission per day.

But Rick Atkinson was not amongst them – February saw him at Nee Soon Barracks on a Malay language course. However, he was able to practise his new-found skill for only a few months – in July an exchange posting sent him to the AAC at Middle Wallop to fly the Sioux. Bizarrely, he missed out on the General Service Medal (GSM) with Borneo bar. To qualify there had to be a total of thirty days' service in Borneo before the cut-off date of 11 August 1966. Rick had done just twenty-eight.[62]

Meantime, his 110 Squadron colleagues still in the Far East had a tale to tell about Jinx, Rick's canine passenger from Labuan. On three occasions they had been tasked to fly from Kuching up to the 3rd Division, involving a two-and-a-half-hour transit. On the final one of these, fading light on the return leg required a night-stop at Sibu. After landing, even before the engine was shut down, a dog came bounding across the airfield to their aircraft. It leaped into the cabin, jumping on and licking all on board. It was the wayward mongrel, Jinx. The Air Traffic Officer told the crew that the dog had been hanging around for weeks and would appear on the airfield whenever a helicopter came in. At last he had found one with the right people on board. Jinx settled himself in the cabin for the night, refusing to leave. The next morning, his fear of flying overcome, Jinx flew happily on to Kuching where he was reunited with the delighted ground crew.

★ ★ ★ ★ ★

On their return to the wintry UK in November the year before the crews of 230 Squadron had found themselves enduring flying conditions in Odiham that were in some ways as demanding as those in Borneo. While being immersed in re-categorization they were being updated in icing procedures. Until their Whirlwinds had been modified with de-icing kit, there was to be no flying in rain or in visibility of less than 1,000 yards in air-temperatures of plus or minus 5 degrees Centigrade. As those were routine mid-winter conditions in Hampshire that year, the whole squadron was in effect non-operational until 9 January when the mods were completed. But even then the tasking available was limited to routine army cooperation. There was a diversion with the Paris Air Show in May but that was no more than a static display. After the excitements and successes of Borneo the squadron was being reminded of the more humdrum aspects of military life.

★ ★ ★ ★ ★

With 230 Squadron gone and the 110 detachment withdrawn to Kuching, Labuan Airport Hotel was no longer needed as an Officers' Mess, the Membedai Club being sufficient to house the RMAF as they took over.

Colin Cummings was kept busy closing down airstrips and bases over in Borneo until the end of March when he climbed into an Argosy for the long flight up to Hong Kong. RAF Kai Tak, and the Hunters of 28 Squadron, was his next posting.

★ ★ ★ ★ ★

After its successful operational flying in Borneo, the powers-that-be decided that 66 Squadron, now based at Seletar, would remain *pro tem* very much on a war footing with full participation in Commonwealth Brigade exercises. Dave Lanigan expands:

> Flights were laid on to familiarize our crews with Royal Navy ships' helidecks, and their ratings with a helicopter much larger than the Wessex. We flew onto HMS *Intrepid* in Singapore harbour and HMS *Bulwark* on the South China Sea. And we continued to train up New Zealand and Australian soldiers in jungle warfare prior to their deployment to Vietnam. They were initially based at the Jungle Warfare School at Ulu Tiram, Malaya, and needed us to simulate massed helicopter assaults against dug-in enemy positions, with Gurkhas acting as a formidable and realistic enemy. The new era of SH troop insertions was here to stay.

The crowding of Seletar accommodation was eased a little by the transfer of four of the Kuching aircraft to Butterworth and there was a heartwarming

Belvedere embarks HMS Intrepid *in Singapore harbour. (Dave Lanigan)*

event when Squadron Leader Gray returned to Kuching to receive a plaque from the Chief Minister, engraved with: 'In recognition of close ties with the people of Sarawak'.

On 26 October the squadron's final Far East detachment, the one at Butterworth, closed. This marked almost five years since the first one opened, at Labuan in December 1962 when the four Belvederes had made that pioneering eight-hour flight in support of the action in the Brunei Rebellion. Since then 66 Squadron had totalled over 10,000 flying hours in Borneo, Singapore and Malaya.

The squadron flew on from its Seletar base until 20 March 1969, the day of both its disbandment and the end of the service life of the Belvedere – the year before, negotiations had begun to acquire the American Chinook as the twin-rotor medium-lift support helicopter for the RAF. On the day before the final parade, the squadron mounted an eight-ship formation to make a farewell flight around the island.

Dave Lanigan was on both that flight and that parade, having totalled 935 hours on the FEAF Belvederes and gained a 'High Average' rating. After a couple of weeks and a few parties he and Ann were on their way to the UK in a VC10. He was to be a helicopter pilot, both military and civilian, for the next thirty years.

★ ★ ★ ★ ★

From May 1967 operational life for 110 and 103 Squadrons at Seletar became easier – 1st and 2nd line servicing were again de-centralized and serviceability of the Whirlwinds, as well as the morale of the men, was noticeably boosted. In their rostered month's duty in Kuching, tasking for 110 increased as the RMAF Alouettes were temporarily grounded. In the four weeks the 110 men acquired the title of 'Flying Doctor Service of 1st Division', lifting no fewer than fifteen *Dayak* medical cases from outlying villages into Kuching Hospital.

In June it was VIP work at Seletar that formed a mainstay of 110 Squadron tasking at no less than 20 per cent. That same month the crewmen of 103 had something extra to celebrate – one of their number, Flight Sergeant Thatcher, was awarded the Air Force Medal, a landmark for the trade. In the same announcement, the squadron learned that two of their former pilots had been rewarded for services in Borneo – Mike McKinley had been Mentioned in Despatches and Brian Skillicorn had won the AFC.

★ ★ ★ ★ ★

August 1967 saw 103 Squadron preparing for their Fiftieth Anniversary celebrations which duly took place at Seletar on 1 September. The band of the 1st Battalion the Royal New Zealand Infantry Regiment played for the parade and four Whirlwinds mounted a flypast, the squadron flag resplendent under the lead machine. At dusk the pipes and drums of 2/10th Gurkha Rifles beat the retreat as the squadron hosted several military and parliamentary dignitaries.[63]

Within three weeks the excitement mounted even higher as an advance party of two-dozen ground crew left by air for Hong Kong, tasked with preparing the way for a squadron detachment in that exotic British colony. October saw six of the squadron Whirlwinds, after a five-day transit on HMS *Triumph*, hauling bale after bale of barbed wire up into the New Territories where it was needed to secure the border ridge against refugees from the turmoil of Chairman Mao's Cultural Revolution. After a brief interruption for the three days that Typhoon Clara roared into the bay and up into the hills, the work continued into November.

Meanwhile, 110 Squadron had maintained the Kuching detachment until 1 November. The Alouettes had become serviceable again and, on that day,

Last RAF rotaries in Borneo, 110 Squadron Whirlwinds, bid farewell to Istana and Kuching.
(Crown Copyright)

the Whirlwinds flew off to the docks for the last time. Since its first Borneo action, the Rebellion in Brunei, 110 had served in Borneo almost continuously for close on four years, the longest for any RAF squadron. With their departure the RAF rotary presence in East Malaysia was finally at an end.

★ ★ ★ ★ ★

BORNEO BOYS

Fred Hoskins's 103 Squadron detachment in Hong Kong flew 150 tasks in November 1967, varying from straightforward troop deployment and re-supply to bomb disposal and medical evacuation. One of the latter was dramatic by any standards. Early in the month a Convair 880 of Cathay Pacific Airways aborted its take-off from the Kai Tak runway and skidded into the sea. No call for help had been received but, although it was a Sunday morning, three 103 Squadron Whirlwinds were airborne within fifteen minutes to assist in the evacuation of casualties. After seven of the more seriously wounded had been lifted to Queen Elizabeth Hospital, there was some doubt whether all had been evacuated. So a crewman, Flight Sergeant Robbins, was winched down onto the floating fuselage to carry out a search of the cabin, which he found to be clear of crew and passengers. Needless to say, all concerned congratulated the RAF helicopter crews on their prompt and efficient action.

By the end of the month the 103 Detachment withdrew to Seletar as 110 Squadron relieved them at the beginning of a planned six-weekly rotation. But in December a Whirlwind accident on the Queen's Flight in England resulted in a worldwide programme to replace suspect main-rotor shafts and all were grounded. Despite celebrations at Seletar for the Fiftieth Anniversary of 110 Squadron and, although their shared Hong Kong detachment with 103 was to become established in March 1968 as 28 Squadron, for the ex-Borneo Whirlwinds, 1967 ended with something of a whimper.

* * * * *

December 1967 was the month that Harold Wilson's Labour government decided to remove £100M from the British defence budget and implemented a plan for military withdrawal from east of Suez which, in effect, meant from Malaysia and the Persian Gulf. The Conservative government that came to power in 1970 under Edward Heath did nothing to reverse the situation.

The course of that pullback is mirrored in the final history of HMS *Albion*. In March 1971 she sailed again for South East Asia. The Suez Canal being closed, she took until 12 May to reach Singapore where the embarked Wessex of 848 NAS mounted a flypast to mark the disbandment of the Far East Fleet. She was there again in October that year for the withdrawal from the Naval Base, thirty-four years after its opening. On the 29th of the month there was a Farewell Parade by 40 Commando Royal Marines and another 848 flypast to mark the closure of Sembawang before, two days later, the base facilities were handed over to ANZUK forces and *Albion* left Far East waters for good. On the way home she went to the aid of British fugitives from the Indo-Pakistan war – her last act in service. After seven months in Fareham Creek, she was put up for sale. No one wanted the Old Grey Ghost and by November 1973 she was in the breaker's yard at Faslane, twenty-nine years since her keel plates were laid at Swan Hunter in Newcastle-upon-Tyne.

★ ★ ★ ★ ★

In all the internecine mayhem of the British withdrawal from Empire, the Federation of Malaysia stands out as a shining example of order and economic success. The Borneo Campaign (the last British campaign in Asia until Afghanistan at the turn of the century) had successfully defended the nascent nation against the bullying aggression of a giant neighbour. The Right Honourable Denis Healey had the following to say to the Commons:

> When the House thinks of the tragedy that could have fallen on a whole corner of a continent if we had not been able to hold the situation and bring it to a successful termination, it will appreciate that in the history books it [the Borneo Campaign] will be recorded as one of the most efficient uses of military force in the history of the world.

That was a ringing endorsement for the brilliance of Generals Walker and Lea and their joint-service, multi-national Security Force, as well as for the Far East Fleet. It shines out in contrast with what was happening for the Americans and their allies in Vietnam.

Any number of casualties is too many, but by any reckoning those sustained in Borneo were mercifully light. British and Commonwealth troops lost 114 in action and 181 were wounded. There were thirty-six Malaysian civilians killed, fifty-three wounded and four captured. For the record, it was estimated that 590 Indonesian soldiers died, 220 were injured, and 771 were captured.

A total of 439 gallantry awards were made to the British and their allies, headed by the Victoria Cross to Gurkha Lance Corporal Rambahadur Limbu. Those awards signify the bravery and endurance of the serving men who fought in and flew over the jungles.

There were many key contributions to the military success. As far as the airborne elements were concerned, V-bombers and fighters kept the enemy's heads down, maritime crews unceasingly patrolled the Borneo coasts and transports shuttled the troops to and from the jungles, keeping them in fuel, bullets and bully beef while they were in it.

But the achievements of the rotaries in Borneo cannot be over-stated. They were up for almost any task, from winching tracker dogs down to the ground to positioning a radar station halfway up the precipitous gorges of Mount Kinabalu. They not only saved lives and reduced suffering through casevac but also offered the troops flexibility and the element of surprise, minutes in a helicopter as against hours or days on foot. Immune to ambush, and clever enough mostly to avoid small-arms fire, they were able to operate in the lower air close to the fighting and alongside the soldiers – minimal 'dead' flying hours meant a quicker response to their needs. And the hearts and minds campaign – winning the confidence of the local people in a land of dense jungle, fast-flowing rivers, steep hills and mountains – would have been practically impossible without the rotaries.

The number of helicopters available to the Americans and their allies in Vietnam peaked at close on 3,000. In Borneo General Walker had a maximum of a hundred. This meant that there were no 'cavalry charges' as in Vietnam but Walker was not interested in such high-risk operations – his tactics were far more subtle. The support helicopters in Borneo worked so closely with the troops that they were considered to be supplementary pieces of military hardware – and highly effective ones at that.

For the young chopper pilots of the time, extraordinary self-reliance was a must. They were thrown in at the deep end to fly, often alone, across endless wilderness and in the worst of weathers. All the Borneo Boys in this story agree that being given the opportunity to show that they could cope was a godsend, something for which they were, and remain, truly grateful. The experience gave them the kind of self-confidence which prepared them for any challenge presented by the military or business worlds. And in the process of providing that springboard for their future careers they had helped to win the Borneo Campaign and leave Malaysia intact for its people.

Appendix 1

Post-Borneo Curricula Vitae

Borneo Boys in order of appearance in the story

Colin Ford – Whirlwind pilot, 110 and 103 Squadrons RAF
On repatriation in 1966, for his time on 103 Squadron, Colin Ford was awarded the Queen's Commendation for Valuable Services in the Air. He completed the four-month QHI course before marrying Jan, his Seletar fiancée. A number of ex-FEAF helicopter pilots, including Ian Morgan and Mick Charles, attended the wedding and, instead of swords, they formed an arch with *Iban parangs*. The wedding pictures were a gift from the same photographer who had taken the ones for the *Day in the Life Of* advertisement out in the Far East.

'Old Rotors' visiting 815 NAS (Lynx) hangar on Royal Naval Air Base Yeovilton, May 2011. Left to right: Rick Atkinson, Bob Turner, Dick Holmes, Mike McKinley and host Lt Ed Barham RN. (Author)

Colin enjoyed being a flying instructor, converting both *ab initio* and experienced fixed-wing pilots to the rewarding joys of helicopter flying. Among those he taught was an old friend who had been a fellow student and room-mate thoughout flying training and who was converting from the V-force.

In 1968 Colin volunteered at very short notice for a posting to Hong Kong as Training Officer on the newly formed 28 Squadron, flying Whirlwinds out of RAF Kai Tak. Within a few hours his boss at Tern Hill turned up with a bottle of bubbly, three glasses and the good news that Colin had the job. Next morning he reported for met briefing dressed up in his old jungle-green combats.

Following his Hong Kong tour he returned to CFS(H) where he converted to the Sioux and became a tutor to QHI students. Later he was appointed the CFS(H) project officer for the introduction of the Gazelle helicopter and, together with a colleague, wrote the *Instructor Handbook* and *Student Study Guide*.

Promoted in 1974 to Squadron Leader, he was appointed OC 22 Squadron based at RAF Thorney Island, West Sussex, with responsibility for SAR across the south of England. He again returned to Tern Hill in 1976, this time as the CFS Helicopter Examiner, responsible for the categorization of all QHIs in the three Services as well as by invitation advising several foreign air forces on rotary flying skills. He flew many helicopter types in all parts of the world.

Colin had transferred to the General List in 1964 while on 103 Squadron in Singapore, giving him the opportunity to retire at the age of thirty-eight. In 1979 he waived the option and, effectively, his flying days were over. He spent the remainder of his RAF service working in a variety of staff appointments in the MoD in Whitehall, which was within easy commuting distance from his home in Maidenhead. When he retired in 1996, aged fifty-five, he started his final journey in the RAF from Platform 1 of Paddington Station – the very platform from which he had set off in 1960 for South Cerney and together with Sam Smith in 1963 had journeyed to Lyneham, Singapore and Borneo.

Since leaving the RAF Colin has had no desire for further employment and, with two grandchildren so far, he and Jan have found full satisfaction in their domestic and family life. 'Boredom,' he says, 'is not in our vocabulary.'

Mick Charles – Whirlwind pilot, 110, 103 and 225 Squadrons RAF

After the QHI course at Ternhill Mick spent a year on the staff during which he renewed his acquaintance with Jen, a girl who had grown up in the same village as he had.

From May to December 1967 he did a tour on SAR Whirlwinds in Khormaksar Base, Aden, and, out there, converted to the Wessex – twin-engined, and with a cruising-speed of 115 knots compared to the Whirlwind's 90. It was also robust, as Mick found out when his aircraft was peppered with lead by a group who had just mortared the airfield. On return to the UK in 1968 he and Jen were married, spending their first three years together at ETPS at Boscombe Down – Mick a qualified test pilot, flying the Puma and the Queen's Flight Wessex.

They then changed climates for three years, with Mick taking up an exchange posting to Canada as a test pilot in Canada at AETE Cold Lake – it was minus 40 degrees Centigrade on their arrival. While there Mick was promoted Squadron Leader and he and Jen had a daughter. In 1972, he was awarded the AFC. 1975–77 saw Mick appointed a Flight Commander on 33 Squadron (Pumas) and his one and only ground tour was in 1978–79, as TF1c heli training at Adastral House, London, commuting from Hampshire.

At the thirty-eight-year point, he seamlessly migrated to the CAA and on to the Accident Investigation Board, first in Victoria Square and later at Farnborough. He retired at the end of 2001 but kept his ATPL current until 2006. He still lectures at Cranfield on AIB subjects, using the Lockerbie investigation, which he drove, as his case-study. He serves one day a week in the Witness Service at Winchester Crown Court, drawing on his AIB experience of working sympathetically with witnesses to air accidents. His hobby is silversmithing, for which he attends the courses and workshop at West Dean College, Chichester.

Mick reckons that no one could ask for a better first tour than his in Borneo: 'Lovely country and people, all the responsibility that you could ask for at age twenty-one, plenty of flying – and making a difference.' Even today, he still wears the watch he bought in Changi Village.

Ian Morgan – Whirlwind pilot, 110, 103 and 225 Squadrons RAF

Following his time on the staff at CFS(H) Ian moved on to instruct on the Wessex OCU at Odiham, thence to 72 Squadron, also at Odiham, as Training Officer before a brief spell as Wing Examiner.

Then, in 1969, he was selected for an exchange posting to the USAAC at Fort Rucker, Alabama training pilots on Huey helicopters for Vietnam. It was a strange situation in that many of the instructors were warrant officers and Ian, although still a Flight Lieutenant, had the seniority to be appointed second-in-command of a US Army training regiment with some eighty-eight aircraft on strength. It was a challenge which he thoroughly enjoyed.

After promotion to Squadron Leader, Ian had just one more flying tour, as Deputy CFI Middle Wallop. He married at thirty-five and took his new wife to Hong Kong and a staff job in the Joint Secretariat, working on a range of sensitive issues with the Hong Kong government.

He attended Staff College in 1979, after which spells at HQ 38 Group and at HQ STC preceded three tours at MoD. He was promoted to Wing Commander and moved to Air Plans where he co-ordinated the RAF's long-term costs. In his final MoD appointment, with responsibility for drafting the RAF Management Plan and a system for Performance Reporting against its required standards, he took an MBA.

Armed with that he retired from the RAF at the age of fifty-five and became CEO of a professional association of lawyers, accountants and bankers specializing in Private Client Trust Law, with offices in Jermyn Street. A move to the field of private equity saw him working on the acquisition of a number of corporate and family businesses until 2008 when the international credit crisis led him to head for final retirement.

He has a son and daughter and lives contentedly between the Pennines and the Dales in Yorkshire.

John Davy – Whirlwind pilot, 103, 225 and 110 Squadrons RAF

After the instructor's course at CFS, and before reaching the age of twenty-four, John had put in a stint at No 2 FTS, RAF Syerston, and then returned to CFS to join the staff. In 1974 he became one of the youngest squadron leaders in the RAF and 1976 found him at Valley as OC the SAR Training Squadron, reunited with the Whirlwind 10 (and also managing to get airborne in the Hawk jet trainer).

He married his schooldays' sweetheart (Chunky Lord stood up as his Best Man) and when, in 1982, he took his thirty-eight-year option to retire (resisting all blandishments to stay and gain promotion) he had completed twenty years of service – his flying skills well outweighing all the black-marks for individualism that had been amassed on his F1369 Personal Reports.

His entrepreneurial career then took off. In his last posting, at the MoD, he had managed, in the evenings and at weekends, to set up Specialized Flying Training Ltd, commuting Friday evening to Monday morning to the Middle East. When he left the Service he eventually based the company in Carlisle, operating Gazelle helicopters and the Slingsby Firefly. He acquired the Slingsby company and developed the turbine version of the Firecracker. He was responsible from 1980–87 for Iraqi Army Air Cooperation, employing many who had been his bosses in the RAF (including Chunky in 1983). In another twist of fate, in the Helicopter Museum at Weston-super-Mare, there's an ex-Queen's Flight Whirlwind on display, one that was once owned by the Davy Enterprizes.

In 2011, his usinesses continue to flourish and he spends some of his leisure time flying a Hornet Moth out of White Waltham.

David Reid – Whirlwind pilot, 225 and 110 Squadrons RAF

After leaving the Far East at the end of 1966, David's four-month instructor's course at Tern Hill was on the Sioux helicopter. His brother happened to be on an exchange posting at CFS(H) from the AAC at the same time, and flying

Dave Reid at rotary simulator consoles, RAF Benson, March 2011 (still there at time of writing). (CAEATS)

the Sioux, they flew together in the Sioux *Tomahawks* aerobatics display team. He found his true niche in instructing, gaining the coveted A1 Instructor Category and flying 450–500 hours a year.

And it got even better. David completed the Empire Test Pilot's Course in 1971 and remained at Boscombe Down to become the lead test pilot on the Gazelle development and Release to Service flying programme. In 1975 he moved to RAF Odiham to join 33 Squadron as the Training Officer, flying the Puma, and after a further two years he was posted as an RAF Exchange Officer Test Pilot to the Canadian Forces Flight Test Centre at CFB Cold Lake, Alberta, Canada.

Shortly after his arrival at Cold Lake, David had another close shave similar to his Borneo experience with the Whirlwind. Whilst waiting in dispersal for his first flight in a Canadian Forces Twin Huey, the crash bells rang – the helicopter he was to fly in had lost a rotor and the crew had been killed. Subsequently he completed a successful flying tour in Canada and returned to ETPS in 1980 as a Tutor and then Senior Tutor, for which he was awarded a Queen's Commendation and the Royal Aeronautical Society's Alan Marsh Medal for services to test flying.

In due course he attended RAF Staff College at Bracknell, brushing up on reading and writing skills, before putting in two tours in Whitehall. He worked on Operational Requirements for new RAF aircraft programmes including NH90, Lynx Mk 7 and 9, SAR Sea King Mk3a, Merlin Mk3 and Islander for the Army Air Corps. After a further two tours in MoD he retired at fifty-five as a Wing Commander.

In his RAF career David completed over 5,000 flying hours and flew some fifty aircraft types (thirty-eight rotary and eleven fixed-wing). In 1992 he was the first UK Military Test Pilot to fly the Bell XV-15 proof-of-concept Tilt Rotor, the lead-in programme for the V-22 Osprey Tilt Rotor which is currently operated by the US Marine Corps.

In the late 1990s David, along with Fraser Skea and Rick Atkinson, was recruited onto the Serco team engaged to run the Medium Support Helicopter Aircrew Training Facility at RAF Benson, set up under a Private Finance Initiative between the MoD and the Montreal-based CAE Aircrew Training Services plc. He instructs on the Merlin simulator (at MoD he'd written the OR for the aircraft) and most months operates a control-console on a day-long joint-service exercise, the 'Thursday War', passing on lessons learnt from as far back as the 1960s' Borneo Campaign to today's rotary crews.

David takes a standards test every two years and his next will be in 2012. All being well he'll be operating helis well past his seventieth year – another half-century of aviation for a Borneo Boy, and counting. He finds the job at Benson highly rewarding but has no fears about facing retirement in due course. He vows to find something to keep him out of his long-suffering wife's hair: 'British Legion, golf, anything where I can interact with a group of people'.

Fraser Skea – Whirlwind pilot, 225 and 110 Squadrons RAF
Following his arrival home from Borneo in December 1966, Flying Officer Fraser Skea visited his parents for Christmas. But he had no time for repatriation blues as it was straight back to work in January and, as he says, 'In any event Tern Hill was not the real Air Force – it was more relaxed.'

He duly gained his Helicopter Instructor qualification on the Whirlwind 10, on which he totalled over 1,000 hours. He remained on rotaries – including an exchange tour with the USAF as an instructor on the Sikorsky HH 53, the 'Super Jolly Green Giant' – before retiring from the RAF as a Squadron Leader at his eighteen-year Option Point in 1979. He then flew with British Helicopters on North Sea operations for three-and-a-half years before spending no fewer than sixteen as a police helicopter pilot for the Sultan of Oman.

His Swedish wife, Kerstin, whom he had met while on an RAF tour in Cyprus, followed him on all those adventures, becoming mother to their two girls. In 1999 he moved to two years of less stressful duties as a lecturer on meteorology to APLH candidates at Kidlington Groundschool, near Oxford, before joining the Serco staff on the opening of the simulator facility at RAF Benson, as an instructor on the Puma. On retirement at the turn of 2012, Fraser, a grandfather to two little girls, had been continuously in helicopter-related work from 1963 – just short of fifty years.

Fraser Skea (right) retired in early 2011 and Rick Atkinson (left) followed him in March 2012. (CAEATS)

Ron Hepburn – Whirlwind pilot, 230 Squadron RAF

When Ron arrived at Odiham from Borneo in June 1965, he took repatriation leave until the end of July when, there being no Whirlwinds on base, and his Short Service Commission due to complete in September, he was allowed to begin studying for his commercial licences. He already had an arrangement with Alan Bristow Helicopters and, on demob, started with Bristow on the Hiller 360 on a contract to train AAC pilots at Middle Wallop.

In RAF service Ron had accumulated suficient fixed-wing hours to take a post with BEA in Glasgow on the Heron Air Ambulance and later on the Viscount. He got his first command in 1978 and captained with BEA and BA the Tristar, the BAC111 ('swooping over East Berlin en route Tegel at full noisy 'one-eleven chat') and the Boeing 757. After four more years with Bryman, out of London City with the Dash7, followed by Air Bristol back on the BAC111, he retired in 1999. In a moment of bathos his final commercial flight ended up with his aircraft being impounded at Shannon as surety against the company's unpaid fuel bills.

Meantime Ron had begun flying with 12 Air Experience Flight (12AEF) at Turnhouse and 6AEF at Benson, on the Chipmunk and Tutor. He flew with them until December 2000 by which time he had flown with some 4,500 cadets in over 2,000 hours. So, until final retirement, this Borneo Boy flew for a living for no fewer than thirty-nine years, accumulating over 17,000 hours in all. And his logbook is not complete yet – he is now a member of a group of ex-BA pilots flying a Chipmunk at Old Warden, a Chipmunk that was once with Glasgow UAS.

Pete Chadwick – Whirlwind pilot, 230 Squadron RAF

When Pete Chadwick left 230 Squadron at Labuan at the end of 1965, after having survived no fewer than three fuel-computer run-downs, he was posted to 202 Squadron at Leconfield and immediately assigned to the Whirlwind SAR Flight at Acklington. In February 1967 a mishap to the coach bringing young ladies from Morpeth Hospital to an Officers' Mess ball resulted in a fleet of cars driven by gallant pilots rushing to the rescue. Pete was one of them and Joan, chaperone to the girls, chose to climb into his passenger seat. They were married in October the same year.

SAR formed the basis of Pete's thirty-one-year RAF career. He introduced the Sea King to the RAF and ran the newly-formed OCU while still only thirty-two years old. He then was appointed to command 202 Squadron where he earned an AFC. After Staff College and a job at the RAF College, in 1985 he was promoted Wing Commander and became OC SAR Wing at Finningley for the three years 1988–90. After three more years on the staff at 18 Group, he took an offer of redundancy in 1994, aged forty-nine. But, being a self-reliant Borneo man, he built a new career in Health Centre Management and found a niche as an RAF AEF pilot until the age of sixty-five. He and Joan have a married daughter, and a son who is himself an RAF wing commander (his wife is also a pilot, on the Tristar fleet). There are three grandchildren.

Hugh Lake – Whirlwind pilot and Training Officer, 225 and 103 Squadrons RAF

After leaving Seletar on 21 December 1965, fifty weeks after arriving, Hugh did the one-year course at ETPS during which his wife presented him with a daughter. In a tour of three years at Boscombe Down he spent time in France as test pilot on the new Puma helicopter, for which he earned a Queen's Commendation. He handed this work over to a 225 Squadron colleague, Mick Charles, before going on a two-year accompanied exchange to the AETE test centre in Canada. There he was promoted, before returning to Boscombe as senior Pilot on D, the helicopter test, Squadron. Other colleagues from 225 Squadron, Dave Reid, Martin Mayer and Brian Skillcorn also joined D. For his work on testing de-icing systems for rotaries, Hugh was awarded the MBE.

There then followed a long spell at MoD – first in Flight Safety and then on helicopter OR where he was heavily involved in negotiating within MoD and with Boeing in the US for the purchase of the first Chinooks for the RAF – twenty-six of them at £3m each. He also worked on the development of the SAR Sea King Mk3 and, promoted to Wing Commander, became Project Officer for Puma Development. He attended the Air Warfare course before returning for projects relating to the new UK Air Defence System: radars and sensors and equipping the bunker at High Wycombe. He retired in 1979, after twenty-six years' service and 'not many dull moments'.

The many Whitehall tours had proved right the decision to acquire a house in Camden (where Hugh's wife worked as head of the Maths Department in a girls' school) from which he could lay the groundwork for a subsequent entrepreneurial career. He had been headhunted to join the burgeoning computer-based systems industry from where he launched his own risk-management consultancy. This he sold in 2006, setting up a supplement to his pension 'quite nicely'.

Hugh says that Borneo and especially 225 Squadron had, as with many others, left a permanent impression on him. He can point to three legacies in particular. First, the incident with the melons was not only a lesson about weighing up a cargo before starting off, it also highlighted the huge mark-up on goods as they proceed along an inefficient wholesale/retail chain from producer to consumer – useful knowledge for a management consultancy career. Second, the need in the Whirlwind to keep full left pedal applied in the hot and high hover resulted in his 'left knee still giving me gyp'. And lastly, 'If you train young people properly and don't tell them that it is difficult they will just get on and do it – very well!'

Mike McKinley – Whirlwind pilot, 225 and 103 Squadrons RAF

When Mike was posted from 103 Squadron in December 1965 he qualified as a fixed-wing instructor on the Chipmunk at CFS and returned to the RAF College Cranwell Flying Training Wing. In 1967 he joined the Examining Wing at CFS and served there through to 1970. After a tour on Pumas at Odiham he had a spell in Northern Ireland where, of particular interest, was the continual resupply of the base at Crossmaglen. There his young brother was in the Royal Green Jackets and he once took Mike on foot patrol.

It was in Ulster that he was among the first to use the latest in Infra-Red equipment, sending back pictures of bodies lying in lofts, tunnels being dug in the Maze prison and hostiles meeting in farmhouses. To some extent that echoed his experiences with the SS11 missiles that were the latest kit in Borneo.

Following retirement at the thirty-eight-year point in 1979, Mike worked in publishing. In the late 80s he spent five years in residence in Singapore but then a series of happy coincidences brought him back to the world of aviation in 1990. He got a year's work instructing *ab initio* AAC pilots on the Chipmunk at Middle Wallop and six years as an assessor of army aircrew candidates at the same base. By the turn of the century two of their four daughters had presented him and his wife Clare, comfortably retired to Oxfordshire, with five grandchildren. But still his flying career continued, instructing on Chipmunks and Tiger Moths at local airfields. Mike McKinley is another Borneo Boy with close on half a century of piloting to his name.

Bob Turner – Whirlwind pilot, 225 and 103 Squadrons RAF

After Tern Hill in 1966, and a spell in helicopter instruction, Bob Turner returned in 1969 to the SH force with postings as QHI on 18 and 72 Squadrons at Odiham, operating the Wessex. In 1972 he moved to Hong Kong as the Whirlwinds there were replaced with the Wessex. Next came ground tours at HQ 38 Group and the MoD followed by an exchange tour with the USAF flying the large Sikorsky HH53 in the combat rescue role. After this he attended the Royal Navy Staff College Course at Greenwich and then was appointed Personal Staff Officer to the AOC 38 Group and later AOC 1 Group. He found this work particularly fascinating in that it involved operating transport, SH and ground attack aircraft and also because his tour encompassed the Falklands War.

By 1984 Wing Commander Turner was commanding 230 (Tiger) Squadron at Gütersloh in West Germany operating the Puma, once again in the army support role. In 1986, after this succession of superb postings, Bob thought that 'his future in the RAF couldn't be any better than his past', so he decided to exercise the option he had to retire from the RAF on his forty-fourth birthday.

After moving back to the UK and settling in Clevedon, he realized that after twenty-two years of married life in the RAF, with so many house moves and several lettings of their own house, he had acquired considerable expertise in property management. He set up a management company operating from home and rapid growth meant that within a few years he was employing five people in his backroom. This resulted in the purchase of a proper office building in Clevedon and, when Bob retired for the second time in 2009 and the agency was sold, it had grown to ten employees and was managing some 500 properties.

However, the main purpose of the business was to finance his first interest – aviation. As a longstanding keen aeromodeller, he had seen in Germany that many model clubs there had their own small airfields and he resolved to create a similar facility in the West Country. A newspaper advert in 1987 to initiate the project attracted some seventy local enthusiasts who each agreed to invest £100 towards the purchase of suitable land. After considerable work, in 1989 Woodspring Wings Model Aircraft Club opened its own mini airfield and now, with twenty-seven acres, runways, taxiways, club house and car park, it is one of the best-equipped clubs in the UK. Bob and the club have organized annual air displays since 1990.

Bob and Carole are proud of their family. Their son Andrew followed his father into the RAF and arrived on 230 Squadron as a junior pilot about a year after Bob had left as CO. He has progressed rapidly and was Station Commander at Odiham from 2007 to 2009 and, in 2010, the initiating Commander of the Joint Aviation Group in Afghanistan before becoming Air Commodore on the staff at the UK's Permanent Joint Headquarters (PJHQ).

In 2002 Andrew and the family arranged a Tiger Moth flight for Bob as a gift for his sixtieth birthday. The wheel had come full circle.

Dick Holmes – Whirlwind pilot, 230 Squadron RAF

Dick left Borneo with fond memories of the Whirlwind, not least its reliability, and that of its Gnome engine. He points out that in his year in Confrontation there were no fatalities and the squadron lost only one aircraft – that due to engine failure in the high hover.

Back in the UK, and CFS(H), he qualified as an instructor while still only twenty-one before an exchange tour with the FAA, on the Wessex with 845 NAS. His next step was to introduce the Puma to RAF rotary service, first as a QHI at the OCU and then as Training Officer on 33 Squadron at RAF Benson.

In 1976 Dick returned to Borneo with his wife and child for two years of Huey operation with the Royal Brunei Malay Regiment and re-acquaintance with the Sabah and Sarawak mountain ranges – this time with a great deal more power to spare.

Returned to the RAF, he joined No 72 Wessex Squadron. After a year, in which he was 'close to being blown up by the IRA' at Warrenpoint, he became the pilot on the SD Flight. After eighteen months the flight converted to the Puma helicopter on 33 Squadron. That was not a success and Dick ended up instructing on Pumas on 240 OCU for a couple of years.

After a stint of training at Shawbury on the Gazelle, he put in his one staff tour – at the old enemy, 38 Group – before four years back on the Puma at 33 Squadron and five more of VIP flying on 32 Squadron Gazelles and Twin Squirrels out of Northolt.

It only remained for Dick to spend two years on the ground with the Handling Squadron at Boscombe Down producing Pilots' Notes, 'hanging on', as he says, 'to get my pension'. He then retired at fifty-five years of age in the rank of Flight Lieutenant, having served and survived close on thirty-eight honourable years as RAF professional rotary aircrew.

On retirement, he and his wife bought a 250-year-old converted grist mill in the West Country and, on a self-build basis, added a workshop, a sun room, and a small hydro-electric turbine producing power for the mill and the National Grid. They also made a garden out of an acre of wheat field. With two daughters and three grandchildren, Dick's life is never dull.

Martin Mayer – Whirlwind pilot, 225 and 103 Squadrons RAF

After the instructor's course on the Whirlwind 10 at Tern Hill in early 1967, Martin joined Number 2 Training Squadron as a QHI and married Jennifer, a WRAF officer he had met at Seletar. He achieved an A2 Category and, in July 1968, was moved to CFS(H) as a tutor.

Two years later, and still a Flying Officer, he was on the course at ETPS, unique in making it to Test Pilot School having flown just the two types, the Jet Provost and the Whirlwind 10. By 1972, now a Flight Lieutenant, he had added

many more types to his list including the Puma. He was Project Pilot for the acceptance trials which
earned him the AFC before becoming an instructor on the OCU at Odiham.

From 1975–76, as a Squadron Leader, he was a Flight Commander on 18 Squadron with the Wessex 2 (equivalent to the RN Wessex 5) at Gütersloh before returning for two years to ETPS as a tutor. 1979 saw him doing well at Staff College and in 1980–81 he served as PSO to the AOC 38 Group at RAF Upavon. His next tour was as the Wing Commander OC 7 Squadron (Chinooks) before becoming Naval and Air Advisor at the British High Commission in Nairobi in 1985–88, coupled with Defence Advisor to Tanzania and Zanzibar.

There was a milestone in 1989 when Martin became the first with a rotary background to command ETPS. In that job he had thirteen aircraft types to fly and was qualified to instruct test-pilot students on five rotary and three fixed-wing types of aircraft.

Then, aged fifty-two, he saw an advert in *Flight Magazine* for an AEF commander at RAF Woodvale. He applied and, eschewing promotion to group captain, took post as OC 10AEF, until final retirement in 2002.

He is a Fellow of both the Royal Aeronautical Society and the Society of Experimental Test Pilots. He had had almost forty years of a thoroughly rewarding and fulfilled flying career and, with children coming along in 1968, 1970 and 1976, declares himself the 'luckiest and happiest man in the world'.

Fred Hoskins – Whirlwind pilot and OC, 103 Squadron RAF

Fred Hoskins handed over command of 203 Squadron at the end of March 1968 and reported for duties as a General Staff Officer 2 at Headquarters Army Strategic Command, Wilton. After organizing army exercises overseas and air support for exercises in the UK for a little more than a year, he was back at Tern Hill for refresher flying on Sioux and Whirlwind before converting to the Wessex at Odiham and becoming familiar with the Scout at Middle Wallop. All that was in preparation for taking post from October 1969 to November 1970 as Officer Commanding Flying Wing for the Gulf Air Force, based in Sharjah.

While there, on 1 January 1970, he was promoted Wing Commander and the first six months of 1971 saw him a student on Number 21 Air Warfare Course, RAF College of Air Warfare, Manby. Next came the Helicopter Operational Training Squadron at Odiham and conversion to the Puma HC1, prior to taking command of 33 Squadron and seeing service in Northern Ireland.

From August 1973 to September 1975 Fred was immersed in Whitehall, working on Operational Requirements for helicopters and fixed-wing transport aircraft. In this post he was responsible for preparing the Air Staff Requirement for the Search and Rescue Sea King helicopter.

That task completed, Fred took premature voluntary release in November 1975 having, after thirty years and three months' RAF service, accumulated 3,665 flying hours in a score of aircraft types.

Following the RAF, he became a solicitor until final retirement in Dorset in 1996 when he devoted his efforts to charitable organizations, including SSAFA. For these, long after he left the RAF, he was awarded an OBE in the Civil Division.

He was Chairman of the RAF Cranwell Apprentices' Association from 1996 to 2004, and has become 'Honorary Father' of the Old Rotors.

Paul Moran – Engine Fitter, 230 Squadron RAF

Following 230 Squadron, Sergeant Paul Moran's RAF career led from the Andover at Thorney Island to the Hercules at Lyneham and Colerne. He worked on XV179, the ill-fated Hercules shot down in Iraq in January 2005 but well before that calamity, in December 1979 and after twenty-five years' service, Paul had left the RAF in the rank of Chief Technician. He joined the staff of Wiltshire College as Principal Technician and part-time lecturer, spending another twenty-five years there until retirement to Chippenham, Wiltshire in 2004.

David Lanigan – Belvedere pilot, 66 Squadron RAF

Dave's next flying tours were on SAR, first on the Whirlwind at RAF Leconfield in Yorkshire and then the Wessex from RAF Valley in Anglesey. He found the Wessex particularly exciting, especially in the mountains in cloud or at night. As in Borneo, the trick was to approach slowly and sideways (the Wessex could fly at 30 knots sideways) before creeping up the slope, looking out for references from the open cockpit window. He was pleased to have two engines again. He became the display and VIP pilot, and authorizing officer.

He completed over 200 rescue missions during seven years on SAR before deciding, still a Flight Lieutenant at his thirty-eight-year option point, that the military was not for him. He approached the civilian rotary market and, finding himself almost spoilt for choice, decided that Bristows, the largest operator in the sector, would provide support and security. He had twelve years with them on North Sea ops before going freelance, working under contract to BA in the Falklands and the UN in Croatia. His last flight was in 1996 when, aged fifty-five, he retired to deepest Dorset, and an Open University degree. He now keeps busy with Royal Aeronautical Society and Christchurch Aviation Society business, and active on local rambles with his wife, Ann. He keeps up to date on helicopter affairs and is proud to see the achievements of the Chinook, in so many ways the heir to the Belvedere twin-rotor legacy.

Rick Atkinson – Whirlwind pilot, 110 Squadron RAF

Following his post-Borneo exchange posting to the AAC at Middle Wallop, Rick moved on to West Germany to fly the French Alouette 2 helicopter from the AAC base at Bunde, spending two years 'barn-storming around just about the whole of the country'.

Later on, Rick found himself flying a Wessex on a tortuous ferry trip to RAF Wildenrath in West Germany. Bad weather caused delays and he arrived late on a Friday afternoon, in fading light, to find the base virtually deserted save for an Officers' Mess full of women teachers having a good time. One of those teachers took a shine to him and they eventually married.

He became a QHI and, as well as the Wessex, was to fly anti-tank Gazelles with the Kuwaiti Air Force and Pumas in Belize, commanding 1563 Flight for which he was awarded the AFC. As a staff officer, his final job in the RAF was, as he puts it, 'to switch out the lights and hand the keys to the Chinese military' during the hand-over of Hong Kong in 1997.

Rick is a civilian instructor with the Serco team at the CAE helicopter simulators at RAF Benson. He is the Groundschool Senior Instructor and two of his colleagues are Frazer Skea and Dave Reid who were Whirwind pilots with him in Borneo all those years ago. He also operates in the Instructor Operating Station (IOS) on the Puma Dynamic Mission Simulator (DMS) and for this role all instructors are checked annually by the RAF STANEVAL trappers. Rick is another Borneo man with a record of half a century in rotary aviation.

Colin Cummings – Station Supply Officer, RAF Labuan

In March 1967 Colin left Labuan for a posting to Hong Kong and at the end of that year was involved in the transfer of half-a-dozen RAF Whirlwinds from Malaysia to 28 Squadron RAF at Kai Tak. After a full thirty-year career, he retired from the RAF as a Wing Commander and worked as a management consultant. Following a period in the Reserve, he re-made his links with the ATC, in the Daventry Branch. Nine years ago he was introduced to Rugby School CCF and became a Flight Lieutenant VR(T) and assisted the school's masters by lecturing on aviation subjects. Then, on the departure of the then RAF Section head, Colin took over. He is now the second-in-command of the entire Rugby School CCF. He attends every Thursday in term-time and at weekends when there is a camp. He went on an Air Cadets Leadership Course at Cranwell.

For Colin the wheel has thus come full circle – a circle of fifty-two years. In the years since he joined the ATC in 1958 he served in the RAF from 1963 to 1994 before joining the Reserve of RAF Officers, followed by RAF Reserve Wing Admin Officer and finally becoming a VR(T) officer.

He is the dynamo behind the Old Rotors, which comprise a list of close on ninety names, all held on his computer and all of whom have had some involvement with RAF rotary operations. There are no subs and no AGMs. They meet from time to time, at least annually, usually on a visit to an operational service base.

Colin also finds time to publish under the name of Nimbus Publishing, his subjects including Airborne Warfare, Accident Investigations and Second World War Flying Training.

John Richards – Scout pilot, 656 Squadron AAC

After completing his two-year tour at Kluang, John was posted for a second stint abroad, in West Germany. Staff Sergeant Richards was then seconded to RAF Tern Hill for training as an instructor and, within a year achieved a B1 rating. After a further six months he progressed to A2 and, in 1972, was

John Richards renews acquaintance with Scout at Museum of Army Flying, Middle Wallop, June 2011. (Author)

awarded a Special Regular Commission, in the rank of full lieutenant. Within the next dozen years his career blossomed and by the time his twenty-five years of service in the AAC were up, his final posting being to the Tri-Service Rotary Standards Team, he had been promoted Captain. He had also become qualified to wear not only the British Army Flying Badge but those of Italy, France and the USA.

Then, in 1984, John was approached by the RAF who were keen to use his rotary skills. He transferred in the rank of Flight Lieutenant and served for ten years as a Staff QFI at CFS(H) and as an A Category VIP captain on 32 (The Royal) Squadron at Northolt, ending up as the Squadron Leader commanding the rotary section. By the time he retired, he had accumulated 11,400 flying hours on eleven different types, surviving 3,500 of those on the challenging Scout AH1. Following demob in 1994 John was able to indulge his passion for yachting – but he also took a gliding course at Lasham airfield and celebrated his seventieth birthday with a final solo.

In 2004 the King and Government of Malaysia issued the Pingat Jasa Malaysia (Malaysian Service Medal) intended for British and Commonwealth veterans of the Malayan Emergency and Indonesian Confrontation. This was 'in recognition of their distinguished chivalry, gallantry, sacrifice and loyalty in contributing to the freedom and independence of Malaysia'. In the UK many thousands have been awarded, heroically administered by the Malaya & Borneo Veterans Association. Here, in 2008, Mick Charles receives his from a Colonel of the Malaysian Army. (Mike Marriott)

A Week in the Life of Colin Ford

A week in the life of Colin Ford

Colin Ford, 22, is pilot of a Whirlwind helicopter, stationed with 103 Squadron at Seletar, Singapore. He is a typical Royal Air Force Officer. This is a typical week in his life.

Flying Officer, Royal Air Force

Could this be the life for you?
Read and find out

MONDAY Week starts 700 miles from regular base, "on detachment" in Labuan, North Borneo. Country hereabouts is true impenetrable jungle, movement almost impossible on land, but helicopters can just about go anywhere, land anywhere, do anything. Task for today, supply run for troops near Indonesian frontier. After briefing, fly to forward airstrip to pick up small part of load already parachute-dropped there (in one-ton lots): food for 10 men, letters from home, anti-malaria pills, spare radio batteries, etc. Then deep, deep into jungle to deliver it. Usual warm welcome from Army.

TUESDAY Long flight from Labuan over jungle—map on knee but curious how familiar terrain becomes: you can soon tell one mountain, one valley, one river-bend from another. Objective, a forward platoon location, to put in a new Section of Gurkhas. Wonderful fighting men—small, brown, muscular, and very tough indeed—but they give you a smile that goes twice round their heads.

WEDNESDAY Deep into interior of Borneo, to a point where two rivers meet: a village of the Murut people—to keep regular rendezvous with Army, and convey doctor. (Fever was reported, he wants to take blood samples, etc.) Village is 3 longhouses and 1 soccer pitch; helicopter puts down between goalposts, all 300 inhabitants come out to see. Men (in shorts) endlessly shake hands; women and girls (mostly in tunics and sarongs) hang back, shy and silent, watching; small boys (some in nothing at all) chatter like magpies, cluster round, smiling, laughing, peering fascinated into camera. *Penghulu* (village headman) appears —quick, lively very animated man with intricately tattooed forearm, invites by gesture into his house. Scrupulously clean, but very bare—no furniture. Hot sweet coffee from big black iron kettle. You say '*Terima Kaseh*' (Thank you).

THURSDAY Half-hour flight to Brunei, past new Mosque (*beautiful:* white marble and a glittering gold dome—strange contrast with waterborne town jostling round it— houses on stilts, right over water). Refuel at town airfield and pick up patrol of Special Air Service— the Chindits of the jungle today. They carry weapons and food for 10 days; with air supply may be in jungle that many weeks. Long trip to forward area, where old patrol lean, bearded, pale) waiting on river bank, ready to go back to Brunei. Thence to Labuan airfield, quick lunch, fly back to Singapore by Argosy.

FRIDAY Home comforts again: brick-built Mess, civilised furniture and food (choice is *immense*), air-conditioned 'Ops' rooms, feeling of positive luxury! But serious training to do— two air-sea rescue training assignments: first, pick up 'survivor' from dinghy, transfer to launch; second, pick up same 'survivor' from deck of ship, prepare to rush to hospital. Repeat several times. Evening, check over car: could not take to Labuan, had been standing 4 weeks in garage.

SATURDAY On standby yesterday, so free today. Late breakfast, collect girl-friend, motor to Singapore city. Buy Thai silk to send home, browse through record library, lunch with brother-officer. Bathe in club pool, laze about, back to Mess for tea, shower, change of clothes and off for the evening to open-air eating-house in chinatown.

SUNDAY a day for relaxing. Meet friends and their families coming out of church. Spend whole afternoon in camp pool. Then, 7.30 to 8.30, the usual Sunday-night get-together in the Mess, chatting with Squadron wives and friends. After dinner, open-air cinema. Under the huge clear star-spangled sky, with tropical night-noises all about, movies are strangely remote, realities of R.A.F. Service seem very close. Flying, the supreme exhilaration, is but the means to an end. In small but vital ways, R.A.F. helps new nations to emerge, old neighbours to be better friends, whole world to be a safer place. All this is work that wants doing.

Colin Ford went to Westcliff High School, Leigh-on-Sea, and joined the R.A.F. at 18. Initially, his commission will take him to age 38. Meanwhile, at 22, he has over £1000 a year, and a life that anybody might find fascinating.

Your G.C.E. could be the first step to a career just like his. Think about it. And ask yourself: what other profession could so well *use* the talents you bring to your career—or give you such interest, such variety, such a high standard of living?

Appendix 3

Self Athorisation Certificates

R.A.F. Form 1150

MEMORANDUM

FROM	TO
OC 103 SQN (DET)	Fg. OFF. C. FORD
RAF KUCHING	103 SQN

Our ref. _____ Your ref. _____
Tel. No. _____
Ext. _____ Date 24 Sep 65 Dated _____

SUBJECT: FLIGHT AUTHORISATION

You are hereby empowered to authorise flights from Red 37 by yourself or any other pilot of this squadron detached from Kuching to Red 37 as follows:

a. Operational tasks as required

b. Training recce sorties

c. Night medevac or casevac tasks provided that:
    1. You are captain
    2. The take off from the LP is before dark.

Signature of Sender _____
Name in Block Letters F.D HOSKINS
Rank/Appointment SQN LDR/OC 103

NOTES
1.—Continue overleaf if necessary, annotating "P.T.O.".
2.—This form is normally to be completed in manuscript.
MsC 51-8371

This certificate allows :—

.... Fg. Off. C. G. Ford .... of 103 Sqdn.
to authorise his own flights whilst away from his present station, under the terms of Air Ministry Flyin. Order No. 4?

This certifiate is valid only while the above pilot is in the Far East Air Force.

Date 8-8-63

_____ AVM
A.O.C. No. 224 Group.

Appendix 4

Mike McKinley's Flying Logbook Extracts

Juy 1965

June 1965 was the month of the 225 Squadron 'stress test', when a total of 885 flying hours was flown. For Mike, the high level and variety of activity continued through the first three weeks of July:

1. The SAS insertion, two-up with John Davy on the 2nd of the month was followed a week later by their extraction. In between 'We speculated what they were up to!'

2. The 'Bako Run' on the 4th would have been a standard, regular re-supply job.

3. The 5th and 9th saw instrument, night and Engine-Off Landing (EOL) practice with Hugh Lake. Mike says, 'For EOL's, although we didn't actually stop the engine we did disengage the rotor – below a certain height there was no going round again.'

4. Training the soldiery in roping, abseiling and winch work was important – as with the Singapore Guards' Regiment on the 15th of the month.

5. Mike says, 'Rescuing each other from greater or lesser dangers was fairly regular but two in one month was unusual.' The SAR mission on the 4th was to lift out an Army Scout crew that had come to grief near the border and the one on the 17th to assist Brian Skillicorn when he lost his tail rotor and landed intact in a very tight clearing.

6. On the 19th Mike flew a trooping mission in the midst of the insurgencies on the Serian road.

Presentations made to 225 Squadron RAF during their two years in Borneo

Shields

1. King's Royal Rifle Corps
2. 3rd Squadron Malaysian Engineers
3. 1st Bn Green Jackets (43rd and 52nd)
4. Argyll and Sutherland Highlanders
5. Queen's Royal Irish Hussars
6. 656 Squadron Army Air Corps
7. 84 Survey Squadron
8. Hadia Daripada
9. 42 Commando Royal Marines
10. 4th Royal Malaysian Regiment
11. 7th KEO Gurkha Rifles
12. 6th Queen Elizabeth's Own Gurkha Rifles
13. 7th Royal Australian Regiment
14. HMS *Albion*
15. A Company, 40 Commando Royal Marines
16. 2nd Bn Parachute Regiment
17. Special Air Service Regiment
18. Scots Guards
19. 2nd King's Edward's Own Gurkhas
20. 10th Princess Mary's Own Gurkhas
21. No. 9 Company Irish Guards

Other

22. Stick presented by 1st Bn Royal Ulster Rifles
23. *Kukri* presented by 1st Bn 10th PMO Gurkha Rifles
24. Picture from 2/2nd KEO Gurkhas

All items, together with three photographs of the Officers and Airmen of 225 Squadron, and the Squadron History, were sent for storage at No.7 MU, Quedgely.

Extracted from RAF F540 Operations Record Book

Notes

1. Of the remaining nine who stayed at Swinderby, one was posted to Hunter fighters, one to Canberra medium bombers, one went to Central Flying School and no fewer than six finished up on the V-Force.
2. The wind was critical. In gusty conditions the Whirlwind's limit for starting rotors was 30 knots.
3. The Mk4 was the main compass, fed by a detection unit in the tail boom. There was an E2B magnetic as a standby. Over level ground these would guide the pilots along timed legs between known points.
4. Search And Rescue Beacon Equipment
5. Fuel stocks were positioned at many forward heavily-fortified airstrips able to accommodate small single-engine aircraft and often manned by army Company HQs and close to hubs of civilian population. Others were small, unmanned and remote, and able to accept only helicopters.
6. Peter Davis was gazetted for the MC in 1947, as a lieutenant in the Gurkhas. Under fire in the turmoil on the North-West Frontier, he'd rescued a wounded soldier – single-handedly.
7. Nowadays, Long Pa Sia sits in a conservation area, protecting the rare *kerangas* heath forest, which grows on sandy soil, supporting orchids, rhododendrons and pitcher plants, many unique to the area.
8. Many such medevacs were flown in the campaign, becoming known as 'stork missions'.
9. Long Banga airstrip was overlooked by a 200-feet tall ironwood tree with root buttresses wide apart, room enough to park a Land Rover. Felling would mean excavating the strip so the tree stayed in place.
10. It took the British and their allies one week at the most to bring troops to the Borneo border from Singapore – for the Indonesians from Java and Sumatra, a similar move could take up to 3 months.
11. Using an estimation of wind-drift to calculate a heading to steer and flying by the compass to make it good – a method used in cloud and all well and good if you're sure of the height of the ground below!
12. For some protection against small-arms fire, a 30lb steel plate had been fashioned to fit under the pilots' seat cushions – detachable and often dispensed with where critical for payload maximization.
13. Geoff is a stalwart of the British Legion and a networker supreme. Every year veterans of Argosy Borneo and Cyprus Detachments, the ARDET, meet under his benevolent care in the Sergeants' Mess at RAF Benson, where he is Patron of the station's Heritage Room.
14. Whirlwind pilots on occasion gave rides to the native kids. Ron Hepworth remembers once carrying more than a dozen of them in the cabin. 'No casual passengers,' he says, 'were ever strapped in.'
15. From that Ba Kelalan op, Colin liberated a 105mm brass shell-case that now serves as an umbrella-stand in his hallway.

16. Colin Ford tells of an earlier familiarization visit to the RCC at Changi. There, logbooks contained many examples of aircraft, some quite large, which over the years had disappeared and never been found despite 'knowing pretty accurately' where they had gone down.

17. The drill for clearing those was to watch out for wires, before abseiling a brave man down to check for mines and other obstacles.

18. According to reports, Sam Smith had a parrot which distinguished itself by going on a mission in a Twin Pioneer – it sat on the luggage rack and got airsick. And a pet macaw kept by another man was a hazard for all – it defended itself simply by rapping any attacker on the skull with its formidable bill.

19. Those 80 inches would have represented a peak month for rainfall. For comparison, in its wettest month (August) Manchester gets an average of some 20 inches.

20. At all the DZs, if there was an airdrop coming, the helis would make themselves scarce to avoid wayward 'chutes. But they'd hang around at a safe distance, on stand-by should one of the transports get into trouble. And both fixed and rotary-wing aircraft had to watch out for possible Indonesian ambush at all DZs and LPs.

21. Colin met his fiancée, Jan at Seletar sick-quarters, where she was a voluntary worker. He'd been at her parents' house – her father was a civil servant on Seletar base – when the switch was thrown on a curfew. He stayed for for two weeks – which became forty-seven years, and counting.

22. In this action, RAF Argosy transports provided airborne radio-relays for the ground forces and helicopters. Then with their Dart turboprops sounding very much like friendly Indonesian Hercules, the Argosies flew low to confuse the insurgents and help the troops flush them out.

23. This is a condition where, on the approach to landing, the helicopter settles into its own downwash. The resulting turbulent flow over a large area of the disk causes loss of rotor efficiency and a plunge to the ground. It is most likely to occur when landing downwind.

24. Bill Oliver was awarded the DFC (Distinguished Flying Cross) in the Birthday Honours List of June 1963, for services in Borneo, which included seeing Sycamore action in the Brunei Rebellion.

25. Fred Hoskins, OC 103 Sqn from September '65, says:, 'The SAS had a theory that the best way to avoid detection was to smell as much like the jungle animals as possible. By the end of a patrol they had acquired a sweet, sort of corpse-like odour.'

26. When in mid-campaign the filters were fitted, according to Colin Cummings, 'They did little else other than altering the aircraft's profile and adding eighty-four pounds in weight, reducing payload.'

27. Dave Collinson had graduated from the same Tern Hill course as Dave Reid and Fraser Skea.

28. The 'abseil tape', a continuous length of nylon, was developed for use in an emergency, complementing Jack Canham's looped multi-hoist system.

29. The shells came two to a box, weighing in at 165lb each, and the Whirlwind could carry ten of those in an underslung net. Reportedly, two Whirlwinds on one occasion spent a long afternoon hauling them between Long Semado and Ba Kelalan, consuming thirty barrels of fuel in the process.

30. Dave Reid and Fraser Skea had to teach him to drive, in the squadron Land Rover.

31. The Westland Scouts had been joined in the AAC by the Agusta-Bell Sioux light helicopter.

32. Colin came off shift at 1pm and then went with Jan to a wedding at Changi followed by the Summer Ball at Seletar. They watched the sun rise the next morning. He admits to having been somewhat tired.

33. A problem that arose from all that power was that the rotor blade did not have sufficient surface area to absorb it all, resulting in a slow turn to starboard on a full-power manoeuvre.

34. Mick Charles was another forced make an emergency landing on a beach, but under power. He was able to pick a spot above the seaweed line to avoid being caught by the high-tide and spent the night in a tropical paradise before watching the splendours of sunrise over the South China Sea.

35. King's Royal Rifle Corps

36. Helicopter support made it possible for the Green Jackets to hold down the whole area from Nibong to Gunong Gajek – a border sector of no less than 120 miles.

37. *The Last Campaign of the Rifle Brigade, Borneo 1965/66*

38. At the time Mike's father was Air Officer Commanding, Malta.

39. After leaving the RAF in 1969 Peter Davis joined the Abu Dhabi Defence Force and then moved to the Sultan of Oman's Air Force. He was awarded the Sultan's Distinguished Service Medal before being shot down and killed on 8 March 1975, aged forty-eight.

40. Fred was somewhat put out at the state of the maps of Borneo. In 1959 he and his colleagues had spent months in Canberras carrying out a major mapping exercise from Changi, evidently to little avail.

41. The Chief Technician who signed off XP237 as serviceable after its major service went before a Court Martial in Singapore. He was found guilty of negligence as it was discovered that there was no wire-locking on the nut. It must have been coming undone as Dave Reid was flying the air test.

42. The 225 Squadron stint in Kuching had already been extended a year. Dave Reid reckons that one of the reasons for its disbandment at the end of 1965 was the difficulty of managing staggered one- and two-year unaccompanied tours.

43. In the New Year's Honours list of 1966, Flight Sergeant Hood was awarded a Queen's Commendation for Valuable Services in the Air.

44. Messrs Bulford and Lord were awarded DFCs in the Birthday Honours 1966, for services in Borneo.

45. In time six of the Whirlwind pilots appearing in this story were to achieve promotion to wing commander, but none made it to group captain.

46. According to reports, they still are.

47. *Renjers* is the Malay for Rangers – Malaysian troops were increasing their Borneo footprint.

48. The full story of this casevac, along with other of Fred Hoskins's Borneo stories, can be found in *From Blue to Grey*, co-edited by Fred Hoskins himself (for details see Bibliography).

49. In 2012 variants of the Gnome are still in service (two powering Royal Navy and

RAF Sea King helicopters) and thus the engine has had well over fifty years of life. It was developed by GE in America as the T58 in the mid 1950s before being manufactured under licence in UK by Bristol Siddeley, who fitted a Lucas Industries-developed fuel control system. BS was absorbed by Rolls-Royce in 1966.

50. Although Kuching Court rolls bear witness to the fact that two babies at least were fathered with local maidens by 225 Squadron boys. All was dealt with properly – paternity was acknowledged and maintenance arrangements were made.

51. Air Transport Operations Centre – the Tasking Authority based at Brunei Joint HQ

52. At smaller forward bases toilet arrangements were more primitive. John Richards of the AAC mentions the hollow bamboo stake topped with a funnel, a device that was nicknamed 'desert rose' as it was constantly being watered and gave off a unique aroma.

53. That attitude had been severely tested in early 1965 when, operating out of Sibu, 845 NAS lost five aircraft between February and April, killing three pilots, two aircrewmen and eleven soldiers.

54. Lt Cdr Craig's diary extract is reproduced here with the kind permission of the Fleet Air Arm Museum Archive and Research Centre, RNAS Yeovilton.

55. Colin Ford makes the point that the RAF in the 1960s operated on the concept of missions from and to an airfield because that is what the overwhelming majority of RAF ops were, and not the independent, 'make-your-own-arrangements' operations that the helicopters found themselves in. The 209 Squadron Pioneers (especially the singles) were the only other RAF aircraft which came close to that type of operation.

56. This S/L John W. Price was known as 'Tail-Rotor' Price (he'd wiped the tail-rotor off both a Sycamore and a Whirlwind), not to be confused with S/L John L. 'Bathroom-Scales' Price (he'd set up the cargo-weighing procedure in Cyprus in 1961 while OC of 103 Squadron and its Sycamores).

57. Paul Moran has since identified his visitor as being 'Gus' Walker, who, in 1966, was Inspector General of the RAF. He was well-known for his genuine interest in the affairs of other ranks. Only a year after his Tawau visit, Sir George Augustus Walker was promoted Air Chief Marshal.

58. The 6,600-foot Batu Lawi was sacred to the *Dayaks*. Nevertheless, despite the twin peaks being a boon to navigation the pilots insisted on finding disrespectful names for it. The RAF transport guys named it the 'Witch's Tit'.

59. Colin Cummings reports General Lea allegedly commenting that as Sumbi had led the British a merry dance for six weeks, the decent thing would be to upgrade his Jungle Warfare School pass to 'First Class'.

60. In 2013 Pen and Sword will be publishing Geoff Leeming's full account of his Borneo adventures, entitled *From Borneo to Lockerbie*.

61. The AAC stayed on in Brunei, however, as part of a British force which remains to this day at the Seria base, the Army operating Bell 212 helicopters.

62. The criteria were relaxed in the latter days of the campaign to 24 hours' service, and 'bottle plus 200 fags plus GSM' runs suddenly became popular. But the change did enable Rick to collect his GSM.

63. Fred Hoskins reports that for parties at Seletar Officers' Mess, the Rothmans' local office, if asked, would send along beautiful Chinese girls bearing Rothman sashes and a supply of free cigarettes for all. But he's at pains to say that they weren't deemed suitable for this rather grand occasion.

Bibliography

Annett, Roger, *Drop Zone Borneo: The Life and Times of an RAF Co-Pilot, Far East 1963–65* (Pen & Sword Books, Barnsley, 2006)

Beattie, John, Jolly, Rick & Howard, Lee, *Fly Navy: The View from a 'Jungly' Cockpit – 1959–2008* (RNHF Publications, 2009)

Bullock, Christopher, *Journeys Hazardous* (Square One, 2004)

Dickens, Peter, *The Jungle Frontier: 22 SAS Regiment in the Borneo Campaign 1963–66* (Malaysian Heritage Series, S. Abdul Majeed & Co Publishing Division, 1984)

Dowling, Wing Commander J. R., *RAF Helicopters: The First Twenty Years, Parts 1 & 2* (Air Historical Branch (RAF), Ministry of Defence, London, 1987)

Fowler, Will, *Britain's Secret War: The Indonesian Confrontation 1962–66* (Osprey Publishing, Oxford, 2006)

Geraghty, Tony, *Who Dares Wins: The Story of the SAS 1950–92* (Warner Books, 2002)

Harclerode, Peter, *PARA: Fifty Years of The Parachute Regiment* (Arms & Armour Press, London, 1996)

Harrisson, Tom, *World Within: A Borneo Story* (The Cresset Press, London, 1959)

Hoskins, Fred, Robson, Richard and Meadley, Brian (Eds), *From Blue to Grey* (Woodfield Publishing, Bognor Regis, 2005)

James, Harold & Shiel-Small, Denis, *The Undeclared War* (Leo Cooper, London, 1971)

Lee, Air Chief Marshal Sir David, *Eastward: A History of the Royal Air Force in the Far East 1945–72* (HMSO, London, 1984)

McCart, Neil, *HMS Albion 1944–73: The Old Grey Ghost* (Fan Publications, 1995)

Smith, E. D., *Counter-Insurgency Operations: 1 – Malaya and Borneo* (Ian Allan, London, 1985)

Trustees of the John Bodley Trust, *The Last Campaign of the Rifle Brigade: Borneo 1965–66* (John Bodley Trust, 2009)

van der Bijl, Nick, *Confrontation: The War with Indonesia 1962–1966* (Pen & Sword Books, Barnsley, 2007)

Unpublished

The National Archives, Kew

F540 Monthly Operational Reports: 66, 103, 110, 225 and 230 Squadrons RAF

Archives of the Fleet Air Arm Museum, Yeovilton

Archives of the Museum of Army Flying, Middle Wallop

Index

General

INDEX